Contents

JEANETTE WINTERSON

A contemporary critical guide

Edited by
Sonya Andermahr

continuum

Continuum International Publishing Group

The Tower Building   80 Maiden Lane, Suite 704

11 York Road   New York

London SE1 7NX   NY 10038

www.continuumbooks.com

British Library Cataloguing-in-Publication Data

A catalogue record for this book is available from the British Library.

ISBN: 0–8264–9274–6 (hardback)
       978–08264–9274–6
       0–8264–9275–4 (paperback)
       978–08264–9275–3

Library of Congress Cataloging-in-Publication Data

Jeanette Winterson : a contemporary critical guide / edited by Sonya Andermahr.
     p. cm.
    Includes bibliographical references and index.
    ISBN–13: 978–0–8264–9274–6
    ISBN–10: 0–8264–9274–6
    ISBN–13: 978–0–8264–9275–3
    ISBN–10: 0–8264–9275–4
  1. Winterson, Jeanette, 1959 – Criticism and interpretation. I. Andermahr, Sonya. II. Title.
    PR6073.I558Z7 2007
    823'.914 – dc22

                                              2007008727

Typeset by YHT Ltd, London

Acknowledgements

For Alice

With thanks to all the contributors for their good ideas and admirable efficiency, and especial thanks to Phil Tew for his help and advice.

Contributors

Sonya Andermahr is Senior Lecturer in English at the University of Northampton. She has written widely on the work of contemporary women writers and is currently completing a monograph on Jeanette Winterson for Palgrave Macmillan. Her books include *A Glossary of Feminist Theory* with Terry Lovell and Carol Wolkowitz (Arnold, 1997, 2000) and *Straight Studies Modifed: Lesbian Interventions in the Academy* with Gabriele Griffin (Cassell, 1997).

Lucie Armitt is Professor of English at the University of Salford. She is the author of several books on women's writing and is currently writing a book on new women's writing with Sarah Gamble.

Ginette Carpenter is Associate Lecturer in English, Manchester Metropolitan University, and is currently working on her PhD on representations of reading in contemporary women's romance. This is her first publication.

Michelle Denby is Research Fellow in Modern Literature at Doncaster University Centre (University of Hull). Her recent research focused on the postmodern fantastic and the representation of identity, sexuality and the body. Her current research project concerns the relationship between spirituality and postmodernism in contemporary fiction.

Helena Grice is Lecturer in English and American Literature at the University of Wales, Aberystwyth. She co-edited a collection of essays on Jeanette Winterson and has published widely on women's writing. Her latest book is *Negotiating Identities* (Manchester University Press, 2002).

Jennifer Gustar has previously published on the work of Jeanette Winterson. She is Associate Professor of English and Gender Studies in the Faculty of Creative and Critical Studies, University of British Columbia Okanagan, Canada. Her research focus is on women's writing in a trans-cultural frame, including contemporary writing from Great Britain, New Zealand and India.

Jane Haslett is a Post-Doctoral Fellow at the University of Alberta, Canada. She is currently working on a collaborative integrated history of British women's writing, the Orlando Project, an electronic research database.

Gavin Keulks is Associate Professor of British Literature at Western Oregon University. He is the author of *Father and Son: Kingsley Amis, Martin Amis and the British Novel Since 1950* (University of Wisconsin Press, 2003) and the editor of the volume *Martin Amis: Postmodernism and Beyond* (Palgrave, 2006).

Sonia Maria Melchiorre is Research Fellow in English Literature at the CICLAMO (Dipartimento per lo Studio delle Civiltà Classiche e Moderne) at the Faculty of Foreign Languages of the Università della Tuscia, Viterbo. While her current research interests are in contemporary British women's writing, a book based on her PhD research, *From Off The Beaten Track: The Bluestocking Ladies Reconsidered* (Settecittà, Viterbo), was published in 2006.

Phil Tew is Professor of English at Brunel University and is the author of numerous books and articles in his chief research area of contemporary British fiction. New publications include studies of Jim Crace (Manchester University Press, 2006) and Zadie Smith (Palgrave Macmillan, 2007), and a collection of essays edited with Rod Mengham, *British Fiction Today* (Continuum, 2006).

Tim Woods is Professor of English Literature and American Studies at the University of Wales, Aberystwyth. He co-edited a collection of essays on Jeanette Winterson and has published widely on contemporary writing, including *Literatures of Memory* (with Peter Middleton, Manchester University Press, 2000) and *The Poetics of the Limit* (Palgrave Macmillan, 2002). His latest book is *African Pasts* (Manchester University Press, 2006).

Introduction: Winterson and her Critics

SONYA ANDERMAHR

As even the most cursory reader of the book pages of the British print media during the last 20 years will be aware, Jeanette Winterson's work and life have attracted a vast amount of critical interest, so much so that it would be possible to fill an entire volume on the subject of Winterson and her critics. However, for the purposes of this introduction to reading her work, my commentary will necessarily be confined to a brief overview of her often fraught and always fascinating relationship with her broadsheet reviewers, before I go on to introduce the main strands within academic studies of her work over the last two decades, and to identify the specific contribution made to the critical understanding of her work by the new essays collected in this volume.

The media view

Just as Winterson's fiction concerns the vicissitudes of romantic love, Winterson's readers often liken their relationship with her novels to a love affair (Pearce 1998). Indeed, the reception of Winterson's work in the print media could be represented, in appropriately Wintersonian terms, as a protracted love story: it began in the mid 1980s on the publication of her first novel with a *coup de foudre*, an instantaneous falling in love, and was followed by a lengthy honeymoon period throughout the 1980s. Then, in the early 1990s, the relationship hit the buffers and became, notwithstanding a few voices of support, an affair of increasing mutual disillusionment and recrimination throughout the 1990s. In the 2000s, some of the magic returned and by 2004 (with *Lighthousekeeping*) the relationship between Winterson and her critical readers appeared to be finally back on track.

As my parody suggests, there was almost universal approval for *Oranges*; in 1985 the novel won the Whitbread prize for a first novel and, as Hilary Hinds reminds us, it cut across the traditional high/popular divide, garnering positive responses from across the mainstream and alternative media:

Most reviewers agreed that *Oranges* was a notable first novel. In the main-stream and alternative presses, words like 'brilliant', 'beautifully written', 'decidedly imposing in [its] originality', and 'moving' recur. Critics delighted in its humour, decided it was 'quirky' and 'eccentric' and proclaimed Winterson a 'talent to watch'.

(1992: 154)

The critical approbation continued with the publication of her third novel *The Passion* (1987), which won the John Llewellen Rhys Memorial prize; and the TV adaptation of *Oranges* in January 1990 established her high media profile, popular success and critical acclaim (see Chapter 9 in this volume). *Sexing the Cherry* was on the whole positively received – it won the 1989 E. M. Forster award – although some people reportedly found it disappointing (Pearce 1998). The divergence in critical views came with *Written on the Body*. Although championed by a minority, the novel was generally seen as over-written, melodramatic and/or derivative, and as insufficiently 'woman-centred' among her – previously loyal – feminist readers and critics (see Pearce 1998). As Lynne Pearce recorded in her reader's diary:

the tide of public and critical approbation that had swept Winterson along for some time … suddenly turned against her. … *Written on the Body*, though, as I'm remembering it, was launched on the market amidst a barrage of negative publicity and criticism. Some of this was to do with the book, most of it was to do with what may be seen as Winterson's own personal slide towards complacency, arrogance and hubris. … What I remember … was the 'quality' newspapers stamping their reservations all over the book: its politics (the issue of the 'genderless narrator'); its form (the slide from narrative towards panegyric with a few recognising it was more like a (courtly love) poem than prose); and, inevitably its ending.

(1998: 31–2)

Some critics, including journalists and academics, subsequently critiqued the negative construction of Winterson as arrogant *enfant terrible*, identifying a sexual double standard and arguing that her behaviour would be deemed (more) acceptable if she were male (Lambert 1998; Stowers 1995). However, the bad press had a lasting effect on Winterson's reputation and thereafter almost universal ambivalence greeted her 1990s work. *Art & Lies* (1994) received an extremely mixed response, including a raft of hostile reviews in which one critic accused her of 'platitude and flashiness', calling her writing 'inflated', 'frivolous' and 'strident' (Ducornet 1995). As Angela Lambert reports, the novel was widely 'castigated for being boring or incomprehensible' (1998), and its reception may well represent Winterson's critical nadir. However, Jeanne DuPrau (1995) called it an 'extraordinary piece of fiction – sometimes exhilarating, sometimes exasperating', defending Winterson's uncompromisingly dense, poetic style. Thereafter, Winterson's collection of essays, *Art Objects*, published in 1995, in which she defended her approach to writing and Art under the banner of high modernism was largely viewed with barely disguised derision by critics and seen (unfairly) as pretentious and pontificating. Responses to her next novel, *Gut Symmetries*, were similarly polarized into those who viewed it as an interesting, linguistically inventive text and those who saw it as too experimental, self-indulgent and inward-looking. Among the decriers Anthony Quinn in the *Daily Telegraph* thought it strained 'for the fluidities of poetry' and was 'mortifyingly dull to read' (1997); while Adam Mars-Jones in the *Guardian* criticized the 'ramshackle plotting' and absence of a 'storytelling element' (1998). On the opposite critical side, Christopher Paddick stated that the novel 'proves Winterson's dynamic sense of language. It is a solid addition to an already stellar body of work' (1997). And Bruce Bawer, writing in *The New York Times*, and echoing the opinion of Winterson's fan base, was effusive in his praise:

> At a time when many publishers expect literary novels to have the relentless forward motion of an Indiana Jones movie, Ms Winterson refuses to shift into narrative drive; eschewing the Interstate, she favors [sic] the bumpy, meandering byways of interior landscapes. At every turn, furthermore, her fresh, vivid way of putting things stops one dead in admiration.
>
> (1997)

Notwithstanding such positive reviews, throughout the 1990s Winterson's reputation as an outspoken public figure and lesbian came increasingly to dominate reception of her work. Accused of being arrogant, self-indulgent and pretentious, her work was subsumed 'under the weight of vitriolic personal attack' (Brooks 2004). No wonder that she refers to the 1990s as 'her dark period' (Brooks 2004). In actuality, Winterson diversified her writing output considerably, writing film scripts, journalism and starting a highly successful website (famously fighting in the courts for her domain name), which increased her popular fan base enormously. *The PowerBook* (2000) was seen as something of a return to form, an inventive work containing literary gems, although Elaine Showalter criticized it for being narrowly focused and out of touch with the 'big subjects' of the day (Showalter 2000). *Lighthousekeeping* (2004), the first novel 'of a new cycle' according to Winterson (2005: 3), was greeted more positively and critics identified a new commitment to narrative and history (see Chapter 10 in this volume). More recently, *Weight* (2005) garnered mixed reviews, from highly favourable to lukewarm, and the children's book *Tanglewreck* (2006) has been generally well received. As Geraldine Bedell commented, 'Writing for children seems to have lent warmth to Winterson's voice and the novel is leavened with a kind of loving, godmotherly assurance that makes it not merely impressive but enormously likable, and fun' (Bedell 2006). There is an unmistakable irony in the characterization of Winterson by the print media and her transmutation from 1985's bright young thing through arrogant lesbian *enfant terrible* of the mid 1990s to kindly fairy godmother in 2006: what a difference a decade or two makes.

Literary critical engagements

In the academy, Winterson's literary critics may have used less emotive language than their journalist counterparts, but they have been arguably no less passionate in their engagement with her work. Theorists of Winterson's oeuvre have utilized two main theoretical approaches, deriving from feminism and lesbian-feminism, and from the discourses of postmodernism and post-structuralism. A third, queer theories, has emerged from the conversation between the two, and has arguably become the dominant paradigm in investigations of her work, exemplified by Laura Doan's 1994 collection, *The Lesbian Postmodern*. Feminist critics divide into those who express reservations about her work and dispute its relation to feminism (Wingfield 1998); those who initially championed her as the feminist writer *de nos jours* but subsequently questioned her status as a woman writer (Pearce 1997); and those who have more or less consistently viewed her writing as radical practice interrogating the discourses of feminism and postmodernism *inter alia* (Doan 1994; Nunn 1996; Lindenmeyer 1999). In addition, a number of other critical approaches have been utilized, drawing on the constellation of (post-structuralist) theoretical concepts associated with the work of Julia Kristeva, Mikhail Bakhtin, Roland Barthes and Michel Foucault among others.

An early feminist reading of Winterson's first novel by Rebecca O'Rourke (1991) was one of the first to point out the politically subversive elements of *Oranges* and identify its lesbian-feminism. A contrasting view is provided by Rachel Wingfield (1998), who claims that while *Oranges* certainly benefited from the strong lesbian-feminist politics of the early 1980s, the novel ultimately espouses a depoliticized liberal individualism rather than (radical) feminism, and ignores the women's liberation movement of the previous decade. For Wingfield, Winterson's work of the 1990s focused increasingly on postmodernism and individualism, 'emptied out' feminism and lesbianism, and exemplified the 'depoliticization of women's writing', 'feminism without women' and 'sexuality without gender' (1998: 65). She concludes, unfairly in my view, by condemning *Written on the Body* as aimed at the 'male literati' (66). Providing a more theoretically nuanced set of readings across a range of works and historical moments, Lynne Pearce (1994, 1995, 1997, 1998) nevertheless comes to a similar conclusion to

Wingfield. In an early work (1994), Pearce commented that many feminist readers felt 'cheated' by Winterson's treatment of gender issues; in a 1995 essay she criticized Winterson's work for its 'universalizing tendency' and 'humanism' (Pearce 1995); and in 1998 she expressed disappointment that her emotional reading relationship with 'her Winterson' had irrevocably changed after the publication of *Written on the Body* and Winterson's adoption of a genderless narrator.

In contrast, Cath Stowers' readings, also strongly informed by lesbian-feminism, find Winterson's work much more compatible with a (radical) feminist perspective, particularly the French School represented by Hélène Cixous and Luce Irigaray (Stowers 1996). She emphasizes Winterson's powerful depiction of communities of women and an alternative female symbolic realm 'beyond' heteropatriarchy and shows how, while existing in the realm of fictional myth, these are politically powerful images for women. In fact, she goes so far as to argue that Winterson's fictional worlds from *Oranges* through *Sexing* can be represented as '*communities built on a lesbian model*' (1996: 77, emphasis in original). Similarly, Lisa Moore's approach accords lesbian poetics a central place in Winterson's oeuvre (Moore 1995).

While Stowers, Pearce and other lesbian-feminist critics place the emphasis on the critique of heteropatriarchy and the privileging of lesbian bonds and tend to evaluate Winterson's work on this basis, critics informed by postmodern and queer theory foreground, rather, the *range* and *deconstructive potential* of sexual identities treated in Winterson's work. Heather Nunn, for example, situates Winterson as a queer/lesbian writer concerned to explore and expand sexual categories:

> While Oranges placed her in legible relation to lesbian desire . . . *The Passion* and *Sexing the Cherry* have attempted to multiply the possibilities of erotic engagement. The lure of her texts . . . [is] the playful enabling of a medley of heterosexual and homosexual/lesbian loves and identities.
>
> (1996: 16)

However, Nunn argues against the feminist tendency to view *Written* as Winterson's watershed post-feminist text (Pearce 1998, and Armitt in this volume), and argues rather that it retains a commitment to lesbian poetics and feminist politics.

Winterson's postmodern credentials have never been in doubt and since her 1985 debut she has been widely appropriated in academe as part of a group – which includes Salman Rushdie and Martin Amis – of British postmodern stylists. As Doan summarizes:

> Eschewing realism, Winterson constructs her narrative by exploiting the techniques of postmodern historiographic metafiction (such as inter-textuality, parody, pastiche, self-reflexivity, fragmentation, the rewriting of

history, and frame breaks) as well as its ideology (questioning 'grand nar-ratives', problematizing closure, valorizing instability, suspecting coherence, and so forth) in order to challenge and subvert patriarchal and heterosexist discourses and, ultimately, to facilitate a forceful and positive oppositional critique.

(1994: 138)

Postmodern readings of Winterson's oeuvre, highlighting the features listed above, are numerous: Catherine Belsey (1994) considers Winter-son's treatment of 'Postmodern Love' (1994), Bente Gade (1999) offers a postmodern reading of *Sexing the Cherry*, Judith Roof (1994) and Paulina Palmer (2001) both examine the intersection of postmodernism and lesbianism in Winterson's work, and Jeffrey Roessner (2002) examines Winterson's writing of a 'history of difference' in *Sexing*.

Significantly, Doan (1994), in contradistinction to Wingfield, sees no contradiction between the aesthetics of postmodernism and the politics of feminism, as one appears to facilitate the other in Winterson's ouevre. Far from disabling feminism, 'The postmodern constructions of such innovative paradigms mobilize and animate a feminist political strategy of resistance, forcing and enforcing new mappings of the social and cultural order through feminist revision and reconsideration, and reconceptualization' (Doan 1994: 154). Indeed, for Doan, Winterson becomes the practitioner *par excellence* of an emergent lesbian post-modern mode, enacting in her writing: 'a sexual politics of hetero-geneity and a vision of hybridized gender constructions outside an either/or proposition, at once political and postmodern' (154). In a similar manner, Antje Lindenmeyer provides a thorough close reading of postmodern concepts of the body in Winterson's *Written on the Body* arguing that the novel provides both a 'feminist critique of androcentric science' and a politically useful postmodern unsettling of 'fixed boundaries and gendered identities' (1999: 60).

However, while this has become the standard 'feminist postmodern' reading of Winterson's oeuvre, it is one that Winterson herself would almost certainly demur at. Winterson has always placed her work in the *modernist* rather than *post*-modernist tradition and, rather than invoke the authorial fallacy to dismiss her view, from a literary critical per-spective it has much to recommend it: Winterson shares both the formal experimentalism, the Eliotean reworking of tradition of the modernists *and*, significantly, their privileging of Art and the *logos*, as may be seen in her modernist manifesto *Art Objects*. Politically she is more radical – certainly in terms of gender – than her (male) modernist predecessors, although a tradition of the exploration of sexual politics can be traced through Woolf, Mansfield and Richardson up to Winterson. It seems that the preponderance of the 'post' in accounts of her work may be due after all to her historical location as a writer of the late twentieth and early twenty-first century, rather than to any clearly identifiable aesthetic criterion. A few critics have explored Winterson's modernist aspects, including Lyn Pykett (1998), and Susana Onega (2006), but there is certainly scope for more analysis.

In addition to the paradigms of feminism and postmodernism, critics have turned to a range of other approaches to study aspects of Winterson's oeuvre. A number of studies use forms of narratological analysis to examine her use of narrative voice. One example is Ute Kauer's (1998) analysis of the first-person narrator in *Written on the Body*, which argues that 'the "I" in this novel plays on sexual stereotypes that constitute our view on love' and that the novel represents a new form of 'female writing questioning gender roles by using the mask of gender ambiguity' (1998: 50). Another significant critical approach is derived from the work of Mikhail Bakhtin, particularly from his notions of carnival, the grotesque and female monstrosity. Lynne Pearce (1994) was among the first to systematically apply Bakhtinian theory to the work of Winterson and other women writers in *Reading Dialogics*. More recently, Lucie Armitt (2000) in her work on the female fantastic has traced the Bakhtinian concepts of the grotesque, hybridity and the chronotope in Winterson's work, and Mary Bratton (2002) provides an interesting analysis of 'the chronotope of the lesbian hero'. In addition, psychoanalytic approaches have produced some valuable readings of Winterson's experiments with language and her major themes of love and desire. Heather Nunn (1996) uses the Kristevan concept of abjection to examine Winterson's exploration of love, desire and the body in *Written on the Body*. Finally, feminist critics have challenged the postmodern tendency to relegate the body to a genderless, a-material realm and have begun to examine more closely Winterson's representation of particular, material bodies and corporal experience (see Andermahr 2005); in particular, Ina Schabert (2001) celebrates what she sees as the 'return of the body' to fictional and theoretical discourse in Winterson's work.

Since the turn of the century, several full-length studies have been published which provide useful overviews of aspects of Winterson's work: Noakes and Reynolds (2003) produced the first student-oriented guide to her best-known novels, which includes a valuable interview with the author; thereafter, Merja Makinen's (2005) introduction to Winterson's novels was published just prior to Susana Onega's (2006) monograph, which provides the fullest account to date of Winterson as a contemporary British experimental novelist, with a particular focus on the modernist tradition represented by Woolf and Eliot among others.

Paddick, Christopher (1997), Review of *Gut Symmetries*, *Review of Contemporary Fiction*, Fall. *http://www.complete-review.com/reviews/wintersj/gut.htm* (accessed 28 September 2006).

Palmer, Paulina (2001), 'Jeanette Winterson: lesbian/postmodern fictions', in Beate Neumeier (ed.), *Engendering Realism and Postmodernism: Contemporary Women Writers in Britain*. Amsterdam and New York: Rodopi, pp. 181–9.

Pearce, Lynne (1994), *Reading Dialogics*. London: Routledge.

—— (1995), '"Written on tablets of stone"?: Jeanette Winterson, Roland Barthes, and the discourse of romantic love', in Suzanne Raitt (ed.), *Volcanoes and Pearl Divers: Essays in Lesbian Feminist Studies*. London: Onlywomen Press, pp. 147–68.

—— (1997), *Feminism and the Politics of Reading*. London: Edward Arnold.

—— (1998), 'The emotional politics of reading Winterson', in H. Grice and T. Woods (eds), *Postmodern Studies 25: 'I'm telling you stories': Jeanette Winterson and the Politics of Reading*. Amsterdam/Atlanta, GA: Rodopi, pp. 29–39.

Pykett, Lyn (1998), 'A new way with words?: Jeanette Winterson's postmodernism', in H. Grice and T. Woods (eds), *Postmodern Studies 25: 'I'm telling you stories': Jeanette Winterson and the Politics of Reading*. Amsterdam/Atlanta, GA: Rodopi.

Quinn, Anthony (1997), Review of *Gut Symmetries*, *Daily Telegraph*, 4 January. *http://www.complete-review.com/reviews/wintersj/gut.htm* (accessed 28 September 2006).

Roessner, Jeffrey (2002), 'Writing a history of difference: Jeanettte Winterson's *Sexing the Cherry* and Angela Carter's *Wise Children*', *College Literature*, 29, (1), Winter, 102–22.

Roof, Judith (1994), 'Lesbians and Lyotard: Legitimation and the politics of the name', in Laura Doan (ed.), *The Lesbian Postmodern*. New York: Columbia University Press, pp. 47–66.

Schabert, Ina (2001), 'Habeas corpus 2000: The return of the body', *European Studies*, 16, 87–115.

Showalter, Elaine (2000), 'Eternal triangles', *Guardian*, 2 September. *http://www.books.guardian.co.uk/reviews/generalfiction* (accessed 21 July 2003).

Stowers, Cath (1995), 'Journeying with Jeanette: Transgressive travels in Winterson's fiction', in M. Maynard and J. Purvis (eds), *Hetero(sexual) Politics*. London: Taylor and Francis, pp. 139–59.

—— (1996), '"No legitimate place, no land, no fatherland": Communities of women in the fiction of Roberts and Winterson' *Critical Survey*, vol. 8, no. 1, 69–79.

Wingfield, Rachel (1998), 'Lesbian writers in the mainstream: Sara Maitland, Jeanette Winterson and Emma Donoghue', in Elaine Hutton (ed.), *Beyond Sex and Romance: The Politics of Contemporary Lesbian Fiction*. London: Women's Press, pp. 60–80.

Winterson, Jeanette (1985), *Oranges Are Not the Only Fruit*. London: Pandora.

—— (1987), *The Passion*. London: Bloomsbury.

—— (1989), *Sexing the Cherry*. London: Bloomsbury.

—— (1992), *Written on the Body*. London: Jonathan Cape.

—— (1996) [1995], *Art Objects: Essays on Ecstasy and Effrontery*. London: Vintage.

—— (1998) [1997], *Gut Symmetries*. London: Granta.

—— (2000), *The PowerBook*. London: Vintage.

—— (2004), *Lighthousekeeping*. London: Fourth Estate.

—— (2005), 'P.S. From innocence to experience: Louise Tucker talks to Jeanette Winterson', *Lighthousekeeping*. London: Harper Perennial.

—— (2005), *Weight*. London: Canongate.

—— (2006), *Tanglewreck*. London: Bloomsbury.

—— Personal website. *http://www.jeanettewinterson.com* (accessed 29 October 2006).

CHAPTER ONE

Storytelling and Feminism

LUCIE ARMITT

Chapter summary: Lucie Armitt considers Winterson's relationship to feminism and identifies, across her work, an increasing 'severance' from feminist storytelling and a gradual abandonment of a woman-centred perspective. Increasingly committed to a postmodern 'genderlessness', Winterson's work, it is argued, begins to substitute the lover's *body* for the woman's *voice*. The chapter concludes that while Winterson's place in the feminist story will remain a significant one, it remains to be seen whether her work will re-establish the idea of a primary attachment to women.

Key texts: *Oranges Are not the Only Fruit; Sexing the Cherry; Written on the Body; The PowerBook; Lighthousekeeping*

Key words: feminism, storytelling, the woman writer, women readers, female identity

Jeanette Winterson is a writer who, especially in the 1980s and 1990s, quickly attracted iconic status for feminist critics. To some extent my own sense of myself as a feminist literary critic is bound up in her moment of emergence. *Oranges Are Not the Only Fruit* (1985), hereafter *Oranges*, was published the year after I graduated, which was also the year I went to my first women's writing conference, where I bought it from the bookstall and, as they say, the rest is history. That moment of 'becoming' is crucial because a mixture of nostalgia combined with personal indebtedness encourages me to situate 'the Winterson of that time' right at the heart of the story of Second Wave literary feminism – and yet I know this to be a sense of belonging that Winterson herself would actively and assertively resist, as well as being one that, from *Written on the Body* (1992) onwards, I equally feel ill befits her.

In truth, I no longer consider Winterson to be 'a woman writer' in the way that I do Angela Carter or Sarah Waters but, unlike many readers, for whom the term 'women's writing' proves problematic or dangerous, I acknowledge that shift in Winterson's stance with a sense of loss – women's writing shaped me as an academic and I remain proud of the responsibilities it taught me (to further the professional cause of other women, to deconstruct the politics of canon formation, to mistrust received opinion, to tell the stories of women's lives and longings). This chapter sets out to place Winterson's work – in particular her fascination with storytelling – within a broader sense of literary feminism and in relation to some of the stories through which feminism can be and has been understood, using readings of five of her novels to do so: *Oranges*, *Sexing the Cherry* (1989), *Written on the Body*, *The PowerBook* (2000) and *Lighthousekeeping* (2004).

Whenever I have tried to define the difference between writing written by women and Second Wave feminist women's writing – and I still believe there is both literary and political value in making the distinction – what I find myself doing is trying to find words to articulate a gut reaction: 'I am attached to these books' sounds feeble, but I am using the word 'attachment' more assertively than as a simple expression of sentiment. I mean it in the sense of being 'tied, threaded, bound' to them, intellectually and politically. Nor am I alone in tracing out a personal intellectual and academic journey in relation to Winterson's oeuvre. Lynne Pearce has offered detailed accounts of her shifting views of Winterson's work and has mapped those responses onto an ongoing awareness of her development as an academic reader. In *Feminism and the Politics of Reading* (1997), Pearce begins by documenting her 'reader's "romance"' with Winterson's third novel, *The Passion* (1987), a romance sparked by the recognition that, in Villanelle's story, 'despite the historical-fantasy location, the discourse on love and passion made profound humanist contact with me. It was that special sense of having your own thoughts and feelings written out for you' (1997: 89).[1] From here, Pearce notes that her sense of identification with the text began to overstep the usual narrative boundaries: 'I . . . allowed myself to play projection/introjection with the reconstructed author of this text . . . Winterson was to become the public embodiment of my own literary aspirations as a writer/scholar . . . my intellectual "other": the "one who understands"' (89). After *Written on the Body*, however, the romance starts to pale as Pearce finds (not unusually in longer-term relationships) obligation taking over. Responding to others' enquiries about her view of the book on first publication, following much negative advance publicity in the media, she notes: 'I did the honourable thing and defended it – and her . . . and this responsibility [was] the first obstacle to a more honest re-engagement' (89–90). It was, she says, only later that she was able to acknowledge:

> The 'I' who approached the text in 1992 clearly had enough faith in her power as a reader (and in her commitment to Winterson) to believe that the text could be made to satisfy her expectations . . . By the time of my re-reading [for the purposes of writing *Feminism and the Politics of Reading*], however, all such conviction has disappeared, and anxiety predicated upon hope is replaced by the fear (certainty?) of disappointment.

(141)

Among feminist scholars, Pearce has contributed perhaps the greatest amount to our understanding of reading as a politicized process – one in which we not only project ourselves most absolutely into a narrative ('we do indeed *move about texts* ... looking for ways in which we might make them respond to us' (25)), but in which she refuses to cloak her own persona behind the mask of academic discourse:

> my use of the autobiographical 'I' ... [partly] support[s] the theoretical and pedagogical principles of what is now known as 'personalist' criticism ... [as well as exploring] the process of reading as a dialogic 'I-thou' relationship: a grammatical recognition that each and every act of reading is the site of potential intimacy and engagement.
>
> (25–6)

Not surprisingly, considering this affirmation of intimacy, implicit in Pearce's approach is an attendant sense that the responsibility she formerly felt she owed to 'her' author should be mutually reciprocated. On one level, a direct attachment to her reader appears to be a responsibility Winterson happily embraces. How else does one interpret her own oft-quoted words from *The Passion*: 'I'm telling you stories. Trust me' (1987: 5). Nevertheless, as we will come on to see, strategies of disengagement are equally built into Winterson's narrative stance to simultaneously and categorically distance her from at least my understanding of Second Wave feminism.

Here, then, we have Winterson's work singled out for use as a screen across which readers' personal journeys into and through subjectivity are established. Again, this is an identification process that Winterson's early books appear to encourage. In *Oranges*, Winterson's central character, Jeanette, shares the author's name, a conscious invitation to an autobiographical reading later dismantled from within the narrative by the intermeshing of realist and anti-realist narrative modes. Towards its end, we encounter the apprenticeship test set for Winnet Stonejar (a near anagram of Jeanette Winterson) by a sorcerer. Placing Winnet in a chalk circle, he refuses to release her until she tells him her name. Responding by challenging him to a game of 'Hang the Man', in which he must free her if he fails (she believes her name too unusual to guess), the sorcerer demonstrates he knew it all along. Winterson may give her reader a little rope here, teasing her with the anagram to encourage her to believe she is 'in on the game', but in fact to scramble the name is to point out the *limitations* of the character/author identification. The success of this distancing technique seems assured in a comment made by Winterson herself in an interview on BBC2's *The Late Show* in 1992: 'I get countless letters about *Oranges*, saying "How could you know that I feel like that, you were writing about me, weren't you?" And of course I wasn't, but then of course I was'.[2]

Telling one story in the process of appearing to tell another's is also the key technique used in Carolyn Steedman's highly regarded feminist study, *Landscape For a Good Woman* (1986). A book about her mother, class identification and the result of both on the author's own sense of identity construction, this is both more and less than an (auto)-biography, a book in which its narrator acknowledges the 'deep and ambiguous conflict' between 'personal interpretations of past time' and 'the official interpretative devices of a culture', while affirming, nevertheless, the existence of a 'biographical and autobiographical core' as its structure (1986: 6–7). It is also more than an (auto)biography because it acknowledges its own existence as an act of political responsibility. As with Pearce, one of Steedman's key methodological overtures is to assert the importance of tying the choice of personal pronoun to this commitment: 'The first task is to particularize ... so that the people in exile, the inhabitants of the long streets, may start to use the auto-biographical "I", and tell the stories of their life' (16). Like Winterson, Steedman simultaneously disrupts that willed proximity between protagonist and implied author through the intrusion of other registers (social documentary, theoretical evaluation) to complicate the personalist stance. Here we locate the voice of the academic historian who both is and hence is not the 'child' of this text.

Most pertinent for our purposes, however, is Steedman's own emphasis on the centrality of storytelling to the construction of a sense of 'who we are', irrespective of whether the 'we' in question is particularized or (as is the case of feminist discourses) collectivized. Hence, Steedman recognizes that 'What historically conscious readers may do with this book is to read it as a Lancashire story, see here evidence of a political culture of 1890–1930 carried from the North-west' (22). Equally strong, however, and here is where the importance of Steedman's account lies, is a matching counter-impulse to resist collectivity, for otherwise the mother will be reduced from character to representative. Hence, repeated reminders of distinction and individuality are made ('my mother rejected the politics of solidarity and communality, always voted Conservative' (47)), combined, on the level of scholarship, with a call for more rigorous attention to be paid to similar nuances on the level of 'group identity':

> The point of being a Lancashire weaver's daughter, as my mother was, is that it is *classy* ... if you were going to be working class, then you might as well be the best that's going, and for women, Lancashire and weaving provided that elegance, that edge of difference and distinction.
>
> (23)

Striking similarities are in evidence between Steedman's and Winterson's approaches. Most evident, of course, is their shared identification with Lancashire, with the working-class cultures from which each emerged into the middle-class intellectual milieu which enabled their voices to be not just heard, but hung upon by others with both similar and different stories to tell; in the fact that, like Steedman, Jeanette in *Oranges* has a mother who, 'At election time in a Labour mill town ... put a picture of the Conservative candidate in the window' (1985: 3) and who, more obviously still, is the dominant force in a household in which, as Steedman puts it, 'A father like mine dictated each day's existence ... But he didn't *matter*' (1986: 19). Additionally, both are motivated by a fascination with history and share the view that it is not a transparent window into a truth, but a source of stories that can, in themselves, be woven into a narrative that simultaneously reveals and conceals, speaks of and hides the self, and hence provides the lacunae which allow for this telling of others' tales.

Steedman says, 'When I look in the mirror I see [my mother's] face, but I know in fact that I look more like [my father]. A real Lancashire face' (49). Close attention to these words reveals more about story-telling. Firstly, the mirror, that object supposed only to show us who *we* are reveals, to this first-person narrator, not one but two imposters, the revelation of the first providing the catalyst for a second story ('I look more like my father'). Clearly neither story is true (she has neither her mother's nor her father's face, but her own), and yet both have cred-ibility (we are each the product of both biological parents and our face is imprinted with that combination). This passage also inspires a personal response in me. On reading the second sentence, a powerful family longing of my own is provoked. I do not know what 'A real Lancashire face' is, but my late father (himself a working-class Mancunian) would have done. The longing takes a two-stage route: firstly, I want him alive again to heal my sense of ignorance; secondly, I recognize this longing to be only partly about facts; primarily it is about stories. In providing information, my father – a good storyteller – would have spoken about himself while appearing to speak of others. Equally, though I would have processed and archived his story as 'truth', I recognize the unlikelihood of it matching Steedman's version, had she given it. Herein lies the authoritative trickery of storytelling: we have to believe stories, because our pleasure in the tale necessitates their success.

Searches for the self framed as quests for others run throughout Winterson's writing, as do first-person narrators. Later, this will become a useful device for concealing the face of the point-of-view protagonist but, in *Sexing the Cherry*, her fourth novel, the boundaries between characters shift and blur as stories merge. Hence the first description we have of one of the two central narrators, Jordan, is shrouded in mist:

My name is Jordan. This is the first thing I saw ... The fog came towards me and the sky ... was covered up ... I tried to find the path ... I began to walk with my hands stretched out in front of me, as do those troubled in sleep, and in this way, for the first time, I traced the lineaments of my own face opposite me.

(1989: 1–2)

Like the daughter's encounter with mirrored otherness in Steedman's text, here Jordan is blocked from plotting a course into self-awareness by the intrusive presence of a mirror-double. And, just as Steedman's protagonist perceives that reflection to shift between differently gendered faces, so the opening to a later passage, this time narrated by his elusive beloved Fortunata, reveals her to be this reflected 'other half': 'My name is Fortunata', she said. 'This is the first thing I saw' (104). Such dislocations between self and others continue to inspire the many journeys that Jordan, a sea-voyager, undertakes:

> Curiously, the further I have pursued my voyages the more distant they have become ... I begin, and straight away a hundred alternative routes present themselves ... Every time I try to narrow down my intent I expand it ... Perhaps I'm missing the point – perhaps whilst looking for someone else you might come across yourself unexpectedly...
>
> (115–16)

This sense of characters-in-process remains a typical feature of Winterson's work and one that suits well her determination to render her point-of-view protagonists 'incomplete'. To finish a character is to fix her and, from Jeanette in *Oranges* onwards, her protagonists are always engaged in journeys that remain unfinished. Surely, herein lies a message for feminism, which must, as Sarah Gamble observes, be prepared to 'adapt to respond to the exigencies of a changing world' (2001: 52), and the worlds of Winterson's novels are ever changing (in time, in substance, even in terms of their physical properties). Nevertheless, that is not the full story. One criticism Mary Russo makes of feminism in the 1990s is that it tried too hard to appeal to the patriarchal mainstream, with the result that it diluted its own strength: 'What is often forgotten in these strategies of reassurance is that the normal is not the same as the ordinary' (1994: vii). What I like most about Dog Woman, the gloriously shocking heroine of *Sexing the Cherry*, is her utter refusal to pander to patriarchal sensitivities: 'How hideous am I? My nose is flat, my eyebrows are heavy. I have only a few teeth and those are a poor show, being black and broken. I had smallpox when I was a girl and the caves in my face are home enough for fleas' (1989: 19). 'Accosted' by a man in the street, he coerces her into providing him with what he thinks will be sexual favours:

> 'Put [my penis] in your mouth ... Yes, as you would a delicious thing to eat.' I like to broaden my mind when I can and I did as he suggested, swallowing it up entirely and biting it off with a snap. As I did so, my eager fellow increased his swooning to the point of fainting away, and I, feeling both astonished by his rapture and disgusted by the leathery thing filling up my mouth, spat out what I had not eaten and gave it to one of my dogs.
>
> (40–1)

A complex caricature of villainy, sexual naivety, brutality and endearing charm, Dog Woman's primary virtue, nevertheless, is her willingness to take responsibility: for her actions, for her foundling 'son' Jordan, for her cause. Note also how, in using the first person again, Winterson allows Dog Woman's primary responsibility to tell her own tale – one detailing the power of the female form.

At this point in her writing career Winterson seems a champion of feminist resistance, but after *Sexing the Cherry* everything changes. Of course, plenty of female flesh remains on offer, but on the whole it is far more carefully circumscribed and controlled – not to mention far more palatable to patriarchy. *Written on the Body* (a watershed novel in Winterson's oeuvre, as it is with this novel that her experiments with ambiguously gendered or incomplete narrators begin) epitomizes this trait perfectly. Here, the adored object, Louise, is 'powerfully' seductive, but only because her lover allows her to be so. Objectively, she is simply the reflection of a desiring gaze – subject to the same kind of chivalric fascination that suits the Arthurian Knights who intermittently travel on horseback across Winterson's pages:

> *You* laughed and waved, *your* body bright beneath the clear green water ... *You* turned on your back and *your* nipples grazed the surface of the river and the river decorated *your* hair with beads. *You* are creamy but for your hair *your* red hair that flanks *you* on either side.
>
> (1992: 11, my emphasis)

This passage returns us to a consideration of pronouns and their political implications. Here, the repeated use of the second-person pronoun has a strangely dislocating effect. On one level it produces proximity (at least by comparison with the third-person 'norm'), but it also pushes the woman away (she is not 'I' but 'you'). In this sense the floating body is a particularly useful metaphor as it almost drifts at the whim of the desiring 'flow' of the gaze, towards and then away from the viewing subject. The real problem for me here is that in denying a woman's voice to the active lover/narrator, the only roles left for the unambiguously female character are the more objectifying ones Louise especially epitomizes: beloved on a pedestal, femme fatale ('There was a dangerously electrical quality about Louise ... Superficially she seemed serene, but beneath her control was a crackling power of the kind that makes me nervous when I pass pylons.' (49)), adulterous married woman, dying wraith ('I couldn't find her. I couldn't even get near finding her. It's as if Louise never existed, like a character in a book. Did I invent her?' (189)).

As early as 1929 Virginia Woolf (a figure to whom Winterson attaches herself as to no other) writes, in *A Room of One's Own*, of the shortcomings of the hypothetical male author, Mr A, for his inability to endow his female characters with genuine physical presence: 'Is that a tree? No, it is a woman. But ... she has not a bone in her body, I thought, watching Phoebe, for that was her name, coming across the beach' (1929: 95). Furthermore, elsewhere she implies that female authors have a specific duty to right these wrongs: 'One might read the lives of all the Cabinet Ministers since the accession of Queen Victoria without realizing that they had a body between them' (1920: 218). Second Wave feminism offered a series of answers to this observation, including, at its most extreme, French-school feminists such as Hélène Cixous exhorting women to 'write the body': 'why don't you write? Write! Writing is for you ... your body is yours, take it' (1976: 246). But it is one thing to exhort and quite another to transform that exhortation into narrative presence. Again, one finds Winterson playing tricks of a 'now you see it, now you don't' kind. In the very title 'Written on the Body', the work of theorists such as Cixous is evoked. But, at the same time, so are their shortcomings, for as the narrative progresses, and Louise falls victim to cancer, the vitality of her body is supplanted by the clinical language of anatomy: 'THE AURICLE IS ... COMPOSED OF FIBRO-ELASTIC CARTILAGE ... THE PROMINENT OUTER RIDGE IS KNOWN AS THE HELIX. THE LOBULE IS THE SOFT PLIABLE PART AT THE LOWER EXTREMITY' (1992: 135). As Winterson cautions, writing on the body can actually make women disappear.

Again we return to responsibility for, as Pearce reminds us elsewhere, even romantic love beyond books 'is a narrative discourse ... the experience of "being in love" depends entirely upon the stories *we find ourselves able to tell*' (1995: 154–5, my emphasis). This perhaps explains why a writer such as Winterson, a powerful personality whose narratives are constructed in terms of longing, especially in relation to the search for romance, adopts an active point-of-view character identification with the suitor through the intrusive 'I' of the implied author, while simultaneously seeking out storytelling modes that dismantle any unified relationship between the teller of the tale and the tale itself.

What happens, then, when the very identity of the author constructing the text comes up for grabs? This is one of the questions Winterson addresses in *The PowerBook* (2000), the final novel of what she calls her first 'cycle of work' (2004: 'Afterword', 18). At the start of the twenty-first century, of course, the word 'attachment' acquires greatest resonance in relation to email – communication that glories in physical severance from the addressee – and this may explain why it is actually in relation to this novel, which explores the games one can play with the internet, that Winterson's discontinuous narrative mode seems to me to work best. Winterson's style has become more Spartan as her writing project has developed, but this novel is written particularly sparely. In effect, this is a book that hides the author within her own text and, in doing so, draws self-conscious attention to the manner in which the author *beyond* the text can be masked by the personae s/he creates inside and beyond it.

In the aforementioned *Late Show* interview, Winterson described language as 'a racehorse [that] needs riding; it needs handling' and goes on to assert her drive to 'work with language at that pressure, at that ... intensity'. In my opinion it is in *The PowerBook* that she best achieves this aim, for on entering this apparently Spartan world, the enormity of the material placed under this extreme stylistic compression is not only apparent but also, through the act of reading, almost detonated. Take, for instance, the novel's opening. The main protagonist starts by 'unwrap[ping]' an email message. That virtual connection immediately transforms the constraints of terse electronic communication into a pleasure dome in which the 'unwrapped' may wrap themselves up again in a variety of disguises and, in the process, unravel their core self-definition, all in the quest for '*Freedom, just for one night*' (2000: 3).

Freedom is surely the watchword of feminism, but the freedom in question here is freedom *from* responsibility. In terms of feminist theory, it is Third Wave feminism that shares most common ground with this novel, in particular the work of theorists such as Donna Haraway or Sadie Plant, both of whom explore the implications of the freedoms supplied to women by cybernetics and virtual technologies. Most freeing, Haraway would argue, is severance from our origins – we can construct a whole new persona in virtual worlds. But an important question for women remains: if we jettison origins, then we similarly jettison our mothers, hence reproduction gives way to replication, the projection of the self into 'otherness'.[3] As Winterson's narrator suggests, 'This is where the story starts. Here, in these long lines of laptop DNA. Here we take your chromosomes, twenty-three pairs, and alter your height, eyes, teeth, sex. This is an invented world' (4). At its best, then, virtual worlds offer utopian possibilities – anchorage in a 'no-place' where we become anybody (or, perhaps, 'no-body'). Unlike previously, therefore, when Winterson's characters (like Steedman's) have progressed in relation to a matriarchal family structure, now the membrane denoting intimacy between characters is not made of flesh, but of glass; a screen reflecting back at the face of the protagonist the name 'user'.

In truth, Winterson seems most 'at home' with severance. When she talks of her conviction that the traditional view of character in a novel is excess 'ballast' or 'scaffolding' that can be 'pull[ed] away' from a text, what she is articulating is a desire to lose unwanted baggage. Hence, in *The PowerBook*, Winterson further develops the narrative experiment she began in *Written on the Body*. Reminding ourselves of Pearce's observation that romantic love itself is 'a narrative discourse', Winterson takes this to a literal level: 'What is it that I have to tell myself, again and again? ... I can change the story. I am the story. Begin' (4–5). Here, the protagonist casts herself in the roles of both teller/sender *and* reader/recipient. Precisely because we are dealing in a virtual reality, not only does the biological identity of the point-of-view protagonist remain shifting and unclear, so does that of the beloved. Thus the 'particular' gives way to the universal throughout, romance becoming a story about reciprocated or, at times, repudiated desire, rather than the narrative of two characters. Thus, while physical descriptions of the beloved are given, they tend to focus on her gestures or her clothes: 'she seemed confident and poised in soft black jeans, white shirt, a slash of lipstick, and a handbag ... Her sweater was a ribbed cashmere crewneck, tied like a sack, hanging like a dancer' (34). In other words 'she' is simply the means by which narrative desire becomes parcelled, abstractly fitted to an unspecified 'other'. Where Steedman emphasizes the importance of seeing the particularity of the individual, in *The PowerBook* to particularize would be to rob desire of its universality. Hence, also, the fluidity of gender identification: 'Your cock is in my cunt. My breasts weigh under your dress. My fighting arm is sinew'd to your shoulder. Your tiny feet stand my ground' (69).

It is surely inevitable that a writer who takes storytelling so seriously will situate a progressive narrative development at the heart of her first novelistic cycle. Nevertheless, even as her reader moves from book to book, moments from previous novels tug at one's consciousness, pulling us back to what has gone before. So what is, in *Written on the Body*, 'I know the calcium of your cheekbones. I know the weapon of your jaw ... Myself in your skin, myself lodged in your bones' (1992: 120) becomes, in *The PowerBook*, 'What if skin, bone, liver, veins, are the things I use to hide myself?' (2000: 15). And, in *Sexing the Cherry*, where the huge physiognomy of Dog Woman is transcended by fantastic/supernatural means, 'I was invisible ... I, who must turn sideways through any door, can melt into the night' (1989: 8), so, in *The Power-Book*, Ali is 'So slender ... and so slight, that I can slip under the door of a palace, or between the dirt and the floor of a hovel, and never be seen' (2000: 11).

Similarly, despite her determination to forge a new relationship between novelist and the novel, Winterson has always paid tribute in her novels to the past. This returns us briefly to Steedman, who sees our personal pasts as determining of how we project ourselves into the future. Crucially, for Steedman, what matters most is for our mothers to be 'good enough' and, to attain this, comparatively little beyond the basics are required: 'I believe that as an infant I was handled and loved enough, looked at enough, was seen, and saw that I existed ... [Hence,] I was able to create in myself the wish for a child, which is the wish to see oneself reproduced and multiplied' (1986: 91). This 'good enough' mother features recurrently in Winterson's novels, from Jeanette's mother in *Oranges*, to Dog Woman in *Sexing the Cherry*, to Mrs M, the woman who, along with her husband, runs a 'Muck Midden' in *The PowerBook*. Mr and Mrs M adopt an orphan, whom they name Alix because they dream about finding treasure among the dirt, and so 'they wanted a name with an X in it, because X marks the spot' (2000: 138). Parented by avarice, Alix's existence to this couple is primarily utilitarian. Nevertheless, what she learns from them is the importance of looking towards the future: 'I had to find the treasure too' (146).

This is an aim retained in *Lighthousekeeping*, the first novel of Winterson's second cycle. Importantly, however, here the primary source of story is not a mother but a literary forefather, Robert Louis Stevenson, who, in Winterson's novel, appears as a character indebted to stories told to him by Blind Pew, the lighthousekeeper, and his charge, the little girl Silver, before he goes on to write *Treasure Island* (1883). Outside this text, another story of mutual literary influences tells itself: namely, that Stevenson's novel will surely have played its own role in the development of a new storytelling venture for Winterson, the writing of her new children's novel, *Tanglewreck* (2006). Whatever the convolutions, those powerfully compelling mothers of the earlier, more woman-centred novels have now been upstaged by two surrogate fathers: one inside and one outside the text. In fact, to say mothers are upstaged is putting it mildly – in *Lighthousekeeping*, the mother gets 'ditched'.

Silver is a child born out of wedlock to a lone mother, living on the edge of the remote Scottish coastal town of Salts, where her origins result in ostracism from the rest of the community. Though Silver is not longed-for, attachment to her mother is necessitated here by the precariousness of their existence: 'I lived in a house cut steep into the bank. The chairs had to be nailed to the floor, and ... [w]e ate food that stuck to the plate' (2004: 3). One day, returning together from a shopping trip, mother and daughter start to scale the cliff, harnessed together, when the mother loses her footing and falls. As Silver struggles to find a foothold, clinging to the spiny shrubs on the cliff-face, 'all the weight behind me seemed to lift ... My mother had gone ... She had undone the harness to save me' (7). In this extreme case, being a 'good enough' mother requires setting the daughter free from mothers altogether.

There are some important comparisons between *Lighthousekeeping* and *Oranges* beyond their shared placing as first novels in two respective cycles. Both Jeanette and Silver are children who lack any real father figure (Jeanette's is ineffectual and Silver's is lost at sea), and this, combined with their shared exclusion from the company of other children, leads to an over-reliance on a reluctant mother. The primary difference between the two, however, derives from the different degrees of adhesion apparent in the cementing of the mother–child bond, revealed in the literary use of the rope image (an obvious metaphorical version of the umbilicus). A further distinction resides in the axes employed for the reeling in and out of the rope. As we have seen, *Lighthousekeeping* employs a vertical axis. Even after the death of the mother, Silver goes to live in a lighthouse on a headland '368 feet high, wild, grand, impossible. Home to gulls and dreams' (12). In *Oranges*, on the other hand, the axis employed is largely horizontal (hence the potency of the magician's chalk circle). Jeanette is a 'feet on the ground' character who, ultimately deciding to forgive her mother's over-controlling intolerance and return home, retraces her journey by train, tube-train and on foot, thereby continually maintaining contact with solid earth, a fact that makes 'bags in the aisle', 'three feet of snow' and the lack of wellington boots credible grounds for complaint (1985: 162). The choice of axis has clear implications for the relative degrees of severance involved. In *Lighthousekeeping*, the vertical axis makes the mother's removal instant and irreversible. In *Oranges*, on the other hand, the horizontal axis enables the return journey to be contemplated, executed gradually and of a temporary (not to mention, reversible) nature.

Furthermore, in *Oranges* it is equally important to remember that Jeanette's roots are not just firmly bedded in the mother, but in a larger close-knit female community comprising Elsie Norris, 'Auntie' Alice, 'Auntie' May, Mrs Arkwright, Mrs White, Miss Jewsbury, Auntie Betty, Nellie, Doreen, 'them two at the paper shop' (76), not to mention, of course, her two lovers, Melanie and Katy. Collectively, this enables the narrative to accord with what Adrienne Rich has called the 'lesbian continuum', defined as 'a range – through each woman's life and throughout history – of woman-identified experience, not simply the fact that a woman has had or consciously desired genital sexual experience with another woman' (1980: 26). Conversely, by the time we get to *Lighthousekeeping*, despite the inclusion of a lesbian love affair later on in the text ('Perhaps it was the light on your face, but I thought I recognised you from somewhere a long way down, somewhere at the bottom of the sea' (200-1)), the only two female characters in it with any *real* shaping influence on Silver's story – Miss Pinch and the librarian – both prove wholly disappointing.

As Winterson enters into this new phase of her writing we wait to see how her female characters will fare as individuals and whether the idea of a primary attachment to *women* (as opposed to an individual woman) will take on renewed relevance. Irrespective of whether it does or not, Winterson's crucial role in the shaping of contemporary literary feminism will certainly remain strong, for in the very power of her writing and her presence as an author of high renown she undoubtedly plays a key role in maintaining the wider collective reputation of contemporary women's writing. Nevertheless, and precisely because of that influential role, what still concerns me is the possibility that those generations of women readers (present and future) who already express scepticism about the need for an ongoing feminist debate may look to Winterson's prioritizing of 'the genderless' as proof of feminism's redundancy. With this cautionary note in mind, my final word goes to Steedman. For despite her awareness of the reductive dangers of collectivism, she nevertheless affirms that we do indeed understand ourselves (past, present and future) primarily 'through the agency of social information, and that interpretation ... can only be made with what people know of a social world and their place within it' (1986: 5). Stories, not just of 'becoming' or 'attachment', but also 'belonging' in relation to other women must continue to matter to women who write and read because – to slightly rephrase a point made earlier on in this chapter – our very belief and pleasure in them ensures their/our success.

Notes

1. In this book Pearce alternates between two different fonts to differentiate between eva-luations of readings she constructed formerly (printed, as here, in sans serif) and readings reflecting her present position (printed in normal typeface).
2. 'Profile of Jeanette Winterson', *The Late Show*, BBC2, first broadcast 10 September 1992.
3. For a fuller discussion of these points see, for instance, Haraway, Donna (1991), *Simians, Cyborgs and Women: The Reinvention of Nature*, London: Free Association Books.

Works cited

Cixous, Hélène (1976), 'The laugh of the Medusa', trans. Keith Cohen and Paula Cohen, in Elaine Marks and Isabelle de Courtivron (eds) (1981), *New French Feminisms: An Anthology*. Brighton: Harvester, pp. 245–64.

Gamble, Sarah (2001), 'Postfeminism', in S. Gamble (ed.), *The Routledge Companion to Feminism and Postfeminism*. London: Routledge, pp. 43–54.

Pearce, Lynne (1995), ' "Written on tablets of stone"?: Jeanette Winterson, Roland Barthes, and the discourse of romantic love', in Suzanne Raitt (ed.), *Volcanoes and Pearl Divers: Essays in Lesbian Feminist Studies*. London: Only-women Press, pp. 147–68.

—— (1997), *Feminism and the Politics of Reading*. London: Arnold.

Rich, Adrienne (1980), 'Compulsory heterosexuality and lesbian existence', in Mary Eagleton (ed.) (1996), *Feminist Literary Theory: A Reader, Second Edition*. Oxford: Blackwell, pp. 24–9.

Russo, Mary (1994), *The Female Grotesque: Risk, Excess and Modernity*. New York: Routledge.

Steedman, Carolyn (1986), *Landscape for a Good Woman: A Story of Two Lives*. London: Virago.

Woolf, Virginia (1920), 'Body and brain', in Mary Lyon (ed.) (1977), *Books and Portraits: Some Further Selections from the Literary and Biographical Writings of Virginia Woolf*. London: Hogarth, pp. 218–21.

—— (1929; 1977), *A Room of One's Own*. London: Grafton.

Winterson, Jeanette (1985), *Oranges Are Not the Only Fruit*. London: Pandora.

—— (1987), *The Passion*. London: Bloomsbury.

—— (1989), *Sexing the Cherry*. London: Bloomsbury.

—— (1992), *Written on the Body*. London: Jonathan Cape.

—— (2000; 2001), *The PowerBook*. London: Vintage.

—— (2004; 2005), *Lighthousekeeping*. London: Harper Perennial.

—— (2006), *Tanglewreck*. London: Bloomsbury.

CHAPTER TWO

Winterson's Dislocated Discourses

HELENA GRICE AND TIM WOODS

Chapter summary: The chapter examines Winterson's work in relation to postmodern theories of narrative, history, subjectivity and science. It explores how Winterson's 'dislocated discourses' call into question a whole host of cultural binaries such as fact/fiction, art/lies, history/ story, science/magic and male/female. While generally approving of Winterson's use of deconstructive strategies, the authors argue that in *Gut Symmetries* her usually careful deconstruction of material and metaphysical realities is undermined by a stereotypical binary opposition between masculine science and feminine intuition.

Key texts: *The Passion; Sexing the Cherry; Gut Symmetries*

Key words: dislocated discourses, deconstruction, postmodernism, binary oppositions, gender relations

I know I am a fool, trying to make connections out of scraps but how else is there to proceed? The fragmentariness of life makes coherence suspect but to babble is a different kind of treachery.

(Winterson 1997: 24)

Storytelling is a way of establishing connections, imaginative connections for ourselves, a way of joining up disparate material and making sense of the world. Human beings love patterns; they love to see shapes and symmetries. We seem to have a need to impose order on our surroundings, which are generally chaotic and often in themselves seem to lack any continuity, any storyline.

(Winterson 2005b: 4)

The workings of narrative or storytelling have always been the key to Winterson's writing. Her fiction frequently calls into question assumptions about narratorial identity, fictional artifice and objective reality, as these are shaped and fashioned by stories. Her novels may be described as 'historiographic metafictions' (Hutcheon 1989: 5), narratives that foreground the recognition that narrative is not objective and that any representation of history is always an ideologically laden discourse.

Indeed, many of Winterson's fictions are engaged in an ironic rethinking of history. For example, in *The Passion*, Henri's narrative is punctuated with a distrust of stories that he relates to the reader. When Patrick describes seeing a man's skin lifted off his back, Henri warns 'Don't believe that one' (Winterson 1987: 23). Again, *The PowerBook* continues Winterson's trademark work at the intersection between the real and the imagined, as the book shifts between the spaces of London, Paris, Capri and cyberspace, fusing cover-versions, fairy tales, contemporary myths and popular culture in a narrative that almost seems to write itself. More recently, the constant request by one of the protagonists in her recently acclaimed novel *Lighthousekeeping*, is to 'Tell me a story, Silver' (Winterson 2005a: 225), which is part of a concerted and sustained investigation of narrative as a means of embracing a wider, non-restricted sense of the world. Everywhere, Winterson constantly foregrounds narrativity, whether it be the patterns of narrative or the fictionality of history. In one interview, she has said: 'People have an enormous need ... to separate history, which is fact, from storytelling, which is not fact ... and the whole push of my work has been to say, you cannot know which is which' (Harthill 1990). Winterson's telling refrain throughout *The Passion*, 'I'm telling you stories. Trust me', fits her fiction squarely within historiographic metafiction's assertion, 'that its world is both resolutely fictive and yet undeniably historical, and that what both realms share is their constitution in and as discourse' (Hutcheon 1989: 142). It is Winterson's exploration of this paradoxical assertion, that narrative embodies and connects lies and truths, that provides the fuel that drives the motor of her fiction (see Grice and Woods 1998).

Winterson's aesthetic of postmodernism

It is this paradoxical assertion that fiction undoes the links between lies and truths, stories and trust, a relationship upon which Winterson preys, that we want to explore as symptomatic of Winterson's 'dislocated discourses'. Jean-François Lyotard argued in *The Postmodern Condition* (1984) that we had entered into what he called a 'crisis of legitimation', meaning that one could no longer conceive of societies as being structured according to certain 'grandes histoires' or 'grand narratives', such as the Enlightenment. Somewhere after the Second World War (some say even earlier), the power of these narratives as socially structuring narratives began to break down. They were replaced by what Lyotard called 'petites histoires' or mini-stories, which were considerably more local in their influence and effect. In this context of crisis, all sorts of certainties have also broken down, or at least been put under severe pressure. In her novel *Sexing the Cherry*, Winterson writes:

Matter, that thing the most solid and well-known, which you are holding in your hands and which makes up your own body, is now known to be mostly empty space. Empty space and points of light. What does this say about the reality of the world?

(Winterson 1989: 8)

We might pose the question slightly differently, asking about the reality or 'reality' of the world. Reference in narratives has always been a thorny issue. The extent to which there is an extralinguistic dimension which can be tangibly known without recourse to textual representation is one of the key areas of debate within the contemporary philosophical and aesthetic currents of postmodernism. Jeanette Winterson's prominence as a contemporary British writer who self-consciously explores the equivocal status of an objective reality is largely due to her persistent metafictional interrogation of the assumptions about narratorial identity, fictional artifice and objective reality. She produces fictions that deconstruct entrenched cultural binaries and hierarchical discourses, showing a crisis of legitimation that is constantly being repaired by recourse to narrative elastoplast.

It is in such an equivocal ontological and uncertain epistemological environment that Linda Hutcheon can write:

> The centre no longer completely holds. And, from the decentred perspective, the 'marginal' and what I shall be calling the 'ex-centric' (be it in class, race, gender, sexual orientation, or ethnicity) take on a new significance in the light of the implied recognition that our culture is not really the homogeneous monolith (that is middle-class, male, heterosexual, white, western) we might have assumed. The concept of alienated otherness (based on binary oppositions that conceal hierarchies) gives way, as I have argued, to that of differences, that is to the assertion, not of centralized sameness, but of decentralized community – another postmodern paradox. The local and the regional are stressed in the face of mass culture and a kind of vast global informational village.
>
> (Hutcheon 1989: 12)

Within this context, narratives begin to emerge that demonstrate an 'incredulity towards grand totalizing narratives', and all those assumptions that used to be embedded in conventional notions of narrative. Indeterminacy and dislocation became watchwords for postmodernism, as various diverse concepts emerge, such as ambiguity, discontinuity, heterodoxy, pluralism, randomness, revolt, perversion, deformation. Through all these signs move a vast will to unmaking and dislocation, a challenge to any system that seeks to unify, control or categorize.

Linda Hutcheon defines 'historiographic metafictions' as a mode in which 'its theoretical self-awareness of history and fiction as human constructs (*historio*graphic meta*fictions*) is made the grounds for its

rethinking and reworking of the forms and contents of the past'
(Hutcheon 1989: 5–6). Hutcheon is talking about how History is a fictional construction; and that once one has made this realization, then it
becomes the basis for rethinking the nature of the past, and how we
relate to it. Hutcheon describes postmodern fiction as a mode which
self-consciously problematizes the making or writing of fiction and
history. Postmodern fiction reveals the past as always ideologically and
discursively constructed. It is a fiction that is directed both inward and
outward, concerned with its status as fiction, narrative or language, and
also grounded in some verifiable historical reality. Postmodernism
tends to use and abuse, install but also subvert, conventions, through
the use of either irony or parody. Pushing at and playing with the limits
of fictionality, the stories and narratives of authors such as John Barth,
Robert Coover, William Gass, Thomas Pynchon, William Gaddis and
Angela Carter increasingly became elaborate forms of complicity
between author, text and reader. Their fiction displays a plurality of
forms, scepticism towards generic types and categories, ironic inver-
sions, a predilection for pastiche and parody, and a metafictional
insistence on the arbitrariness of the text's power to signify. For
example, John Barth's *Lost in the Funhouse* begins with a 'Frame-tale'
that works like a mobius strip:

> Once upon a time there was a story that began
> once upon a time there was a story that began.
>
> (Barth 1969: 1–2)

The tale establishes a parodic model for stories that turn in on themselves, endlessly repeating themselves in increasingly convoluted and
inverted fashion. This play with fictional conventions recurs throughout
the collection of stories:

> I see I see myself as a halt narrative: first person, tiresome. Pronoun sans ante
> or precedent, warrant or respite. Surrogate for the substantive: contentless
> form, interestless principle; blind eye blinking at nothing. Who am I? A little
> *crise d'identité* for you.
>   I must compose myself.
> Look, I'm writing. No, listen, I'm nothing but talk; I won't last long.
>
> (Barth: 33)

In this story, Barth improvises with the notion of whether the existence of a self can or cannot be separated from writing, as well as
exploring ideas of authorial control over the text, and the illusions of the
self-writing or a *writing*-of-the-self embedded in the form of *auto*-
biography. Clearly, this realization of the self as part of a narrative, that
the 'I' is a position mapped out for us by language and narrative
structures, informs our understanding of Winterson's fiction in a
number of ways. For like so many of these postmodern narratives,

Winterson's fiction such as *The Passion, Sexing the Cherry* and *Gut Symmetries* are novels that no longer seek to render the world, but to *make* one from language: fiction is no longer mimetic, but constructive. Representation is no longer to be conceived of as a form of mirror-like *reflection* (the emphasis on this word), but more a form of construction, of making. Indeed, there is a profound consequence to this realization: for if it is recognized that narratives are now the bases upon which societies and worlds exist; and if one can alter the narrative, and get that alteration accepted, then one can actually alter the world. Rather than just being perceived as the creative imaginations and records of daily life, narratives and stories now become the important sites of political and social action. Everything is now seen to be mediated, textualized, or, to go back to our opening, reality is now put in quotation marks – 'reality'. The problem of reference is consequently foregrounded. As one contemporary critic of postmodern fiction states:

> [Postmodernism] revises, indeed transforms, the conventions and norms of historical fiction itself ... with the postmodernist strategy of apocryphal or alternative history. Apocryphal history contradicts the official version in one of two ways: either it *supplements* the historical record, claiming to restore what has been lost or suppressed; or it *displaces* official history altogether. In the first of these cases, apocryphal history operates in the 'dark areas' of history, apparently in conformity to the norms of 'classic' historical fiction but in fact *parodying* them. In the second case, apocryphal history spectacularly violates the 'dark areas' constraint. In both cases, the effect is to juxtapose the officially-accepted version of what happened and the way things were, with another, often radically dissimilar version of the world. The tension between these two versions induces a form of ontological flicker between the two worlds: one moment, the official version seems to be eclipsed by the apocryphal version; the next moment, it is the apocryphal version that seems mirage-like, the official version appearing solid, irrefutable.
>
> (McHale 1987: 90)

So, postmodern fiction seeks to insert into the crevices of history, overlooked, censored, forgotten, marginalized, or otherwise eccentric aspects, and makes its narratives by, in a sense, supplementing history, filling it out.

Dislocated spaces in *The Passion*

The Passion demonstrates a 'dark area' of apocryphal history, producing a history that 'flickers' between historical and imaginative versions of Napoleonic Europe. In terms of a narrative that supplements 'official' history, we get the rise of Napoleon from the singular perspective of the young French peasant Henri, the Emperor Napoleon's chicken-chef; and the stories of Venice from Villanelle, a sort of magical figure with webbed feet, certainly not from the conventions of realist narrative. The magic is a way of decentring the realism, or suggesting an alternative way of life. Winterson is always interested in those aspects that are covered up by narratives. At the beginning of her novel *Sexing the Cherry*, the protagonist states: 'Every journey conceals another journey within its lines: the path not taken and the forgotten angle. These are journeys I wish to record. Not the ones I made, but the ones I might have made, or perhaps did make in some other place or time' (Winterson 1989: 1). In Winterson's mock-historical novel, *The Passion*, her two main protagonists argue about the usefulness of maps to negotiate early-nineteenth-century Venice. Villanelle responds to Henri's request for a map to negotiate the labyrinthine twists and turns of the city by saying: 'It won't help. This is a living city. Things change' (Winterson 1987: 113). The social space of the city is created by the journeys that people make, and, as such, is not represented on any map: 'The cities of the interior do not lie on any map' (114). Any secure cognitive knowledge of the city is completely unrealizable and rebutted, as each journey creates a new route:

> This city enfolds upon itself. Canals hide other canals, alley-ways cross and criss-cross so that you will not know which is which until you have lived here all your life. Even when you have mastered the squares and you can pass from the Rialto to the Ghetto and out to the lagoon with confidence, there will still be places you can never find ... be prepared to go another way, to do something not planned if that is where the streets lead you.
>
> (113)

As a labyrinthine space, it becomes a subjective space, a city constructed by its inhabitants and their pedestrian trajectories. The volatile city of Venice refuses the totalizing effects of mapping. J. B. Harley, a cartographer urging the necessity of deconstructing the textuality of maps, has argued that 'All maps employ the common devices of rhetoric such as invocations of authority' (1989: 11). In her later novel, *Sexing the Cherry*, Winterson is even more sceptical:

> A map can tell me how to find a place I have not seen but have often imagined. When I get there, following the map faithfully, the place is not the place of my imagination. Maps, growing ever more real, are much less true.
>
> (Winterson 1989: 81)

Although maps purport to accurately represent places, they actually produce ideological spaces, and in so doing ignore human experiences of spaces. Maps have invisible spaces within them, unspoken and unwritten places: 'every mapped-out journey contains another journey hidden in its lines' (Winterson 1989: 23). Harley makes a similar observation, by asking 'where is the space-time of human experience in such anonymized maps?' (1989: 14). Harley is particularly concerned with the way in which traditional and scientific cartography is predisposed to lose its hold on the lived world. Maintaining that cartography is ineluctably a form of power, Harley persuasively argues that maps are motivated by an impulse to synthesize alterity, to tame it and bring it back to the knowable, in the desire to contain and represent lived experience with abstract notions of space. Henri's prior experience of space has been derived from the military campaigns of the French emperor who initiated Haussmann's rationalization of Parisian space; it is a rational, fixed dimension that can be mapped, located and occupied: 'Where Bonaparte goes, straight roads follow, buildings are rationalised, street signs may change to celebrate a battle but they are always clearly marked' (Winterson 1987: 112). Winterson's Venice represents a promise of possibility lying untapped in the history of space, which has been displaced from the contemporary world.

It is these possibilities, untapped because ignored or censored, or marginalized, that Winterson seeks to revitalize or reinvoke. Yet Winterson is interested not only in how narratives cover up things, but also in the journey as a metaphor for encountering the unnatural, the strange, or the other. So in *The Passion*, she writes:

> How is it that one day life is orderly and you are content, a little cynical perhaps but on the whole just so, and then without warning you find the solid floor is a trapdoor and you are now in another place whose geography is uncertain and whose customs are strange?
>
> Travellers at least have a choice. Those who set sail know that things will not be the same as at home. Explorers are prepared. But for us, who travel along the blood vessels, who come to the cities of the interior by chance, there is no preparation. We who were fluent find life is a foreign language.
>
> (Winterson 1987: 68)

Here is another example of the 'dark area' of history: how things transmute from the familiar into the unknown and unexpected in a quick flash; or how rather, looked at from one perspective, things are familiar, whereas looked at from another perspective, they are completely unknown. So we get the constant refrain throughout the novel: 'I'm telling you stories. Trust me'. But by now, we realize that stories are a very problematic basis for trust, since they are fictions. Winterson (and postmodern fiction generally) can have it both ways, since postmodernism has argued that fictions are also the *only* basis upon which to create a world – so what else is there?

Displaced subjectivities in *Sexing the Cherry*

Consider the two epigraphs to *Sexing the Cherry*: one from the Sapir-Whorf thesis about the extent to which the world is constructed by a culture's language; the other about the substance of the world and its reality. Both point to representation as a powerful and vital tool in the world. As we have argued, Winterson's fiction constantly makes insertions into History (for example, *Boating for Beginners*, in which the story of Noah and the Ark is treated from a specifically feminist angle). Frequently history and myths are rewritten to highlight the gender bias in their perspective, and to address the question of 'what about the women?'. *Sexing the Cherry* describes how the narrator constantly feels her subjectivity escapes her, how it is 'squashed between the facts', 'trying to catch myself disappearing through a door just noticed in the wall' (Winterson 1989: 10). Yet the protagonist is later caught wondering about the epistemological and ontological necessity of plotting space: 'But does it matter if the place cannot be mapped as long as I can still describe it?' (15). The narratorial 'I' in the novel shifts, from the Dog Woman to her son Jordan, searching for the dancer. In Jordan's adopted guise of a woman, he learns about the female world-view, one in which his world is decentred by no longer being the principal actor and by hearing masculinity gulled and trivialized by women who see men as 'children with too much pocket money' (32). Explorations into the nature of subjectivity lead to theories of the self as able to transcend time and space in (the imagination?) the construction of a new concept of time and space as flexible and at the command of the self: 'Time has no meaning, space and place have no meaning, on this journey. All times can be inhabited, all places visited. In a single day the mind can make a millpond of the oceans' (80). *Sexing the Cherry* concerns spaces that remain as yet undiscovered despite the explorations made by humanity on the face of the earth. This in turn affects the conception of time in the novel, as it repeatedly dislocates our conventional under-standing of time, questioning the metaphysical conceptions of time erected by language (89–90). Within this dislocation of space-time, the novel asks one of the central postmodern questions about the relativity and certainty of epistemology: 'Maps are being re-made as knowledge appears to increase. But is knowledge increasing or is detail accumu-lating?' (81). If you want a catalogue of the propositions which a defi-nition of postmodernism might contain, then it would embrace those areas listed as 'lies' (83). They are propositions that subvert the nature of any essentialist theories, objectivist theories, totalizing theories, onto-logical theories. Winterson's world is not simply one of facts, but one of stories and narratives, which are folded within each other; hence, the realms of the aesthetic and the imagination assume a new importance. This is a novel that extols the realm of the aesthetic, set against the pure empirical world, releasing the realm of the imagination to form other important and acceptable places that need exploring. Like so much of Angela Carter's fiction (for example, *The Infernal Desire Machines of Doctor Hoffman*), *Sexing the Cherry* is about the insertion of fantasy into what is taken to be reality, or history, and the supposed fixed opposition of these two categories. What appears to be a history of the English Civil War, and the early seventeenth century, turns out to hide the myths of the Dog Woman and the 12 dancing princesses.

Gut forces and gut feelings

Structuralism was a movement in the 1960s that invited readers to see patterns in discourses. It was in fact what one might call a unified theory, seeking to combine structure with figure. It sought to make explicit the hidden structures of narratives, structures which were only evident on the recognition of the functionality of discourses. In Roland Barthes's hands, structuralism made the latent manifest. Yet post-structuralism demonstrated the limitations and fallacies of such an entrenched view of a rationalizable world, ushering in a new post-modern lexicon of slippage, fluidity and dynamism to counter the discursive concepts of fixity, encompassment and immobility.

In a review of *Gut Symmetries*, Katy Emck cogently describes the 'three voices' of Jeanette Winterson: firstly, the 'fairground conjuring act', that translates as Winterson's predilection for magic realist embellishments of her work; the 'human textbook', those postmodernist views of history, narrative, reality, and those Grand Theories cribbed from Newton, Einstein, Hawking and co.; and, finally, 'the voice of lyric love', concerning the triangular love plot between Jove and his wife Stella, and their independent yet mutual lover, Alice (Emck 1997: 21). This voice of lyric love speaks in all of Winterson's novels, from Villa-nelle's (the very name a form of lyric) to Lothario's, Jeanette's to Jordan's. With these three voices speaking loud and clear, *Gut Symmetries* occupies familiar Winterson postmodern territory, territory already charted and demarcated by the literary explorations of earlier novels like *Sexing the Cherry* and *Written on the Body*. The novel broaches a series of Grand Theoretical Concerns, that coincide with many of the preoccupations of contemporary critical and scientific theory: the nature and nostalgia of history, the binary structure of Western thought, the space–time continuum, desire, 'reality', fictionality, chance and prediction. Yet, as with Winterson's previous novels, these concerns constitute only part of the narrative, that which serves as a portentous and erudite commentary upon the main preoccupations of the story. *Gut Symmetries* is another reworking of the urge to discover a fundamental structure to all the natural phenomena in the universe. Playing with patterns at every turn in this novel, Winterson sets up a world that is torn between an essential structure and a denial of totalizing patterns. Beginning with the 'Prologue' and the introduction of the medieval alchemist Paracelsus, who 'was a student of Correspondences: "As above, so below"' (Winterson 1997: 2), who thought that 'The zodiac in the sky is imprinted in the body. "The galaxa goes through the belly"' (2), Winterson establishes a complex and elaborate set of parallels and connections between ancient and medieval theories of matter, Newtonian physics, contemporary cosmology, numerology, the Tarot and astrology. *Gut Symmetries* involves an extended pun on 1) the twentieth-century search for a 'Grand Unified Theory' (a 'GUT') of scientific forces in theoretical physics, begun with Einstein and continued today in the discoveries of 'Superstring Theory'; and 2) 'gut feelings', or something felt in the gut, i.e. intuitively. This establishes an opposition between thinking and feeling, rationality and mystery, materiality and metaphysics. In this respect, Winterson's novel is something of a large conceptual linguistic game; yet it is a novel that sometimes loses itself in the trickeries of its playful parallels, and ultimately produces a narrative that falls apart rather than falls together.

Jove, the central male character, is a theoretical physicist studying at the Princeton Advanced Institute for Physics, and his field is 'Superstring theory' and the search for a 'GUT'. The most fundamental theory of this sort that is largely confirmed by experiment is the 'Standard Model' of three interactions: electromagnetic, weak and strong nuclear. Yet the trouble with the Standard Model is that it does not incorporate that most fundamental force known to science: gravity. This search is motivated by the urge to discover a fundamental theory underpinning all natural phenomena. This urge is not new, since even ancient Greek science sought to reduce the world to the elemental 'earth, air, fire and water' structure. Twentieth-century science now works on smaller particles, but the urge is still evident.

The development of a unified theory has preoccupied cosmologists since Einstein, and, if discovered, would entail a great deal of mathematical consistency and inner beauty. String theory has finally emerged as a promising candidate for a unified theory, based as it is on an elegantly simple but beautiful notion (for a brief layperson's guide to 'Superstring theory', see Anthony 1985; for a more sophisticated treatment, see Hawking 1988). Instead of many types of elementary point-like particles, it has been suggested that there is a single variety of string-like objects. As with musical strings, this basic string can vibrate, and each vibrational mode can be viewed as a point-like elementary particle, just as the modes of a musical string are perceived as different and distinct notes. As Alice notes within the novel, 'When gravity and GUTs unite? Listen: one plays the lute and another the harp. The strings are vibrating and from the music of the spheres a perfect universe is formed' (Winterson 1997: 100–1). Once again, the novel hints at a metaphysical solution, this time embedded in a Pythagorean cosmology of a 'harmony of the spheres'.

Winterson has cannily latched on to the recent debates within theoretical physics as a means of providing her with a central metaphor to describe her postmodern sense of the instability and perpetual flux of the universe. In addition to superstrings, Winterson has also appropriated the terminology of quantum physics, the indeterminacy principle and the general theory of relativity, as discourses allied to the postmodern discourse on epistemological insecurity and ontological instability. As the characters constantly muse, their own identities are equally unstable:

> Any measurement must take into account the position of the observer. There is no such thing as measurement absolute, there is only measurement relative. Relative to what is an important part of the question.
>
> This has been my difficulty. The difficulty of my life. Those well-built trip points, those physical determinants of parents, background, school, family, birth, marriage, death, love, work, are themselves as much in motion as I am. What should be stable, shifts. What I am told is solid, slips. The sensible strong ordinary world of fixity is a folklore.
>
> (Winterson 1997: 9–10)

Much of this derives from the impact of quantum physics, which has destroyed the security of 'the mechanistic, deterministic mind/matter of cosmic reality' (Winterson 1997: 11). The characters' general instability of identity, in which there is no secure knowledge of being, occurs everywhere: 'What or who? I cannot name myself. The alchemists worked with a magic mirror, using reflections to guide them. The hall of mirrors set around me has been angled to distort. Is that me in the shopglass? Is that me in the family photo? Is that me in the office window? Is that me in the silvered pages of a magazine? Is that me in the broken bottles on the street? Everywhere I go, reflection. Everywhere a caught image of who I am. In all of that who am I?' (12).

Winterson's novel is self-consciously written with full knowledge of theoretical discussions concerning the indeterminate slippage of sign and object in post-structuralist philosophy, not least the way in which deconstruction has sought to overturn the metaphysical and ideological hierarchies of binary oppositions that structure our lives. On the one hand, the novel establishes the world as a series of material relations that are always available to scientific rationalization and empirical experiment, even if the conclusions are that of random dispersion and dissipative energies. However, the novel also invokes irrational cosmologies, the non-rational and the metaphysical dimension of life. This is also played out in the dimension of time: 'Past. Present. Future. The rational divisions of the rational life. And always underneath, in dreams, in recollections, in the moment of hesitation on a busy street, the hunch that life is not rational, not divided. That the mirrored compartments could break' (20). Temporal narratives invite us to think

of all discourse as taking the form of a story. The cognitively fragmented world in which Alice lives may excite longings for metanarra-
tives that explain everything, but they actually turn out only to give her
the *illusion* of mending her fragmentation. At another moment, Winterson describes that archetypal scientist, Einstein, as a mystic, someone
in love with the power of numbers, almost a numerologist (23). The
function of the Tarot within the novel is part of this non-materialist
dimension, cards which structure the chapter divisions, as well as
gesturing towards the characteristics of the individual protagonists:
Alice the Fool; Jove the Knave of Coins; Stella the Star. A further
symbolic layer in the novel emerges with the Tarot's connection to the
Jewish mystical Kabbalah, in which arcane and secret mysteries Stella's
father is deeply involved: 'Every blade of grass that grows here on earth
has its corresponding influence in the stars. This is the Mazalot' (77). In
a somewhat romanticized view of enigmatic Judaism, the magic of the
Torah and the Kabbalistic frame of mind match the astrological pat-
terning in the Tarot. Indeed, the Tarot partly has its roots in the Jewish
Kabbalistic tradition. Later in the novel, this parallel is made more
explicit:

> Is truth what we do not know?
>
> What we know does not satisfy us. What we know constantly reveals itself
> as partial. What we know, generation by generation, is discarded into new
> knowings which in their turn slowly cease to interest us.
>
> In the Torah, the Hebrew 'to know', often used in a sexual context, is not
> about facts but about connotations. Knowledge, not as accumulation but as
> charge and discharge. A release of energy from one site to another. Instead of
> a hoard of certainties, bug-collected, to make me feel secure, I can give up
> taxonomy and invite myself to the dance: the patterns, rhythms, multi-
> plicities, paradoxes, shifts, currents, cross-currents, irregularities, irrational-
> ities, geniuses, joints, pivots, worked over time, and through time, to find the
> lines of thought that still transmit.
>
> The facts cut me off. The clean boxes of history, geography, science, art.
> What is the separateness of things when the current that flows through each
> to each is live?
>
> (Winterson 1997: 82–3)

Stella, as a poet, espouses a view of the world that is mystical and
eschews the rigidity of disciplinary thought that seeks to categorize
knowledge in specific pigeonholes. She is far more interested in a fluid
concept of interrelationships between things, in some ways more
attuned to the vibrations of the cosmos than Jove with all his mathematical and theoretical paraphernalia. However, this deconstruction of
the poet and the scientist shatters when it later transpires that the
Kabbalist (Stella's father) was in correspondence with the quantum
scientists (Winterson 1997: 168).

Conclusion

Gut Symmetries thus constantly hinges upon the opposition of the material and the metaphysical, the rational and the irrational. Gradually, the novel establishes positions concerning temporality and epistemology as gender positions (see Grice and Woods, 1998: 121–5). In this deconstruction of heteropatriarchal structures, *Gut Symmetries* is paradigmatic of the ideological critique in Winterson's fiction. Her fiction repeatedly utilizes the devices common to postmodern discourses for its own critical ends, as it attempts to lever open the hypocritical practices of patriarchy, the sources and modes of male sexual power, and whether in fact they should be treated with the hierarchical respect with which men have sought to endow such structures. Her novels are filled with positive female figures, all of whom manage to gull or overcome male restrictions: the dancing princesses, Pope Joan, the Dog Woman, Fortunata and Silver. Yet despite Winterson's attempts to deconstruct binary oppositions in her fiction, she does occasionally lapse into some rather tired gendered stereotypes on a number of occasions. The engendering of science versus mystery in *Gut Symmetries* is a wholly stereotypical gendered structure that certainly does not escape from patriarchal notions of the male as a rigorous thinker, and the female as a vaguely impressionistic feeler. Winterson does try to deconstruct this opposition to some extent, by, for example, throwing a spanner in the works of binary oppositions like male/female or husband/wife, by establishing a triangular structure, a threesome, male/female/female, or husband/wife/female lover. In this way, Winterson seeks to disrupt the orthodox sexual power relations that have been established via the sexual and social hegemony of conventional heterosexual relationships. Yet once again, the novel does seem to lapse into some trite formulations about gender and this triadic structure in its dramatic mention of 'The Eternal Triangle' (Winterson 1997: 200–1). Nonetheless, Winterson's efforts at altering hierarchical structures and gendered assumptions are ultimately driven by an overriding sense that such dislocated discourses are vital to reassert a form of energizing agency in the face of an overwhelming empiricism:

> I believe that storytelling is a way of navigating our lives, and that to read ourselves as fiction is much more liberating than to read ourselves as fact. Facts are partial. Fiction is a much more complete truth. If we read ourselves as literal and fixed, we find we can change nothing. Someone will always tell the story of our lives – it had better be ourselves.
>
> (Winterson 2005c: 20).

Works cited

Anthony, Simon (1985), 'Superstrings: A theory of everything?', *New Scientist*, 107, 29 August, 34–6.

Barth, John (1969), *Lost in the Funhouse*. New York: Bantam.

Emck, Katy (1997), 'Gut symmetries', *Times Literary Supplement*, 3 January, 21.

Grice, Helena and Woods, Tim (1998), *'I'm Telling you Stories': Jeanette Winterson and the Politics of Reading*. Amsterdam and Atlanta, GA: Rodopi.

Harley, J. B. (1989), 'Deconstructing the Map', *Cartographica*, 26, (2), 1–20.

Harthill, Rosemary (1990), 'Writers revealed', Radio 4, Autumn.

Hawking, Stephen (1988), *A Brief History of Time: From the Big Bang to Black Holes*. Toronto: Bantam.

Hutcheon, Linda (1989), *A Poetics of Postmodernism*. London: Routledge.

Lyotard, J.-F. (1984), *The Postmodern Condition: A Report on Knowledge*. Trans. Geoff Bennington and Brian Massumi. Manchester: Manchester University Press.

McHale, Brian (1987), *Postmodernist Fiction*. London: Routledge.

Winterson, Jeanette (1987), *The Passion*. London: Penguin.

—— (1989), *Sexing the Cherry*. London: Vintage.

—— (1990), 'Interview', *Spare Rib*, 209, 26–9.

—— (1997), *Gut Symmetries*. London: Granta.

—— (2000), *The PowerBook*. London: Jonathan Cape.

—— (2005a), *Lighthousekeeping*. London: Harperperennial.

—— (2005b), 'P.S. About the author', Appendix interview with Louise Tucker. *Lighthousekeeping*. London: Harperperennial, p. 4.

—— (2005c), 'Endless possibilities'. Appendix essay to *Lighthousekeeping*. London: Harperperennial, pp. 18–23.

CHAPTER THREE

Winterson's Fabulous Bodies

JANE HASLETT

Chapter summary: Haslett's chapter examines Winterson's treatment of the body from the perspective of feminist and queer theory, arguing that Winterson creates a series of fabulous bodies which defy conventional and frequently oppressive definitions of gender and sexuality. Drawing on Russo's work on the female grotesque, Butler's theories of gender as performance and queer models of transgender identity, the chapter argues that Villanelle's transgendered body, Dog Woman's grotesque body, and *Written*'s genderless narrator are all variously queer bodies, which challenge sexual stereotypes and conceptions of the natural body, and thus foster a new sexual politics based on difference and diversity.

Key texts: *The Passion*; *Sexing the Cherry*; *Written on the Body*

Key words: the body, feminism, the fantastic, gender as performance, the grotesque, queer theory, transgender, diversity

Only by imagining what we might be can we become more than we are.
(Winterson, 1986)

Creating fabulous bodies has become a major industry these days. Cosmetic and reconstructive surgeries are common, and new technologies which allow bodies to be shaped and enhanced in endless ways are proliferating. People are increasingly realizing the power of a positive body image, and taking a proactive part in (re)creating their bodies. Jeannette Winterson was ahead of her time in demonstrating how powerfully bodies, even fictional ones, can affect one's idea of self, and she particularly aimed this message at women. In her first non-fiction text, *Fit for the Future* (1986), Winterson encourages women to have 'a lively, irrepressible and highly personal relationship with your own body' and to cultivate its strength (1). Three of Winterson's subsequent novels, *The Passion* (1988), *Sexing the Cherry* (1990) and *Written on the Body* (1992), contain characters which have this kind of relationship with their bodies, and all have fabulous bodies.

The body of Dog Woman, one of the two main characters in *Sexing the Cherry*, dominates the novel. Dog Woman relates to her body in the way

Villanelle's body continuously questions the nature of passion in various situations where passions for sex, love, religion, food and gambling intertwine throughout the novel, and it appears in a dizzying array of guises. Winterson offers no answers to the questions posed by Villanelle's fabulous body. Instead, she uses it to query a number of diverse and often ambivalent attitudes toward the notion of passion as she explores and interweaves the passions of the soldier Henri, Napoleon, Villanelle, Henri, a casino patron/army cook, and gamblers, in a series of vignettes and stories. Villanelle's body moves among these stories like a will-o-the-wisp, illuminating them fitfully but ambiguously, with her body taking on a different aspect in each situation.

The fabulous body of Villanelle is the only body in the novel with divine attributes. In a Christ-like fashion, she can walk on water. Winterson's representation of Villanelle's body exemplifies aspects of feminist Biblical revisionism (Ostriker 1992). It projects a shameless sexuality, an insistence on sensual immediacy, flesh seen as holy, and a compatibility between flesh and intellect. This body also forces a reader to imagine faith and spirituality extending beyond the Bible and religious institutions into areas eschewed by traditional interpretations of the Bible. Thus, Winterson troubles the traditional dominant reading of Biblical narrative by inscribing difference on Villanelle's body itself. However, Winterson moves even further from a traditional Biblical narrative to inscribe difference on and through Villanelle's body by presenting it as the body of a freak. Elizabeth Grosz, in her unpublished essay 'Freaks', posits:

> [T]he freak is an object of simultaneous horror and fascination because, in addition to whatever infirmities and abilities he or she exhibits, he or she is an *ambiguous* being, a being whose existence imperils categories and oppositions dominant in social life. Freaks are those human beings who exist outside the structure of binary oppositions which govern our basic concepts and modes of self-definition. ... Freaks cross the borders which divide the subject off from all ambiguities, interconnections and reciprocal classifications. They imperil the very definitions we rely on to classify humans, identities, sexes – our most fundamental categories of self-definition.
>
> (3)

Mary Russo links this notion of the freak to the notion of the divine when she comments: 'the tradition of the freak as monster – literally, the de-*monstrater* of the marvelous power of the divine – has a long history in European culture' (1994: 75). Thus Villanelle, who begins life in the midst of a series of omens that all point simultaneously to the monstrous and the divine, has historical antecedents, but Winterson adds further complications to her character: Villanelle's body is that of a hermaphrodite. It is a queer body.

Discussing Villanelle's extraordinary and complex body is a task which stretches the imagination as much as Winterson could wish, but she provides a clue in her character's name. According to *The New Princeton Encyclopedia of Poetry and Poetics*, edited by Alex Preminger and T. V. F. Brogan, a villanelle is a musical and poetic form, originally from Italy, introduced into France in the sixteenth century, and later into England. Dylan Thomas, Theodore Roethke, Sylvia Plath and Elizabeth Bishop, among others, have written villanelles. The villanelle has been described as a plait of gold and silver threads into which is woven a third, rose-coloured thread; the metallic, unyielding character of the refrains is an emotional fact which the rose-coloured thread of the intellect, in the various gyrations of the poem, tries in vain to escape. The lines of the rose-coloured thread have been characterized as attempting to withstand the conspiracy of the refrains and to assert change and mortality, thus having a peculiar poignancy and vulnerability.

Her name thus gives Winterson's Villanelle a form or structure, containing 'refrains' of recurring themes of obsession and destiny, and a 'rose-coloured thread' of change and mortality, which can be seen reflected in her body: her physical body echoes the body of the verse form. The most dominant refrains of Winterson's Villanelle, the 'plait of gold and silver threads', are her webbed feet and games of chance, while her heart is the 'rose-coloured strand' of the villanelle, appearing again and again in different guises, always when Villanelle is attempting to counteract the control over her life maintained by the two dominant refrains.

Villanelle's webbed feet, the aspects of her body that make her a freak, are the most dominant refrain connected with her body. Traditionally only males in a boatman's family have webbed feet. Therefore, at birth, her mother agrees that the midwife should attempt to cut the webs between Villanelle's toes, but this proves unsuccessful. Her distraught mother is not comforted until Villanelle's stepfather points out that with shoes the webs will be invisible. The reactions of horror, surgical intervention and erasure of difference shown here have been typical ones historically for parents and caretakers faced with a sexually ambiguous infant body, and these reactions still exist in our present culture. As Julia Epstein argues,

> the transvestite gesture signals the possibility that the social body is as fluid as the private body's drapery and that the gender definitions regulating the social order may shift and mutate. The anatomically ambiguous individual is even more threatening. Hermaphrodites ... have historically posed epistemological challenges to definitions of natural boundaries and to the very notion of gender clarity itself.
>
> (1990: 100)

Epstein notes that hermaphrodites have traditionally been fitted into teratology (the study of monsters); historically, the mark of ambiguity

originates in the genitals, and hermaphrodites in antiquity were frequently put to death (100-1). Although medical science now understands sexual development anomalies, according to Epstein, 'in a
curious way, the results of total medicalization return us to the semiotics of teratology: individuals with gender disorders are permitted to
live, but the disorders themselves are rendered invisible, are seen as
social stigmata to be excised in the operating room. Difference, again, is
erased' (116). Thus, Villanelle's webbed feet can be read as a metaphor
for male genitalia, and Villanelle's body can be seen as hermaphroditic,
and its reception in the novel replicates that often given to hermaphroditic bodies in present white Western culture. She is prevented from
working on the boats (traditionally work for men, who have webbed
feet) by the erasure of the male aspect of her body which she is forbidden to display. Instead, she finds work in a gambling casino, which
brings her in contact with games of chance and connects the two
dominant refrains of her villanelle. There, however, Villanelle resists an
easy gender categorization by performing the hermaphroditic aspect of
her body. Villanelle's webbed feet may be physically hidden at the
casino, but she, instead of assuming a female identity which would be
upheld by the secondary sex characteristics of her undressed body,
assumes a male identity, upheld only by her invisible webbed feet, by
cross-dressing as a male. She is performing gender in the manner discussed by Judith Butler in her near contemporaneous and paradigm-
shifting text, *Gender Trouble: Feminism and the Subversion of Identity*
(1990).

When Villanelle describes her cross-dressing, she exemplifies the idea
that pleasure is constituted through the often contradictory economic,
political, and ideological production of social life, and its hegemonic
articulation is always precarious (Hennessy 1994). Villanelle's relation
to the pleasure she describes is complicated. She cross-dresses not just
for her own pleasure, but for economic profit:

> I dressed as a boy because that's what the visitors liked to see. It was part of
> the game, trying to decide which sex was hidden behind tight breeches and
> extravagant face-paste. ... I made up my lips with vermilion and overlaid
> my face with white powder. I had no need to add a beauty spot, having one
> of my own in just the right place. I wore my yellow Casino breeches with the
> stripe down each side of the leg and a pirate's shirt that concealed my
> breasts. This was required, but the moustache I added was for my own
> amusement. And perhaps for my own protection.
>
> (1988: 54-5)

Potential violence towards women thus joins economics to further
complicate Villanelle's relation to pleasure and sexuality. Villanelle
knows that one physically repellent but wealthy casino patron comes to
play games of chance with her specifically because of his fascination

with her sexually ambiguous body: 'now and again I wear a codpiece to taunt him. My breasts are small, so there's no cleavage to give me away, and I'm tall for a girl' (56). Although Villanelle knows that this man has a passion for her androgynous body, she feels that physical sexual ambiguity is another matter: 'I wonder what he'd say to my feet' (56). Pragmatically, Villanelle considers marrying him: 'He has promised to keep me in luxury and all kinds of fancy goods, provided I go on dressing as a young man in the comfort of our own home' (63). Villanelle's body thus demonstrates that in the realm of queer politics, because of economics and potential physical danger, women occupy a different place than men, a place that has material consequences for her body. When Villanelle rejects the advances of the casino patron, he rapes her, but later she marries him for his money, even though she despises him (64, 96). When she leaves him, he gains his revenge by selling her as a whore into the French army (99). Economics and the femaleness of her body thus restrict Villanelle from displaying 'in your face' queer defiance, and demonstrate how women and men are positioned differently by their bodies even in a queer culture.

The sexual ambiguity of her body proves attractive also to a mysterious female casino patron. She invites Villanelle to dinner, causing Villanelle to ponder the meaning of her body once again: 'She thought I was a young man. I was not. Should I go to see her as myself and joke about the mistake and leave gracefully? ... And what was myself? Was this breeches and boots any less real than my garters? What was it about me that interested her?' (65–6). Villanelle's sexually ambiguous body is put to the test when the passion between Villanelle and the woman leads to physical intimacy. The woman asks to stroke Villanelle's feet, provoking great alarm: 'Sweet Madonna, not my feet' (70). She then asks Villanelle to take off her shirt, which Villanelle does (71). Villanelle is willing to expose herself as a cross-dresser, but not as a hermaphrodite, and her actions demonstrate that a cross-dresser and a hermaphrodite have very different options open to them. A cross-dresser, with only one gender inscribed on her or his body, can choose to perform it or the opposite gender at will, but if naked, becomes visually a female or male body. A cross-dresser's body becomes queer through choice of clothing. A hermaphrodite's body, containing a mixture of female and male gender characteristics, can perform a female or male gender when clothed, but is discovered when naked to be intrinsically and unalterably queer, subject to shame and rejection. Judith Butler's notion of gender as performance appears to work better with the notion of a clothed, rather than a naked, body, and it also requires an essentialist, heterosexual model of gender for the performance of a gender to have any impact. Villanelle signals such a gender performance when she appears to her female lover in a soldier's uniform, calling it 'fancy dress' (70). Here, she chooses to present her body to the woman she loves as a cross-dressed lesbian body, a normal female body, rather than a hermaphroditic body, the body of a freak, a queer body. Similarly, when Villanelle later meets Henri, a soldier in the French army who falls in love with her, she displays the same willingness to expose her lesbian desire while telling the story of her life to the soldiers (94). However, she will not display her webbed feet, the mark of her queer sexuality, despite Henri's curiosity, and he wonders why she never takes her boots off, even in bed (109).

Villanelle's determined and continued erasure of her biological difference relates to the desire of people stigmatized as 'queer' to disappear into normal society. According to Sandy Stone, many transsexuals engage in the process of 'constructing a plausible history – learning to lie about one's past. What is gained is acceptability in society. What is lost is the ability to represent authentically the complexities and ambiguities of lived experience' (1992: 164, emphasis in original). Villanelle echoes this idea when she comments: 'I began to feel like Sarpi, that Venetian priest and diplomat, who said he never told a lie but didn't tell the truth to everyone. Many times that evening as we ate and drank and played dice I prepared to explain. But my tongue thickened and my heart rose up in self-defence' (1988: 70). Stone goes on to state 'The most critical thing a transsexual can do, the thing that constitutes success, is to "pass". Passing means to live successfully in the gender of choice, to be accepted as a "natural" member of that gender. Passing means the denial of mixture' (1992: 165–6). Having a hermaphroditic body is, of course, not the same thing as being a transsexual; it does not mean that one has lived one gender for a time, and then switched to another. It does, however, mean suppressing the truth of one's body, and 'passing' as a gender that is not ambiguous; it does entail the denial of mixture, the erasure of difference, and the obliteration of bodily complexity. When Villanelle takes off her boots and walks on the water in full view of Henri, she performs a political act that Stone urges transsexuals to accomplish: 'to be consciously "read", to read oneself aloud – and by this troubling and productive reading, to begin to *write oneself* into the discourses by which one has been written – in effect, then, to become a ... posttranssexual' (1992: 168). In an afterword, Stone points to the subsequent development of a specifically transgendered positionality which has changed the situation of the transsexual both on the street and in the academy (1992: 168).

Similarly, Anne Bolin argues that transsexualism challenges the biological basis of gender and provides an alternative to a polarized system (with transsexuals and transvestites dichotomized as variant women and men): a system in which a continuum and a multiplicity of social identities are recognized and encouraged. She sees *transgenderist* as a community term denoting kinship among those with gender-variant identities, supplanting the dichotomy of transsexual and tranvestite with a concept of continuity (1994: 461). From this perspective, Villanelle's body can be termed a transgendered body, and her body, coupled with her lesbian desire, elaborates Bolin's view that: 'The transgenderist has pushed the parameters of the gender paradigm even further by disputing the entire concept of consistency between sexual orientation and gender' (1994: 485).

An important part of Villanelle's transgendered body – her heart – plays a major and complicated role in *The Passion*. It is through the metaphor of Villanelle's heart, the 'rose-coloured thread' of her villanelle, that the reader views her struggles to deal with the 'plait of gold and silver', the obsession and destiny, of her webbed feet and games of chance, the inescapable influences in her life. The journey of her heart takes her towards self-discovery, and an understanding of her own lesbian passion. It begins in the casino, where her first introduction to passion is watching the gamblers: 'I like to smell the urgency on them. Even the calmest, the richest, have that smell. It's somewhere between fear and sex. Passion I suppose' (1988: 55). Villanelle sees herself as exempt from a gambler's passion, and immune to the passion of love:

> Passion is sweeter split strand by strand. Divided and re-divided like mercury then gathered up only at the last moment. You see, I am no stranger to love. ... I am pragmatic about love and have taken my pleasure with both men and women, but I have never needed a guard for my heart. My heart is a reliable organ.
>
> (59–60)

Therefore, when Villanelle meets a captivating masked woman at the casino, she believes that gambling with her heart is no different than gambling for any other wager and comments naively, 'You play, you win. You play, you lose. You play' (66). Later, a chastened Villanelle realizes what she has lost: 'It was a game of chance I entered into and my heart was the wager. Such games can only be played once. Such games are better not played at all' (94). Villanelle's married lover does not return Villanelle's passion in kind, and Villanelle realizes that gambling on love can be a disastrous enterprise: 'The gambler is led on in the hope of a win, thrilled with the fear of losing, and when he wins, he believes his luck is there, that he will win again ... all the time losing bit by bit that valuable fabulous thing that can never be replaced' (95–6).

The loss of her heart causes changes in Villanelle's body which signal that her body, the barometer of her emotions, is out of control. She is distracted, cannot eat or sleep regularly, loses weight, and is cold (62–3). Even her heart itself is no longer a reliable organ: 'If you should leave me, my heart will turn to water and flood away' (73, 76). Instead, Villanelle's heart becomes physically possessed by her female lover, who plans to weave it into a tapestry where she could keep it imprisoned forever. Through the very different stances taken by Villanelle's married lover and the soldier Henri towards Villanelle's heart, Winterson exemplifies alternative attitudes towards romantic love. Her lover lives up to an impression Villanelle had of her when they first met, that her passion is gained 'out of passion's obstacles' (71). She prefers to keep her economically comfortable married status, viewing love between women as a temporary form of physical pleasure without commitment. She would keep Villanelle's heart as a trophy, a remembrance of past pleasure. On the other hand Henri risks much danger to retrieve Villanelle's heart, and although he is deeply in love with her and wants to marry her, he freely gives her heart back to her, feeling that it is hers to give as she pleases (120–1). He respects Villanelle, her married lover does not.

Her heart's loss and recovery brings Villanelle to respect both her transgendered body and her love for women, and she gains the knowledge that her passion deserves better than her married female lover can give her. When games of chance enter her life again in the form of the unpredictable wild card, Villanelle meets her lover, whose husband has left. Villanelle acts on her own acquired wisdom: 'I was angry because she had wanted me and made me want her and been afraid to accept what that meant. ... [P]assion, because it is noble, will not long accept another's left-overs' (145). She chooses not to see her lover again.

In the end, what can the complexities of Villanelle's body do to affirm a woman in the construction of her own subjectivity? Her fabulous body offers us clues. Mary Daly suggests:

> Those who are really living on the boundary tend to spark in others the courage to affirm their own unique being. ... Jesus or any other liberated person who has this effect functions as model precisely in the sense of being a model-breaker, pointing beyond his or her own limitations to the potential for further liberation.
>
> (1973: 75)

Villanelle's fabulous body is a model-breaker, through its refusal to fit into most notions of 'woman' considered appropriate in white Western culture. She encourages women whose bodies do not fit this culture, such as Jess in Leslie Feinberg's *Stone Butch Blues* (1993) who describes her body as that of a he/she. Whatever her physical anomalies and her problems, Villanelle carries on, like the women Henri remembers from his village: 'They go on. Whatever we do or undo, they go on' (1988: 27). Written against the grain of the traditional heterosexual romance plot, Villanelle's story tells us that there can be more tragedy in following traditionally accepted social practices than not; she marries for convenience once, but will never repeat that disastrous experience. Her story points out that we all struggle with obsession and destiny, so in a sense each of us is structured like a villanelle. Even if our bodies are not like Villanelle's, we struggle with our own 'plaits of gold and silver' as they intertwine with the 'rose-coloured threads' of our hearts.

Moreover, Villanelle's body exemplifies the ambiguity of the boundary-crossing being that Grosz discusses in 'Freaks', able to imperil categories and oppositions dominant in social life. In *The Passion*, Winterson gives us a myth full of the heart-food, colours and folly that to her provide beauty and a pointer for living, and she does much of this through her representation of Villanelle's fabulous body. As Winterson warns, we should not use any myth as a handbook for living, but we can use myth to enrich our imaginations and stretch our thinking beyond its present limitations.

In this context, perhaps we can see Villanelle's body addressing the fears and anxieties arising in the debates around women's bodies that are currently raging in our present white Western culture – for example, the debates around the ethics of reproductive technologies; cosmetic surgery; current research on personality-altering drugs; and the emergence of the transgendered community from the closet. Sociologist Chris Schilling notes that for people who have lost faith in religious authorities and grand political narratives, the body initially appears to provide a firm foundation on which to reconstruct a reliable sense of self in the modern world. But Schilling notes emphatically: *'We now have the means to exert an unprecedented degree of control over bodies, yet we are also living in an age which has thrown into radical doubt our knowledge of what bodies are and how we should control them'* (1993: 3, emphasis in original). He goes on to argue, 'the more we have been able to control and alter the limits of the body, the greater has been our uncertainty about what constitutes an individual's body, and what is "natural" about a body' (4).

This uncertainty has been prominently reflected in current feminist debates around sexual difference. Rosi Braidotti discusses the importance of 'the political will to assert the specificity of the lived, female bodily experience, the refusal to disembody sexual difference into a new allegedly postmodern anti-essentialist subject and the will to reconnect the whole debate on difference to the bodily existence and experience of women' (1994: 174–5). Braidotti, moreover, asserts that feminist theoreticians should reconnect the feminine to the bodily sexed reality of the female, refusing the separation of the empirical from the symbolic, or of the material from the discursive, or of sex from gender, arguing for the ontological basis of sexual difference (177). This position should include the ability for a woman to say, ' "I" have been a woman – socially and anatomically – for as long as "I" have existed, that is to say, in the limited scale of my temporality, forever' (186). Braidotti's argument becomes problematic if one considers a hermaphroditic or transgendered body such as that of Villanelle, and limits the category 'woman' to those persons born with only female genitalia. I believe that a rethinking of the category 'woman' is necessitated by the emergence of the transgender community as a political entity into our culture, and that we can no longer think in terms of a physical definition of 'woman' as defined by her body, or continue to react with horror, surgical intervention and attempts at erasure when faced with bodily differences.

Perhaps we should consider that whatever genitals a person possesses, that person can choose to exist at whatever point on a gender continuum that s/he deems appropriate. From this perspective, Villanelle, who places herself at various points on this continuum at different times, can be seen as a liberatory figure. If gender were more difficult to 'read', and seen as more of a continuum, it would be more difficult to favour one gender and oppress the other. Elizabeth Grosz, in *Volatile Bodies*, argues:

> Sexual difference, though, cannot be understood, as is commonly the case in much feminist literature, in terms of a comparison and contrast between two types of sexual identity independently formed and formulated. Instead it must be seen as the very ground on which sexual identities and their external relations are made possible. . . . [S]exual difference is a framework or horizon that must disappear as such in the codings that constitute sexual identity and the relations between the sexes. Sexual difference is the horizon that cannot appear in its own terms but is implied in the very possibility of an entity, and identity, a subject, an other and their relations.
>
> (1994: 208–9)

Sexual difference might be seen from this perspective as mutable. It exists, but more as a notion against which an individual can project a notion of sexual subjectivity that fits with a personal notion of sexuality. We already can no longer look at any body and know for certain that it is the body of a 'woman' or a 'man'. Such sexual fluidity can be seen as leading to a politics of extreme individualism, but it could also mean that identity politics might give way to more global politics on a sexual level. The notion of 'queer' is politically effective because it envisions possibilities for very different individuals to work together and promote social change. Anthony Slagle notes:

> Queer Nation has reconceptualized the notion of identity in such a way that it does not essentialize those who take on a queer identity. Queer Nation develops a collective identity based on the idea that queers are unique not only from the mainstream but from one another. For this reason, the movement can be understood as an identity politics (collective identity) based on differences and diversity (individual identities).
>
> (1995: 98)

The fabulous bodies of Dog Woman, the sexually indeterminate lover of *Written*, and Villanelle all fit in well with this notion of identity, and demonstrate that however one's body is physically constructed, one can be loved for oneself, not measured against a physical ideal. Villanelle's lover Henri makes an insightful comment about Villanelle, which illuminates one aspect of the passion of love: 'Her. A person who is not me. ... My passion for her, even though she could never return it, showed me the difference between inventing a lover and falling in love. The one is about you, the other about someone else' (1988: 158). These bodies, therefore, in all their postmodern complexity, are all queer bodies, deconstructing notions of a stable bodily identity and a 'natural' body, and they afford a female reader the confidence to participate in being part of, or relating to, the differences that surround us at the end of the twentieth century. Wendy Brown observes that we live in a world of cultural chasms, social fragmentations and political disintegrations, and we need to develop an oppositional politics within these postmodern political conditions (1991). Winterson's fabulous bodies work toward developing such politics; through these bodies, Winterson encourages us to relate to each other in our material realities, no matter what differences our bodies project. Her message transfers very appropriately from the pages of her novels to the street, where the ideological battles of our culture are fought by actual human bodies instead of fictional ones.

Works cited

Bolin, Anne (1994), 'Transcending and transgendering: male-to-female transsexuals, dichotomy and diversity', in Gilbert Herdt (ed.), *Third Sex Third Gender: Beyond Sexual Dimorphism in Culture and History*. New York: Zone Books, pp. 447–85, notes pp. 589–96.

Braidotti, Rosi (1994), *Nomadic Subjects: Embodiment and Sexual Difference in Contemporary Feminist Theory*. New York: Columbia University Press.

Brown, Wendy (1991), 'Feminist hesitations, postmodern / exposures', *differences: A Journal of Feminist Cultural Studies*, 3, (1), 63–84.

Butler, Judith (1990), *Gender Trouble: Feminism and the Subversion of Identity*. New York: Routledge.

Daly, Mary (1973), *Beyond God the Father: Toward a Philosophy of Women's Liberation*. Boston: Beacon Press.

Epstein, Julia (1990), 'Either/or-neither/both: sexual ambiguity and the ideology of gender', *Genders*, 7, Spring, 99–142.

Feinberg, Leslie (1993), *Stone Butch Blues*. New York: Firebrand Books.

Grosz, Elizabeth. 'Freaks'. Unpublished essay.

—— (1994), *Volatile Bodies: Toward a Corporeal Feminism*. Bloomington and Indianapolis: Indiana University Press.

Hennessy, Rosemary (1993), *Materialist Feminism and the Politics of Discourse*. New York and London: Routledge.

Marvel, Mark (1990), 'Jeanette Winterson: Trust me. I'm telling you stories', *Interview*, 20, 164–8.

Milton, John (1957), 'Paradise lost', in Merritt Hughes (ed.), *John Milton: Complete Poems and Major Prose*. New York: Macmillan, pp. 207–469.

Ostriker, A. S. (1992), *Feminist Revision and the Bible: The Unwritten Volume*. Oxford: Blackwell.

Rich, Adrienne (1977), *Of Woman Born: Motherhood as Experience and Institution*. Toronto and New York: Bantam Books.

Russo, Mary (1994), *The Female Grotesque: Risk, Excess and Modernity*. New York and London: Routledge.

Schilling, Chris (1993), *The Body and Social Theory*. London: Sage.

Slagle, R. Anthony (1995), 'In defense of Queer Nation: From identity politics to a politics of difference', *Western Journal of Communication*, 59, Spring, 85–102.

Stone, Sandy (1992), 'The empire strikes back: a posttranssexual manifesto, *Camera Obscura*, 29, May, 151–76.

Preminger, Alex, and Brogan, T. V. F (eds) (1993), *The New Princeton Encyclopedia of Poetry and Poetics*. Princeton, NJ: Princeton University Press.

Winterson, Jeanette (1986), *Fit for the Future: The Guide for Women Who Want to Live Well*. London: Pandora Press.

—— (1988), *The Passion*. London: Penguin Books.

—— (1989), *Sexing the Cherry*. London: Vintage.

—— (1992), *Written on the Body*. Toronto: Alfred Knopf.

Wittig, Monique (1985), 'The mark of gender', *Feminist Issues*, 5, (2), Fall, 3–12.

CHAPTER FOUR

Language and the Limits of Desire

JENNIFER GUSTAR

Chapter summary: Jennifer Gustar's chapter examines the central importance of the relationship between language and desire in Winterson's work through the lens of psychoanalytic theory. It argues that Freud's classic theory of mourning and melancholia, Lacan's notion of language as a signifying chain that endlessly incites and defers desire, and Julia Kristeva's concept of abjection, can all illuminate Winterson's own foregrounding of love and loss in her fiction.

Key Texts: *The Passion; Written on the Body; Weight*

Key words: language, representation, desire, psychoanalysis, loss, abjection

All literature is engaged in a perpetual conversation about desire.

(Flieger 1991: 244)

Jeanette Winterson's language is strikingly spare: always honed, polished like silver. Such language opens up imaginative possibilities rather than delimiting them, perhaps because, as Winterson writes, 'the important things are often left unsaid' (2004: 135); rather, they are inferred, between the lines, or written on the body. Additionally, they may echo, uncannily, with the unknown – the unconscious. In part, this is because Winterson most often avoids the conventions of realism as for her they point 'to a terror of the inner life, of the sublime, of the poetic, of the non-material, of the contemplative' (2005a: xv). Rather, writing such as Winterson's 'takes for granted that the process of representation can never be the reconstitution of presence ... it variously celebrates or struggles with the opacity of the signifier ... The subject is what speaks, writes, reads, signifies, and it is no more than that. Silence is death. Desire lives, then, in its inscription' (Belsey 1994: 77). Winterson pursues this inscription through the realms of the poetic, the fantastic, the imaginary and the magical. Her work evinces a commitment to revivify and transform language; and reveals evidence of an 'other' language, one that expresses desire by keeping language in motion, rather than simply preserving language as a prison house of repetition that maintains the status quo. This site of eruption lies in the changing contexts of any reception; whether reading or writing, we bring to language our inarticulate and unconscious desire. When we '[t]urn down the daily noise ... at first there is the relief of silence. And then, very quietly, as quiet as light, meaning returns. Words are the part of silence that can be spoken', writes Winterson (2005a: 135). Literature and art may be the best intimation of that which is radically unknowable.

Although Winterson's themes range widely, attesting to the richness of her imagination, there is always one theme to which she invariably returns: the power of stories to shape our desire, to defend us against the weight of inevitable loss, to move us to love. Desire demands expression. In *Written on the Body*, she writes, 'Love demands expression. It will not stay still, stay silent, be good, be modest, be seen and not heard, no' (1993: 9), but these words follow almost immediately on the opening line: 'Why is the measure of love loss?' (9). Winterson, in this instance as in so many others, draws our attention to the links between language and loss, writing and desire. Writers such as Winterson have never needed Freud in order to explore psychic space, but Freud's theories and their subsequent revisions by contemporary theorists can assist our understanding of the relationship between language, literature and desire. As Winterson writes in *The Passion*, 'the cities of the interior do not lie on any map' (1989: 114); yet we do so desire to map them. For Julia Kristeva, literature explores the ways in which language is structured over a lack. Poetic language, in particular, is limned with the abject fear of loss: it is 'a language of want, of the fear that edges up to it and runs along its edges' (1982: 38). As human subjects, we are necessarily subject to language, the language which is a measure of our loss and our desire to defend against it, as '[t]here's no choice that doesn't mean a loss' (Winterson 1985: 172). Arguably, what separates the human animal from its non-human others is our capacity to make meaning, primarily, but not exclusively, through language. And language is an act of repetition. Famously, Jacques Derrida argues that iterability is inherent to language, but the contexts of any iteration are limitless:

> Every sign, linguistic or non-linguistic, spoken or written ... can be *cited*, put between quotation marks; in so doing it can break with every given context, engendering an infinity of new contexts in a manner which is absolutely illimitable.
>
> (Quoted in Ulmer 1985: 58)

Derrida's insight is clearly shared by Winterson, as one of her most characteristic narrative strategies is to place language in quotation marks, as it were, and, in so doing, to reframe meaning. She writes:

My work is full of Cover versions. I like to take stories we think we know and record them differently. In the re-telling comes a new emphasis or bias, and the new arrangement of the key elements demands that fresh material be injected into the existing text.

(2005a: xiv)

Importantly, then, while meaning is contextually bound, contexts are boundless. As Winterson insists, 'there is no limit to new territory. ... Reality is continuous, multiple, simultaneous, complex, abundant and partly invisible. The imagination alone can fathom this and it reveals its fathoming through art' (2005b: 255).

Winterson has remarked that Art has the capacity to allow us to apprehend more than the visible world (2005b: 247). In her work, she explores desire, the 'valuable, fabulous thing' (1989: 150) that remains difficult to articulate. Although Winterson may dispute Freud (2005a: 139), psychoanalysis is in fact based on a similar apprehension of the non-visible. It theorizes an unconscious that cannot be known outside of its effects, but the notional idea of the unconscious has considerable explanatory power for those of us who understand that, despite the fact that we are born into a language that already proscribes our identities, our perpetual desire empowers us to make new meanings. Freud's notion of desire was inextricably linked with prohibition and loss: for Freud, it is the desire to master alienation that produces the drives. For Jacques Lacan, the production of the self is predicated on the desire for an irrecoverable unconscious Ideal, an agency that we imagine pre-exists the I that is 'objectified in the dialectic of identification with the other ... before language restores to it, in the universal, its function as subject' (2005: 549). For Kristeva (1982), the constitution of the self follows on abjection; for Judith Butler (1997) on mourning and melancholia. That which enables the formation of the unconscious is unknowable in an absolute sense, it must, according to these theorists, pass through a process of metaphorization to be seen or heard. Literature is part of this process.

According to Winterson, the signature language motif of *Weight* is 'I want to tell the story again' (2005a: xiv). Given that changes in contexts – in time, in memory, in psychic space, in physical space, in language capacities, in knowledge, in emotions, *et al* – all collaborate in the production of a current sense of self, I have to concur with Kristeva who claims that the self is not a stable entity, but is always, necessarily a self-in-process. This is Villanelle's consolation in *The Passion*: 'I content myself with this; that where I will be will not be where I am' (1989: 150). Moreover, the subject, as we know it in a profound and meaningful sense, is a narrative self. It is always a repetition, a citation of a precedent, an intertextual self, autobiographical and unstable. *Weight* flirts with the vexed notion of autobiography and its relationship to fiction. '*Weight*', writes the author, 'has a personal story broken against the bigger story of the myth we know and the myth I have re-told. I have written this personal story in the First Person, indeed almost all of my work is written in the First Person, and this leads to questions of autobiography. Autobiography is not important. Authenticity is important' (Winterson 2005a: xiv-xv). Which begs the question: how can we guarantee authenticity in light of the fact that our subjectivities are already citational and, yet, not entirely knowable? In the opening preface of *Weight*, Winterson, tellingly, repeats herself:

> The strata of sedimentary rock are like the pages of a book... Each with a record of contemporary life written on it ... Unfortunately the record is far from complete ... The record is far from complete ...
>
> (Winterson 2005a: x, ellipsis in original)

Here she suggests that a 'contemporary' life is a narrative palimpsest that is laid down like a mountainous landscape, and it must be mined for the record, however incomplete: 'obscured as strata become *twisted or folded*, or even completely inverted by enormous geological forces' (x, emphasis in original).The repetition implied in citational identity is inescapable, yet this does not necessarily mean that the repetition lacks authenticity as we unfold the strata of sedimentary rock. As subjects, we are citations of a language that is not of our own making, but we are also citations of what we have made of that language.

This semi-autobiographical narrative that disavows the centrality of the autobiographical is also and at the same time a reiteration of the Atlas and Heracles myth, suggesting an identification of the authorial voice, the 'I' who speaks, with Atlas, or he who holds up the world. In this, Winterson perhaps suggests that the writer, in some sense, carries the weight of the world and the responsibility to expose the limits of the incomplete record. Certainly, this text carries the accumulated weight of earlier texts. When Winterson writes that she wants to tell the story again, to which story does she refer? The story of Atlas and Heracles, clearly, but is she also revisiting the story of *Written on the Body* which she cites and which is also itself a retelling of romance narratives lamenting the narrator's collusion in 'the same story every time'? This reiteration and self-reference suggest that perhaps Winterson is always cunningly engaging in her own literary critique. Certainly, she does so in *Art Objects: Essays on Ecstasy and Effrontery*: 'I know that ideas about the Self can only be approximate but it might be fair to say that the artist is less approximate than other people. But I have said these things in *Oranges Are Not the Only Fruit*' (1995: 188); 'I'm telling you stories. Trust me. But I have said these things in *The Passion*' (189); 'What have I said in *Written on the Body*? That it is possible to have done with the bricks and mortar of conventional narrative ... by building a structure that is bonded by language' (190). She is also pointing to the inescapable 'citational legacy'[1] (Butler 1993: 225) of her own subjectivity in relation to her own body of work. Winterson advocates a new language, or a new use of language, that can engage a level of feeling, beyond 'calling a spade a spade' (1995: 185). Clearly, reading her work, one cannot help but recognize that her new language remains citational; however, the context necessarily changes and thus evokes the intensity of feeling that she might well call passion and that can produce the transformation she herself desires. Writing that can position the reader in a liminal space, between fear and desire, is a rewriting of the language of desire.

This reflexive autocritical stance is a salient feature of Winterson's fiction: '[t]his is the wrong script' (1993: 18); '[h]aving brought no world with me, I made one' (2005a: 141); 'Trust me. I'm telling stories' (1989: *passim*). Recurrent statements such as these draw our attention, not only to the rather conventional *topos* of the problematic relationship between the real and the fictive, but also to the construction of narrative selves as effects of language and desire. 'The ill fit between language and the body introduces wrinkles and gaps that generate desire', writes Tim Dean. 'We might say that the unconscious and desire exist only as a consequence of this disharmony between the structures of language and those of the body' (2000: 59). This unconscious object which escapes signification in the symbolic 'keeps desire in motion' (31). In *Written on the Body*, Louise, and the loss she represents, is the incitement for narrative, for the language predicated on the desire to replace loss. In *The Passion*, Henri writes out his desire from his prison house of language, unable to end his grieving. These narratives figure the means by which language attempts to negotiate the loss of the radical Other – the Real in Lacanian terms – 'because it is only in the imaginary that the Other can be an other – that is an image of another person' (34).

As Belsey writes, '[d]esire was probably always citational' (1994: 82). The unappeasable nature of desire is the condition of living, of becoming a self: 'Life always becoming' (Winterson 2004: 150). Winterson's *Weight* locates its subject with the recurrent phrase, 'desire and boundaries', which is, certainly, a massive theme, and the theme of this chapter: language – the limits of desire. As Winterson writes in *The Passion*, '[w]e gamble with the hope of winning, but it's the thought of what we might lose that excites us' (1989: 89). Desire is thus irrevocably connected to the fear of loss of self, that is, to abjection. As such, while motivated by the past, it necessarily gestures toward the future for its fulfilment or frustration. While 'not a Freudian' (2005a: 139), Winterson nevertheless concurs with Freud's sense of the compulsion to repeat. In the concluding chapter of *Weight*, entitled 'Desire', she writes:

What can I tell you about the choices we make?
I chose this story above all others because it's a story I'm struggling to end. Here we are, with all the pieces in place and the final moment waiting. I reach this moment, not once, many times, have been reaching it all my life, it seems, and I find there is no resolution.

I want to tell the story again.
That's why I write fiction – so that I can keep telling the story. I return to problems I can't solve, not because I'm an idiot, but because *the real problems can't be solved.*

(137, emphasis added)

Winterson thus suggests that the story she is compelled to repeat is one that has no resolution in language. Stories are evidence of their own necessity and their incompleteness guarantees their continued circulation. Narrative is evidence of the problems we can't solve – of inconsolable mourning – but these are the problems that bring us into being: our unanswerable and unconscious desires.

The citation compulsion can be seen in most of Winterson's fictions. *Written on the Body* reframes much of the literature of the romance tradition: beside current clichés of love are allusions to Shakespeare, Charlotte Brontë, Petrarch, Keats, and Donne, among others. Judith Seaboyer (1997) has rigorously explored Winterson's fascination with repetition in *The Passion*, which mimics the genre of memoir and echoes, uncannily, with the poetry of T. S. Eliot, as when Winterson describes the work of dreams: 'In dreams we sometimes struggle from the oceans of desire up Jacob's ladder to that orderly place. Then human voices wake us and we drown' (1989: 74). Recognizing the second line as a quotation of Eliot's 'Prufrock', we are all the more inclined to read Henri's experience of war as echoing Eliot's *Waste Land* and *Four Quartets*, which are, themselves, 'responses to war, as was Freud's *Beyond the Pleasure Principle*' (Seaboyer 1997: 485). The more recent *Lighthousekeeping*, published in 2004, returns us to the tragic romance of Tristan and Isolde, as '[e]very new beginning prompts a return' (209), its signature language motif: 'Tell me a story' (*passim*). *Weight* retells the Greek myth of Atlas and Heracles in relation to the authorial voice. As she approaches the end, Winterson wishes to postpone closure and, instead, 'want[s] to tell the story again' (2005a: 146).

Reading *Weight* when it was released in 2005, I was struck, as if for the first time, by the following phrase: 'Written on the body is a secret code, only visible in certain lights' (141). This phrase has an uncanny effect because it is so very familiar. I have heard this phrase before; indeed, I have cited it (Gustar 2005). These lines do more than point to the title of her earlier text; they actually cite its language: 'Written on the body is a secret code only visible in certain lights; the accumulations of a lifetime gather there. In places the palimpsest is so heavily worked that the letters feel like braille' (1993: 89). This reiteration compulsion is so ubiquitous in Winterson that it provokes in the reader a desire to understand it. We are invited, by Winterson's recourse to repetition, to explore by means of 'certain lights' an undercurrent that recurs in her work. We are encouraged to use 'reading hands' (89) to decipher the braille that is so heavily reworked as reiterations of desire in language.

In *Written on the Body* and *The Passion*, the loss of a beloved is the incitement to narrate. Loss, however, is a problem that cannot always be 'solved' (2005a: 137). However, in both works, mourning passes over into melancholia. As Freud (1957) taught us, mourning becomes melancholia when the love object is not replaced by another, when the subject does not succeed in shifting libidinal investment. Judith Butler writes that 'Melancholia refuses to acknowledge loss, and in this sense "preserves" its lost objects as psychic effects' (1997: 183). It is tempting to explain Henri's refusal to leave his tower in light of Butler's description. Instead of making his escape, he tells the story of his life in order to preserve his love. Henri fails to overcome his loss – to do the work of mourning – and passes into the terrain of melancholia. However, what is crucial to note is that Butler also argues that the failure to mourn effectively, to release and/or replace the lost object of desire, is not psychosis but, rather, is constitutive of each human subject:

> Survival is a matter of avowing the trace of loss that inaugurates one's own emergence. To make of melancholia a simple 'refusal' to grieve its losses conjures a subject who might already be something without its losses, that is, one who voluntarily extends and retracts his or her will. Yet the subject who might grieve is implicated in a loss of autonomy that is mandated by linguistic and social life; it can never produce itself autonomously. From the start, this ego is other than itself; what melancholia shows is that only by absorbing the other as oneself does one become something at all.
>
> (1997: 195)

This insight into the constitutive aspect of melancholia, the incorporation of the other, accounts for what is difficult to explain: our compulsion to repeat loss. Our very existence is predicated on it, and it is this process that Winterson attempts repeatedly to narrativize.

In *Written on the Body*, for instance, the narrator's loss of Louise 'demands expression': the narrative represents language predicated on the desire to replace loss that must be repeated, because 'the real problems can't be solved' (2005a: 137). In the final passage of the novel, we cannot discern absolutely whether the narrator's beloved has returned, or whether it is her figuration in narrative that returns to haunt. We are returned by this haunting image to the beginning to tell the story again: 'This is where the story starts' (1993: 190). Instead of satisfying our desire for a happy ending in the field of romance, the writer demands something other than the typical consolations offered by 'the clichés that cause the trouble' (10), by the promise of living 'happily ever after' (10). Rather, this is a romance that evades the clichés of romance precisely by invoking them, by repeating them in epidemic proportions: the 'Petrarchan ... fragmentation' (Farwell 1996: 190), the illness and death of the body of the beloved, the obstacles that beset and separate the lovers. Because of its repetition of these conceits, *Written on the Body* received a rather mixed response from critics due to its perceived 'unabashed romanticism' (Reed-Morrison 1994: 101). It was accused of hovering 'dangerously on the precipice of device' (Schulman 1993: 20) and viewed by another critic as 'not altogether original' (Hoffert 1993: 195). However, as I have argued elsewhere, the lack of originality is the very point (Gustar 2005). 'Why is it that the most unoriginal thing we can say to one another is still the thing we long to hear' (Winterson 1993: 9), asks the narrator. Moreover, if ' "I love you" is always a quotation' (9), what is not? The text does not simply repeat the romance narrative, but makes the citational legacy of the romance narrative its particular focus by reiterating the conventions of romance in its multiple love plots, motifs and intertextual echoes of the multiple discourses of the body: narrative, biomedical or poetic. Winterson thus demonstrates the failure of language to revivify the body of the beloved, but language remains a necessity – it is the only, if inadequate, consolation for the loss. Of course, language can only remember the beloved as figuration, as substitute. Narrative, then, is the signifier of perpetual desire to recover our loss by means of language. Hence, neither narrator nor reader is liberated from loss at the conclusion, but each is sent back to repeat the story again, or else to remain, as indicated by the blank page following on, deathly silent. The alternative to death is repetition, with a vengeance: the melancholic narrative.

Winterson, of course, has already traversed this ground, in an earlier work, *The Passion*, which structures a parallel through a process of mirroring that sets Henri's grim story of the Napoleonic campaigns and his loss of heart, at the gross abuses of war, beside the story of Villanelle's loss of her heart to the Queen of Spades. These parallel but different narrations of the past intersect and produce the future, in a harrowing and emblematic story told by Villanelle to Henri about the ultimate game of chance: the risk of one's life. What is key to this text is the relationship of love and loss to a game of chance, which is underscored by the oft-repeated phrase – 'You play, you win, you play, you lose. You play' (Winterson 1989: 66, 73, 133) – and by the clear indication that life is a gamble and what we venture is what we most value. The first thing we all venture is attachment and the next may be language.

Winterson herself had not been to Venice when she wrote *The Passion*, but its position as symbolic inheritance in Anglo-American imagination is thoroughly documented by Judith Seaboyer (1997). As Seaboyer notes, Venice, as an imaginative construct, is already a well-established trope, a repetition, as it

> recalls the ancient myth of the labyrinth, a fluid space of transformation and danger that has traditionally stood for the psychic inward journey, and increasingly for textuality itself. Distinguished by death and decay, it is a figure for Kristevan abjection; all border. (485)

Henri deals with his loss by writing. He has not covered his 'heart with barnacles' (Winterson 1989: 146); he may live on a rock, but he has not become stone. Significantly, the narrator of *Written on the Body* similarly narrates 'alone from a rock hewn out of my own body' (Winterson 1993: 9). However, both narrators' insistence on revising, and rereading their narratives of 'self' suggest that what is lost, 'the valuable, fabulous thing' (Winterson 1989: 150 and *passim*) may only be approached, however unsatisfactorily, through reiterations of the language of desire. If, as Henri suggests, 'our longing for freedom is our longing for love' (154), then his consensual imprisonment signals his growing acceptance: 'There's time here to love slowly' (157). However, Henri's prison is an external one. Internally, he feels free to make his own mistakes (157) and aware that if he 'starts to cry will never stop' (159). He continues in a state of melancholic desire that gives him his 'self': 'I review my future and my past in the light of this feeling [of love]. It is as though I wrote in a foreign language that I am suddenly able to read. Wordlessly she explains me to myself'(159). This review is the passion to repeat, to understand the self in light of this desire.

While Winterson had not been to Venice when she wrote *The Passion*, she clearly had read Eliot. In 1995, she writes: 'there is no twentieth-century poem that means more to me than *Four Quartets*' (Winterson 1995: 126). Certainly, the chapter entitled 'The Rock' points to Eliot's poem of the same name, in which we read: 'O perpetual recurrence'.[2] The oft-repeated phrase – 'In between freezing and melting, in between love and despair. In between fear and sex, passion is' (Winterson 1989: 76) – constitutes an explicit allusion to 'The Hollow Men'.[3] However, the one who is 'hollow' in this text is Villanelle, whose heart has been stolen by another and eventually returned to her by Henri. While Villanelle is thus given a reprieve against irreparable loss, one 'such as only the stories offer' (151), Henri is offered no such reprieve so he must, necessarily, keep on telling his story and dreaming the nightmare of his shadow self. In Seaboyer's reading, Henri chooses a second death, a 'death-in-life'; she notes that Winterson's work 'emphasizes the role of repeating in keeping the trauma at bay' (Seaboyer 1997: 490):

> Henri's record of his experiences is a heroic act of bearing witness that refuses the desire for wholeness at the same time as it struggles to construct it, forcing open gaps through which the excluded Real floods back. Contact with the real plunges Henri into the imprisonment of madness, but the text he writes is an expression of the transformative force that operates both in the human psyche and in literature.
>
> (491–2)

However, rather than a 'death-in-life', I would prefer to discuss Henri's experience as a life in the face of death, in the face of abjection.

Kristeva defines abjection as an aspect of mourning:

The abject is the violence of mourning for an 'object' that has always already been lost. The abject shatters the wall of repression and its judgments. It takes the ego back to its source on the abominable limits from which, in order to be, the ego has broken away – it assigns it a source in the non-ego, drive, and death. Abjection is a resurrection that has gone through death (of the ego). It is an alchemy that transforms death drive into a start of life, of new signifiance [*sic*].

(1982: 15)

An uncanny effect becomes a mask for this rift which the lack of stable boundaries produces. The immanence of the strange within the familiar, Kristeva reminds us, accounts for the uncanny's power to contaminate categories because it destabilizes the hierarchy between the known and the unknown, the proper and improper, the same and its other, the story and its repetition. Repetition itself is uncanny, as it feels familiar, homely, domestic, but returns also a difference, a loss of familiarity, an uncanny strangeness, a spectre. We are all strangers to ourselves. Kristeva articulates our fear of loss of self, as, in fact, a fear of the uncanny stranger that constitutes the ego and, at the same time, threatens its dissolution: 'Strangely, the foreigner lives within us: he is the hidden face of our identity' (2002: 264).

Henri knows well the experience of being a foreigner. As he commences his narration from his prison, he has been 20 years far from home. However, home haunts him, as do spectres from his violent past. His abject other returns to haunt his present. As Seaboyer notes, Henri was a cook himself; moreover, he wishes to be Villanelle's husband and thus replace the Cook. When he tears out the Cook's heart, he becomes as murderous as the man he has just killed and he encounters the strangeness in the familiar, in himself. Moreover, he has already returned one heart to its rightful owner. Not only is he thus brought to enact the violence which he witnessed but avoided perpetrating during the war, but by engaging in this act of extreme brutality, he symbolically steals back his own heart and steals himself against renewed loss by consigning himself to the same prison which housed Napoleon (Seaboyer 1997). These repetitions enable us to read Henri's desire to garden as one which would recreate the world in a new context: to bring about renewal where there is only rock. It also accounts for his desire to both write and reread his past: to bring about renewal where there is only abjection: 'I go on writing so that I will always have something to read' (Winterson 1989: 159), he writes.

Abjection transforms the security of the self-regarding 'I': it threatens the boundary between I/other, threatening dissolution of the self. 'Perhaps', thinks Villanelle, Henri 'has lost himself' (Winterson: 150). After he is imprisoned, Henri recognizes that his 'self' as he had known it, in love and war, has repressed a 'shadow' self that he fears and loathes: 'When I fell in love it was as though I looked into a mirror for the first time and saw myself ... And when I had looked at myself and grown accustomed to who I was, I was not afraid to hate parts of me because I wanted to be worthy of the mirror bearer' (155). Believing that he had joined Napoleon's army to set himself and others free, Henri has learned of his bondage to his shadow self. He has confronted the radical other within, as Kristeva describes it, and has figured that 'other' in his writing. 'Words like passion and ecstasy, we learn them', he writes,

> but they stay flat on the page. Sometimes we try and turn them over, find out what's on the other side, and everyone has a story to tell of a woman or a brothel or an opium night or a war. We fear it. We fear passion and laugh at too much love and those who love too much. And still we long to feel.
>
> (155)

It is through Kristeva's sense of the enigmatic draw of the other as both threat and as constitutive that we may best understand what draws us, repeatedly, to literature, and what may, indeed, draw Henri to writing his memoir.

Like *Written on the Body*, this text invokes the genre of retrospective autobiography in confrontation with loss and the narrative that must sustain us. Autobiography, Kristeva reminds us, is always necessarily an act of retrospection, recuperation and, hence, repetition. In his madhouse prison hewn out of rock, Henri communicates with the ghosts of his past, voices that are of his 'own making' (Winterson 1989: 147). While confined in body, he is 'free' in heart, because he writes his loss and confronts the other within: 'Her. A person who is not me. I invented Bonaparte as much as he invented himself. My passion for her, even though she could never return it, showed me the difference between inventing a lover and falling in love. The one is about you, the other about someone else' (158). That someone else may represent a more primal loss: 'To love someone else enough to forget about yourself even for one moment is to be free ... our desire for another will lift us out of ourselves more cleanly than anything divine' (154). As Kristeva writes, the terror of abjection and the recognition of the other within may lead one to the recourse of writing: 'The writer is a phobic who succeeds in metaphorizing in order to keep from being frightened to death; instead, he [/she] comes to life again in signs' (Kristeva 1982: 38). Henri survives the trauma of war, the loss of his best friend and his mother, the loss of Villanelle and the terror of his own capacity to brutally dismember Villanelle's husband, by writing. Henri's notebook, his narration, becomes his passion: 'What you risk reveals what you value' (Winterson 1989: 91).

According to Villanelle, '[t]here's no sense in loving someone you can only wake up to by chance' (122). However, loving is always only by chance; there is always the risk of loss. Love, like life, is a gamble, 'an expression of our humanness' (73) and, hence, a constant threat to the ego. Literature itself threatens the assurance of the ego. It is one of the outsides that subjects us to affect, to the fear of dissolution and thus brings us to the edge of abjection and melancholia. In so far as we are intimately involved in any narrative act, fantasy positions the reader neither in the text nor outside the text but as produced by the affect/effect as between two worlds, inhabiting a border space between the 'real' and the 'imaginary', between the self and other. Language and narrative may be our attempt to fill the gap left by unconscious and unanswered desires, and to ward off our fear of the other, but they do so only imperfectly. These substitutes, 'for what cannot be figured in language, in the symbolic' (Dean 2000: 58), repeat our attempts to replace something other, and, hence, leave always an unanswered excess of desire. We must keep speaking, keep writing, keep repeating stories.

Henri and the narrator of *Written on the Body* both reach the conclusion that stories are our best consolation: this seems also to be Winterson's conclusion. Winterson is the instrument of language and of received narratives, and hence she cannot but repeat; however, she is also an instrument of an unconscious desire. Her work returns to those questions which are impossible to answer: 'I reach this moment, not once, many times, have been reaching it all my life, it seems, and I find there is no resolution. *I want to tell the story again*' (Winterson 2005a: 137). In telling the story again, her work inscribes an uncanny excess so reminiscent of our compulsion to repeat, which is the indication of our melancholic loss. We must repeat, because these experiences of mourning and abjection are integral parts of who we are as subjects of an unconscious other. Because never completely satisfied, desire moves us to language; because language never finally contains desire, we are moved again. The possibilities are vast: 'the cities of the interior do not lie on any map' (Winterson 1989: 114). Trying to map them is Winterson's passion; she has a romance with stories. And romance, says Henri, is not necessarily 'a contract between equal parties but an explosion of dreams and desires that can find no outlet in everyday life. Only a drama will do and while the fireworks last the sky is a different colour' (Winterson: 13). Reading Winterson, in certain lights with our reading hands, we may perceive our own romance with stories. Stories can return us to where we started, so we might once more glimpse intimations of this imaginary place for the first time and begin again to tell the story.

Notes

1. In *Bodies That Matter* (1993), Judith Butler expands on the concept of the citational legacy of subjectivity: 'This not owning of one's words is there from the start', writes Butler; 'however, since speaking is always in some ways the speaking of a stranger through and

as oneself, the melancholic reiteration of a language that one never chose, that one does not find as an instrument to be used, but that one is, as it were, used by' (242).

2. Winterson's chapter 'The Zero Winter' echoes Eliot's 'zero summer', also from 'Little Gidding'. The serious games of chance, the ravages of war, the prison of the self, the quandary of desire are all ideas that revisit Eliot's poetry. Villanelle's Venice, the 'city of madmen' is perhaps an echo of Eliot's 'Unreal City'. See Judith Seaboyer for further allusions to Eliot.

3. 'Between the desire/And the spasm/Between the potency/And the existence/ ... Falls the Shadow', T. S. Eliot, 'The Hollow Men' V: 17–23.

Works cited

Belsey, Catherine (1994), *Desire: Love Stories in Western Culture*. Oxford: Blackwell.

Butler, Judith (1993), *Bodies that Matter: On the Discursive Limits of 'Sex'*. New York: Routledge.

—— (1997), *The Psychic Life of Power: Theories in Subjection*. Stanford: Stanford University Press.

Dean, Tim (2000), *Beyond Sexuality*. Chicago: Chicago University Press.

Eliot, T. S. (1952), *The Complete Poems and Plays*. New York: Harcourt Brace, (reprinted 1980).

Farwell, Marilyn R. (1996), *Heterosexual Plots and Lesbian Narratives*. New York: New York University Press.

Flieger, Jerry Aline (1991), *The Purloined Punchline: Freud's Comic Theory and the Postmodern Text*. Baltimore and London: Johns Hopkins University Press.

Freud, Sigmund, (1957), 'Mourning and melancholia', in James Strachey (ed. and trans.), *Standard Edition of the Complete Psychological Works of Sigmund Freud*. Vol. 14. London: Hogarth, pp. 243–58.

Gustar, Jennifer (2005), 'The body of romance: Citation and mourning in *Written on the Body*', *Aesthethica*, 2, (1), 25–41.

Hoffert, Barbara (1993), 'Review [of *Written on the Body*]', *Library Journal* 118.3, 195.

Kristeva, Julia (1982), *Powers of Horror: An Essay on Abjection*. Trans. Leon S. Roudiez. New York: Columbia University Press.

—— (2002), 'Strangers to ourselves', in Kelly Oliver (ed.), *The Portable Kristeva*. New York: Columbia University Press, pp. 264–94.

Lacan, Jacques (2005), 'The mirror stage as formative of the function of the I as revealed in psychoanalytic experience', in Becky McLaughlin and Bob Coleman (eds), *Everyday Theory: A Contemporary Reader*. Toronto: Pearson Longman, pp. 548–53.

McLaughlin, Becky and Bob Coleman (eds) (2005), *Everyday Theory: A Contemporary Reader*. Toronto: Pearson Longman.

Reed-Morrison, Laura (1994), 'Review [of *Written on the Body*]', *Chicago Review* 40, (4), 101–6.

Schulman, Sarah (1993), 'Guilty with explanation: Jeanette Winterson's endearing book of Love.' *Lambda Book Report* 3.0, 20.

Seaboyer, Judith (1997), 'Second death in Venice: Romanticism and the compulsion to repeat in Jeanette Winterson's *The Passion'*, *Contemporary Literature* 38:3, 483–509.

Ulmer, Gregory (1985), *Applied Grammatology: Post(e) Pedagogy from Jacques Derrida to Joseph Beuys*. Baltimore: Johns Hopkins University Press.

Winterson, Jeanette (1985), *Oranges Are Not the Only Fruit*. London: Pandora.

—— (1989), *The Passion*. New York: Vintage International.

—— (1993), *Written on the Body*. New York: Alfred A. Knopf.

—— (1995), *Art Objects: Essays on Ecstasy and Effrontery*. Toronto: Vintage Canada.

—— (1998), 'The art of fiction'. Interview, *The Paris Review*. 39, 68–112.

—— (2004), *Lighthousekeeping*. Toronto: Vintage Canada.

—— (2005a), *Weight*. Toronto: Alfred A. Knopf.

—— (2005b), 'Imagination and reality', in Becky McLaughlin and Bob Coleman (eds), *Everyday Theory: A Contemporary Reader*. Toronto: Pearson Longman, 246–55.

CHAPTER FIVE

Reading and the Reader

GINETTE CARPENTER

Chapter summary: Chapter 5 focuses on Winterson's representation of reading and the role of the reader in her fiction. It explores the ways in which three novels represent readers and reading, and depict the relationship between the body and the text. It argues that Winterson's novels work to problematize the act of reading and that Winterson asks her readers not simply to gain pleasure from reading her texts but also to engage with the difficulties and contradictions of reading. In Winterson's texts reading, like writing, is a desiring act and, the chapter suggests, it requires the close attention and commitment of a lover.

Key texts: *Written on the Body; Art and Lies; The PowerBook*

Key words: reading, the reader, interpretation, desire, dis/embodiment, complexity

---

Jeanette Winterson's passion for 'the word' is self-confessedly 'evangelical' (2006). Her work has always pushed at the boundaries of storytelling in order to stretch language, to show what language can do. Her concern with the transgressive clearly includes crossing and recrossing the conventional limits of narrative. And as she highlights the fictionality of her work so she also foregrounds the practices of reading. Winterson is archly aware of the fact that her books only take on existence when read; that is, that reading re/creates the text: 'When I talk about writing I have to always come back to reading' (2006). This chapter will explore the ways in which *Written on the Body* (1992), *Art and Lies* (1995) and *The PowerBook* (2000) represent readers and reading with specific reference to the relationship between the corporeal and the textual, between body and word.

It seems unnecessary to state that writing and reading are inextricably linked. The connection is not, however, always explicitly made. Literary criticism's concern with interpretation is, of course, a reading of the text but one which can often fail to acknowledge the feelings and pleasures associated with, or, arguably, intrinsic to, the act of reading: 'The act of interpretation is a search for a language adequate to the intimate experience of reading. Yet the interpretative act can also obscure the emotional experience of reading' (Grice and Woods 1998: 3). In 'The emotional politics of reading', in Grice and Woods' influential collection of essays on Winterson's work, Lynne Pearce criticises reader theorists for 'being blind to ... the complex emotional processes of reading' (1998: 29). Her earlier detailed study of reading as a feminist critic (1997) engages very precisely with these debates and uses Barthes' (1978) exegesis of the language of desire to address the range of sentiments that accompany the process of reading. Thus, like Belsey (1994), Pearce locates reading as a process that effects far more than a merely cerebral response. Winterson's writing is interesting in this regard in that it *insists* upon recognition of these emotional components of reading; her novels demand that the reader is active and engaged. In Barthesian terms her work broadly conforms to the characteristics of the 'writerly' text (Barthes 1975) in that the reader is not a passive recipient of the story but rather participates in the creation of meaning. The reader's relationship with the text shifts and fluctuates and thus interpretation remains open-ended.

In *Art Objects* (1996) Winterson convincingly argues that reading is itself an art, one that is difficult to acquire and has to be practised and refined: 'Learning to read is more than learning to group the letters on the page. Learning to read is a skill that marshals the entire resources of body and mind' (1996: 111). Her novels' non-linear narratives and temporal eclecticism insist that the material reader is conscious of the practice being enacted; indeed, it is difficult to read Winterson without being acutely aware that one is reading. Her evangelicalism about the 'word' (2006) would seem to extend to a mission to ensure that her readers begin consciously to procure the skills needed to really engage with the text and appreciate that 'Art is the realisation of complex emotion' (1996: 111). In addition to the ways in which her novels make the reader work, Winterson's characters themselves are often readers and their reading skills, or lack of them, become central to the unfolding of the story/ies. Thus reading is highlighted in two distinct yet inter-related ways: the texts demand attention and interaction from the material reader; and the texts explicitly represent readers and reading. A third aspect can also be identified: Winterson's own reading and re-presenting of canonical works. Her writing abounds with inter-textuality[1] and literary allusion as she reworks both traditional stories and traditions of storytelling. These three aspects work together to blur the conventional distinctions between author, reader and text. The author is also the re/reader; the reader 'writes' the work; the text is a site that shifts its significance, that is continuously in flux.

In *Written on the Body*, *Art and Lies* and *The PowerBook*, the fore-grounding of the processes of reading is specifically linked to both corporeality and desire. The body is positioned as a text that can be both inscribed and read. Or, conversely, the text is represented as a body and, as such, as an animate object that is constantly changing and that can exert not only intellectual but also physical pleasure, and, conversely, pain, upon the reader:[2]

> A book can separate you from your husband, your wife, your children, all that you are. It can heal you out of a lifetime of pain. Books are kinetic, and like all huge forces, need to be handled with care.
> But they do need to be handled. The pleasure of a book is, or should be, sensuous as well as aesthetic, visceral as well as intellectual.
>
> (Winterson 1996: 122–3)

This physical actualization allows for a direct correlation to be made between the pleasures of reading and bodily pleasures. The relationship between reader and text is located as far more than a cerebral activity; rather it is intimate, embodied and potentially life-altering: 'Passion. The secret passages matter. Where will the book take you?' (124). The text is positioned as 'a total world' (25) and therefore one upon which the reader brings to bear all her desires, including the desire for romance: 'in a total world we fall in love' (25). Ultimately, however, if Winterson's work is about the body then the body that it is primarily concerned with is the body/ies of literature.[3] If it is about romantic desire then it simultaneously inculcates a passion for reading. The different way in which each of the three novels addresses this interrelation between reading and desire and the body will form the basis of the discussion of the rest of this chapter.

The idea that the body can be read and re-read, written and rewritten is the central motif of *Written on the Body*. The novel tells of a love affair between a married woman, Louise, and an unnamed narrator. The gender of the narrator is never revealed, rather her/his identity is deliberately unfixed and shifting; there are times when the reader may be convinced that he is male and others when she seems clearly female. However, despite the discomfort engendered by this fluctuation, in many ways, the novel is a traditional romance. The narrator and Louise fall in love, obstacles are put in the way of their love (the narrator's girlfriend, Louise's husband, their own mistrust of love), the obstacles are overcome and they are able to be together. However, the revelation of Louise's leukaemia returns the relationship to its more precarious state, reintroducing (self) doubt, mistrust and misinterpretation. The narrator has failed to read Louise as fluently as s/he thought. Having revealed the secrets of *her/his* text – 'Your handprints are all over my body. Your flesh is my flesh. You deciphered me and now I am plain to read' (Winterson 2001b: 106) – the narrator has wrongly believed her/his revelations to be reciprocated:

> Louise, in this single bed, between these garish sheets, I will find a map as likely as any treasure hunt. I will explore you and mine you and you will

redraw me according to our will. *We shall cross one another's boundaries and make ourselves one nation.*

(20, my emphasis)

But Louise has not reciprocated; she is not the open book that she seems. The body is not as easily decipherable as it would appear; the surface can conceal far more than it reveals and reading it is a skill that can only be attained over time. The narrator reads for a living, working as a translator from Russian into English. S/he makes understandable that which is incomprehensible, translates one sign system into another sign system, inscribes meaning. Yet s/he lacks the fluency needed to adequately translate her/his lover's body. Elgin, Louise's husband, has access to parts of Louise's text that the narrator has been denied: Elgin knows that Louise is very ill. The narrator discovers her/himself to be deficient where s/he most seeks knowledge. Reading Louise, translating her flesh into meaning, proves deceptively difficult. The slippage that always occurs in translation, the lack of fit between two different sign systems, becomes an insurmountable obstacle – the signifieds slide too far for the narrator to decipher. Her/his difficulties begin when Louise confounds her/his expectations and declares that she will leave Elgin – 'This is the wrong script' (18) – and the reading becomes progressively harder until, faced with an unfamiliar and paralysing state of illiteracy, the narrator can do nothing but leave.

Ultimately, however, it is reading that saves the narrator. The image of her/him holed-up in a ramshackle cottage in the middle of nowhere frantically reading everything s/he can find about cancer serves to reinforce the value of being both able to read, and of being able to read *well*. It is reading that gives the narrator solace and that connects her/him back to her/his lover. Reading is represented as that which allows and promotes understanding but only through application and effort. The narrator must read in order to be able to translate her/his love of Louise into knowledge of Louise. This journey towards understanding is mirrored in the effort required of the material reader to assimilate the novel's unconventional structure, as the narrator explores aspects of human anatomy and translates the generic into the specific. What s/he learns is not what s/he seeks; s/he learns that meaning cannot be forcefully imposed. Leaving Louise has produced a monolithic reading of Louise's body, condemning it to illness and decay: 'If I stay it will be you who goes, in pain, without help' (105). The narrator has to learn to allow for the free play of signifiers, to resist the translator's urge to pindown meaning:

> 'I couldn't find her. I couldn't even get near finding her. It's as if Louise never existed, like a character in a book. Did I invent her?'
> 'No, but you tried to,' said Gail, 'She wasn't yours for the making.'

(189)

Louise herself is represented as a skilful reader: 'I didn't know that Louise would have reading hands. She has translated me into her own book' (89). Louise is clearly aware that, 'It's the clichés that cause the trouble' (10) and avoids rehearsed platitudes or scripted exchanges:

> 'I want you to come to me without a past. Those lines you've learned, forget them. Forget that you've been here before in other bedrooms in other places. Come to me new. Never say that you love me until that day when you have proved it.'
>
> (54)

As such, the character of Louise confirms the novel's premise that the conventional language of romance is an inadequate tool for capturing the complexities of love and desire. Yet 'Love demands expression. It will not stay still, stay silent' (9). The novel pivots upon this paradox: that this love that is purportedly beyond language has to be written and read in the very language that it claims to be beyond. Thus both the narrator and the material reader need to learn to read with courage, to accept that meaning can lurk in the gaps and shadows of discourse. Language features as playful and pliable, as demanding and petty. Linguistic slippage – in the case of this novel, between the discourses of the body, desire and disease – is celebrated as perhaps the one space where love can find expression.

Initially, *Art and Lies* or, *Art and Lies: A Piece for Three Voices and a Bawd*, to give it its full title, seems to be a far more inaccessible novel than *Written*. Its apparent lack of narrative cohesion and immoderate intertextuality can both alienate and frustrate the reader. Clearly, this is not an easy novel and indeed it received much press criticism for what was regarded as its impenetrable quality, 'castigated for being boring or incomprehensible' (Lambert 1998: 4). Winterson herself admits that the novel was a product of a particularly difficult period in her life when she was 'looking inwards' (Winterson, web resource). Nevertheless, this is a novel that rewards persistence and careful reading. Its fruits only ripen and drop into the reader's lap in the final sections. To return to the analogy of the love affair: it is only when the novel reaches its conclusion that the reader realizes how successfully she has been seduced. The complications of the text warrant some narrative exposition. Handel, Picasso and Sappho are on a long train journey. Both Handel, a priest and a breast cancer consultant, and Picasso, a young woman painter, are leaving an unspecified city to escape the restrictions and torments of their lives. What these lives were/are is revealed, tortuously, over the course of the novel. Picasso (christened Sophia) is disclosed as the daughter of entrepreneur Jack Hamilton and his former maid whom he raped. Handel is the doctor that Hamilton's wife suggests that the maid approach to ask for an abortion. Handel refuses and, coincidently, ends up delivering the baby. The maid leaves the baby, Picasso, on

Hamilton's doorstep to be raised by its father and his family. From the age of 9, Picasso is routinely raped by her older adoptive brother. Handel is revealed to be a castrato, taken for the illegal operation before puberty by his elderly mentor and lover, a Catholic cardinal. Sappho is both Sappho the poet and a twentieth-century namesake. Her character works as counterbalance to Handel and Picasso's pain in coming to terms with their pasts and voicing their futures. Sappho has suffered but has the self-knowledge to articulate herself fully and her poetic contributions are unapologetic celebrations of life and love. The twentieth-century Sappho is in love with Sophia/Picasso and is revealed to have been present when Picasso was pushed from the roof of her house by her father.

The train that the three are travelling on is both 'hosed in light' (1995: 33) and journeying towards it. Light and dark feature as metaphors for life and death. And life and death themselves become metaphors for a life filled with art, or a life filled with lies: 'there's only art and lies' (69). In travelling toward the light, Handel and Picasso are clearly embracing art and relinquishing the falsities of their pasts. Their journey is punctuated by reading from an aged, unfinished book that was a gift to Handel from the cardinal. Doll Sneerpiece's story, *The Entire and Honest Recollections of a Bawd* (165), appears in this book alongside canonical works from Homer to Wilde (203–4). But Handel and Picasso read only Doll's tale and her bawdiness throws into relief Handel's asceticism and Picasso's pain. Doll reads life far more fluently than either Handel or Picasso and her skill is reflected in the dextrous way she is able to combine prostitution and self-education:

> She had found that by arching her bottom in a calculating manner, she could prop her forearms on the bed and continue to read undisturbed by the assaults on her hypotenuse. It was in this way that she had come to delight in the elevating works of Sappho.
>
> (29)

For Doll, the text and the body are inextricably linked, not the same but analogous, experience of one allowing easier access to and understanding of the other. This is evinced by her comparison of Ruggerio, the object of her unrequited affection, to a book:

> And if I were to say that I would care to turn the pages of that gentleman one by one, and to run my fingers down his margins, and to decipher his smooth spine, and to go on my knees to enjoy his lower titles, and to upturn that one long volume that he keeps so secret to himself.
>
> (6)

Reading and desire, or, more specifically, sexual desire, become metaphors for each other; the relationship between reader and text is as intimate, as visceral, as that between lovers. Doll's self-assurance in matters of desire is contrasted with Handel's inexpertise. Despite operating as a commentator upon his (and our) contemporary times Handel lacks experience in matters of the heart, turning away the woman he loved when much younger: 'She rightly read the moment while I stumbled through a second-hand text. I loved her and lied' (113). Ironically then, Handel's profession reveals him to be adept at reading women's bodies and soothing their minds, safely inured from his moments of lasciviousness by Catholicism, medical science and, perhaps, his own castration:

> I like to look at women. That is one of the reasons why I became a doctor. As a priest my contact is necessarily limited ... Am I tempted? Perhaps, but I would never break my vows, professional and religious. Isn't that enough?
> (9)

His ascetic surface conceals his passion not only for women but also for his art, for singing, something which has marked his body in the most violent of ways. The grand narratives of science and religion are exposed, through Handel, as purveyors of lies, their jargons and practices disguising their deceptions. Handel spends the train journey symbolically regaining his balls, remembering who he was before he was deadened by priesthood and medical practice.

Picasso's body has been so abused and bruised by her brother and father, she has been so repeatedly deceived, that it is only painting that has prevented her return to hospital. It is the colours that she clings to as she and her brother and play '*Torpedoes and Targets*, ... with his hand over my mouth and his cock between my legs' (153), and the colours she uses to wreak her revenge as Matthew lies 'covered in paint and half-naked on the floor' (157). It is only when Picasso leaves her 'dead' (159) adoptive family that she can learn to read herself without fear of reprisal. The histories divulged at the end of the novel appear as Handel and Picasso begin to harmonize with both themselves and each other. The liberation is represented in the form of communication and song and it seems fitting that the novel ends with nine pages of the score for Strauss's *Der Rosenkavalier* as the protagonists are learning to lose their inhibitions and sing, both literally and metaphorically. Thus, if *Written* is concerned with the wonders that can be revealed by an intimate relationship with the physical body and the textual body then *Art and Lies* is about what happens when the body is denied expression by being constantly misused and misread. If *Written* is a eulogy to the body, even in its sickness and decay, then *Art and Lies* is a cry of pain. Handel and Picasso struggle to read both themselves and others due to the abuse they have suffered, the lies that they have been told. Consequently, it *is* a difficult read because Winterson forces the material reader to experience the disquiet of her two key protagonists. The spiralling, non-linear narrative requires careful deciphering as the dis-jointed structure of the text is used to reflect Handel and Picasso's disease, their dis-comfort. They are learning to read themselves through the unravellings and re-readings of their pasts and their narratives move between third and first person to reflect this process; in contrast, Sappho's voice is almost always 'I'. In the process of learning to read their own lives the two revert to the skills they have always used to make sense of, or to *read*, their worlds: singing for Handel and painting for Picasso. The novel is concerned with how to live life, what path to take. Its unashamed exultation of art is juxtaposed with a passionate repositioning of Sappho, inferring that 'art' itself must be constantly re-read in order that it does not become relocated as lies.

Like *Written* and *Art and Lies*, *The PowerBook* is also concerned with the interrelations between reading, the body and desire but addresses a different mode. *PowerBook* tells of a writer who uses the internet to advertise and promote her work. She is approached via email and asked to provide stories that will provide '*Freedom, just for one night*' (Winterson, 2001a: 3). The tales she tells include a developing story of the affair between a married woman and a woman writer. This embedded narrative steadily becomes more and more indistinguishable from the frame story of the narrator and her customer. The boundary between 'reality' and 'fiction' is being portrayed as unsteady and as easily, and necessarily, transgressed. This is a familiar Wintersonian trope – 'I'm telling you stories. Trust me' (Winterson, 1988: 13) – and works to foreground the ways in which 'reality' is rewritten and re-read. Winterson's insistence upon the insertion of her own biography into the text further blurs this boundary and forces the reader to confront the lazy compartmentalization of fact from fiction.

The narrator's use of the internet as the medium by which she produces and promotes her stories reflects the late-twentieth-/early-twenty-first-century move into new modes and models of reading. The web offers new opportunities for the dissemination and reception of texts and the fragmentation and multi-layering of *PowerBook*'s narrative/s reflects the non-linear way in which we read hypertext.[4] In addition, chat-rooms and email allow a degree of intimacy and feedback previously denied the writer. The 'conversations' between the narrator and her customer mirror the simultaneous intimacy and distance of communicating via the net. Cyberspace produces both absence and presence: the absence of corporeality is counterbalanced by the presence of a more immediate response. Winterson's narrator is not just telling a story, she is also receiving feedback from the customer as the story develops. Thus the fictional reader becomes a complicit companion in the unfolding of the narrative/s and the material reader is constantly aware of the activity of reading.

If the internet works both to reflect and to engender the polysemy of the text, it also allows for the reinvention of identity. New selves can be fashioned and reproduced at the click of a mouse; identity becomes unfixed and fluid, with the potential for endless proliferation: 'This is a virtual world. This is a world inventing itself. Daily, new landmasses form and then submerge. New continents of thought break off from the mainland' (Winterson 2001a: 63). The opening two chapters of *Power-Book* highlight both this potential mutability and the limitations of identity. The customer asks to be changed – 'You say you want to be transformed' (4) – and the narrator complies, offering a different DNA through the discarding of the corporeal for the metamorphic power of storytelling: 'This is where the story starts ... This is an invented world where you can be free for just one night ... Undress. Take off your clothes. Take off your body ... Tonight we can go deeper than disguise' (4). However, this feast of possibilities comes at a price; the loss of corporeality and the expectation of a response weigh heavy upon those used to a more embodied existence: 'I logged onto the Net. There were no emails for me. You had run out on the story. Run out on me. Vanished.' (63). In fact, the frustrations of corporeal distance are clear throughout *PowerBook* and the desire for fleshly consummation runs concurrent with the desire for the freedoms offered by the anonymity of cyberspace. Thus, although the narrator's stories are constructed in hyperreality they are eventually put on display in the shop (235), much as earlier in the novel it is clearly signposted that the relationship between the lovers of the embedded narrative has shifted into 'meat-space' (161).

This tension between the simultaneous pleasures and restrictions of disembodiment foregrounds the fact that reading itself exists in the interstices of the embodied and the disembodied. Reading allows entry to worlds where new identities and lives can be acquired; all that is needed is imagination and the ability to understand the semiology of language. Yet it is clearly more than this, for it also requires a physical presence and some degree of physical interaction. However, if reading happens in the body its effects and pleasures are about consciousness, it enacts a process of transformation that is more than the purely corporeal. Thus, like desire, it finds its execution in a complex interaction of the bodily and the cerebral; both are crucial to its performance. If *PowerBook* operates as both a representation *of* and metaphor *for* reading then the embodied components are foregrounded by the very clear connotations of prostitution, itself another common Wintersonian topos. The action unfolds at night as the narrator plies her trade across the net and is contacted anonymously with the commission to tell stories that will give 'Freedom, just for one night' (3). She provides a service for which she is rewarded and during which she must take account of the desires of her customer and alter her behaviour, i.e. her writing, accordingly. This paradigm positions the reader as cruising client, trawling cyberspace for the best story for the best price. Meanwhile, the narrator plies her trade across the net and the final versions of her stories are exhibited as a display of her assets in order that she may attract more customers for the following night/s. Thus, storytelling features as both economic necessity and sexual titillation, as the narrator works throughout the night to sate the demands of an anonymous punter and finishes the job by pimping her wares in a shop window (235). The writer 'prostitutes' her craft, repeating a tried and tested formula in order to make a living. This model not only positions writing and reading as a process of supply and demand but also as acts that have a clear relationship to the physical performance of desire and its attendant discourses of power and privilege. However, as noted above, desire, like reading, exists in the mind as much as the body and the voyeuristic and erotic elements of text work to highlight this interaction.

This model of economic exchange, of the search for fleeting textual satisfaction, is contradicted in several ways as the novel progresses. The online flirtation and burgeoning love affair between the narrator and customer can be seen as reflecting the developing relationship between reader and text; both very *specifically* in terms of the material reader's relationship to this text, and more generally in terms of the relationship between all readers and the texts that they are reading. However, *PowerBook* not only highlights and interrogates the relationship between reader and text, but also that between reader and author as the narrator anxiously awaits a response from her client. Emails are 'unwrapped' (3) like eagerly awaited presents and stories are churned out to invite a reply: 'I keep throwing the stories overboard, like a message in a bottle, hoping you'll read them, hoping you'll respond' (83). Within this model the dynamic between the writer and her reader is represented as a far more complex interaction than merely one of supply and demand; it is positioned as symbiotic and mutable. The narrator is both paid with and seeks romantic love; the customer repeatedly returns for the love that she is offered by the tales that she is told. The story and the process of storytelling become the means by which seduction is executed. Writing, therefore, is something that tempts and seduces the reader in its promise to indulge and fulfil the desire to read. As the connection between narrator and customer deepens so the merging of the frame story and embedded narrative increases and love operates alongside economics as a metaphor for the relationship between both writer and reader, and reader and text. Textual satisfaction becomes about far more than a quick, furtive fumble behind closed doors. The pleasure of the text derives from the consummation of the desires of author and reader; a coming-together of ideal reader and ideal text which can, at best, achieve transcendence. However, the novel's lack of closure implies that this 'union' never really attains this zenith. Rather, the desire to read is positioned as unquenchable yet in constant need of sating; there is no more a perfect text that provides the perfect reading pleasure than there is the perfect love affair that comes at no cost. The reader is preordained to search through text after text, seeking an ever-deferred salvation.

In all three of these novels, Winterson is insisting that her readers engage with the complications and contradictions of reading, that is, with its *difficulties*. *Written on the Body*, *Art and Lies* and *The PowerBook* all work to problematize the processes of the act of reading, that is, they refuse to locate it as a transparent act, as merely a way of accessing material. Their focus upon the body and desire serves to highlight further the complexity of engaging with a text. Using the body and the enactment of bodily desire/s as a metaphor for the act of reading means that reading becomes, alongside love and art, something that can transform and save, that can change lives:

> The book does not reproduce me, it re-defines me, pushes at my boundaries, shatters the palings that guard my heart. Strong texts work along the borders of our minds and alter what already exists.
>
> (Winterson 1996: 26)

Reading, correctly executed, becomes a challenge, an act that requires fortitude and is not for the weak of body or mind:

> The Word terrifies. The seducing word, the insinuating word, the word that leads the trembling hand to the forbidden key. The Word beyond the door, the word that waits to be unlocked, the word springing out of censure, the word that cracks the font. The Word that does not bring peace but a sword. The word whose solace is salt from the rock. The word that does not repent.
>
> (Winterson 1995: 55)

The 'word' is represented as a harsh mistress and reading as something that antagonizes and disappoints as much as it pleases. Learning to read is an ongoing process that is beset with pitfalls as well as pleasures: 'Reading is not a passive act' (Winterson, web resource). Winterson's writing purposively confounds the reader's expectations and works to deliberately discomfort as the struggles of the characters in the novels are mirrored by the struggles of her material readers. The narrator's difficulty in translating Louise; Handel and Picasso's journey towards self-actualization; the writer and her customer's difficulty in defining their relationship: all serve to reinforce the effort necessarily involved in passionately interacting with the text. Winterson's own re-reading of literary tradition, of literary heritage, confirms reading as an act that consumes energy, upkeep and attention, as that which requires constant nurturing in order to fully divulge its secrets. This acute awareness of the visceral qualities of reading, of the bodily desire/s and pleasure/s engendered by and contained within the text, calls for a new anatomy of reading that demands that feeling be promoted as of utmost importance. Readers are relocated centre stage.

Notes

1. Intertextuality refers to the way in which texts allude to and make use of other texts, both consciously and unconsciously. Winterson is a highly arch intertextual writer – that is, she deliberately reworks other texts in order to re-present and challenge the familiar stories that we tell and are told.
2. Brian Finney (2002: 27) makes a similar point in his detailed and engaged discussion of the language of romance in *Written*: 'Winterson not only describes humans as textual artefacts but also thinks of works of literature as if they were living beings'.
3. Christy Burns (1996: 299) discusses this idea with reference to *Art and Lies* claiming that Winterson 'effects a kind of transubstantiation of body into word'.
4. The term 'hypertext' was first coined by Theodor H. Nelson and used to mean 'non-sequential writing – text that branches and allows choices to the reader, best read at an interactive screen' (quoted in Landow 1997: 3). It now tends to refer to the specific way in which text is presented on the internet, i.e. in juxtaposition with both sound and image and as offering the reader different paths via hyperlinks. Landow convincingly argues that hypertext requires us to read in different and new ways and sees the internet as a way of moving away from Barthes' 'readerly' text, whereby meaning is fixed, towards his 'writerly' text where meaning proliferates (3–5).

Works cited

Barthes, Roland (1975), [1970], *S/Z*, translated from the French by R. Miller. London: Jonathan Cape.

—— (1978), [1990], *A Lover's Discourse: Fragments*, translated from the French by Richard Howard. Harmondsworth: Penguin.

Belsey, Catherine (1994), *Desire: Love Stories in Western Culture*. Oxford, UK/ Cambridge, USA: Blackwell.

Burns, Christy L. (1996), 'Fantastic language: Jeanette Winterson's recovery of the postmodern word', *Contemporary Literature*, 37, (2), 278–306.

Finney, Brian (2002), 'Bonded by language: Jeanette Winterson's *Written on the Body*', *Women and Language*, 15, (2), 23–31.

Grice, Helen and Woods, Tim (eds) (1998), *Postmodern Studies 25: 'I'm telling you stories': Jeanette Winterson and the Politics of Reading*. Amsterdam/Atlanta, GA: Rodopi.

Lambert, Angela (1998), 'Jeanette Winterson', *Prospect Magazine* 27, February 1998, http://www.prospect-magazine.co.uk/article_details.php?id=4295

Landow, George P. (1997), *Hypertext 2.0, Being a Revised, Amplified Edition of: Hypertext: The Convergence of Contemporary Critical Theory and Technology*. Baltimore/London: Johns Hopkins University Press.

Pearce, Lynne (1997), *Feminism and the Politics of Reading*. London and New York: Arnold.

—— (1998), 'The emotional politics of reading Winterson', in H. Grice and T. Woods (eds), *Postmodern Studies 25: 'I'm telling you stories': Jeanette Winterson and the Politics of Reading*. Amsterdam/Atlanta, GA: Rodopi, pp. 29–39.

Winterson, Jeanette (1988), *The Passion*. London: Penguin.

—— (1995), *Art and Lies*. London: Vintage.

—— (1996), *Art Objects: Essays on Ecstacy and Effrontery*. London: Vintage.

—— (2001a), *The Power Book*. London: Vintage.

—— (2001b), [1992], *Written on the Body*. London: Vintage.

—— http://www.jeanettewinterson.com/pages/content/index.asp?PageID =12 (accessed 19 July 2006).

—— (2006), Talk at Manchester Metropolitan University, 22 March.

CHAPTER SIX

Reinventing the Romance

SONYA ANDERMAHR

Chapter summary: This chapter explores Winterson's representation of sexual love, relating it to the tradition of romance writing in general and to the subgenre of lesbian romance fiction in particular. It suggests that while Winterson utilizes and reworks many features of the lesbian romance genre, she ultimately strives to write beyond gender *and* genre to inscribe a new discourse of sexual love capable of speaking to and about all human lovers.

Key texts: *Oranges Are Not the Only Fruit; The Passion; Written on the Body; Lighthousekeeping*

Key words: the romance genre, lesbian representation, queer theory, sexual discourse, literary experiment

Without love what does humanness mean?

(Winterson 1998: 32)

From her first novel, *Oranges Are Not the Only Fruit* (1985), to the more recent *Lighthousekeeping* (2004), Jeanette Winterson has been concerned to represent sexual love between women. Yet, her texts' reluctance if not refusal to use the signifier 'lesbian' has from the outset rendered her work eccentric to the genre of lesbian romance and to lesbian fiction as a whole.[1] Indeed, as Heather Nunn observes: 'The force and challenge of Jeanette Winterson's fiction is in its offering up of an erotic experience that contests the conventional fixity of identity' (1996: 16). Winterson's work is characterized by a strategy of simultaneous universalization and particularization, in which her representations of love and desire oscillate between non-specific universals which could apply regardless of sex and sexuality, and more specific references to pairs of lovers, female and female, male and female, male and male, or to kinds of love: sexual, platonic, familial. This chapter charts Winterson's representation of women's erotic experience, focusing on four of her major novels: *Oranges, The Passion* (1988), *Written on the Body* (1992) and *Light-housekeeping*. It demonstrates how, as Winterson's work has progressed, her treatment of same-sex relations has taken a variety of forms encompassing a coming-out narrative, sexual masquerade, romantic quest, an anti-romantic critique and more recently an almost incidental subplot. Throughout her texts, Winterson may be seen to be simultaneously drawing on and critiquing the subgenre of lesbian romance as well as the Western tradition of the romance more generally. Both utilizing and subverting romantic tropes in the representation of love between women, her work nevertheless gestures beyond lesbian specificity to inscribe multiple sexualities, queer, lesbian and indeed heterosexual. For, as I will show, Winterson is committed to reinventing the discourse of sexual love *tout court*, remaking the language of romance for all of us.

A brief history of the lesbian romance

As Winterson implies in *The PowerBook* (2000), from Tristan and Isolde to Cathy and Heathcliffe, the most striking and naturalized feature of the canonical romance genre is of course its privileging of heterosexual love. And, indeed, as famous same-sex lovers such as Oscar and Bosie, and Vita and Virginia discovered, the increasing hegemony of heterosexual romance coincides historically with the social oppression of same-sex love and its classification as deviant and illegitimate. The conjunction of romance with heterosexuality therefore presents lesbian writers with a problem, which Winterson herself has tackled in a number of ways.[2] The feminist movement of the 1960s and 1970s radically altered the social meanings of lesbian love and identification. The first element to disappear was the 'invert' or 'third sex' invented by the sexologists and popularized by Radclyffe Hall's *The Well of Loneliness* (1983), arguably still the best-known example of the lesbian novel. In the 1970s, lesbianism was dissociated from invertism and masculinity and redefined in terms of woman-identification. Woman-bonding became a way of celebrating and acknowledging femaleness instead of denying it. Radical feminists, such as the group Radicalesbians (1973) and the poet Adrienne Rich (1996), argued that what made lesbians different from other women was the fact that they prioritized women's relationships over relations with men.

Much of the lesbian fiction that came out of the women's movement had the ideological aim of representing lesbianism as a positive alternative to heterosexuality in women's lives. The romance genre was used by lesbian writers to celebrate lesbianism as an attractive lifestyle and to portray erotic feelings and encounters between women. Lesbian romance has served an important function both as erotic fantasy, and as a corrective to images promulgated by mainstream culture of lesbians as sick or sinful.[3] It emphasizes the naturalness and normalcy of lesbian relationships and frequently offers an explicit critique of the institution of heterosexuality. Moreover, at a structural level, the lesbian romance breaks with the narrative trajectory of the heterosexual genre, adopting a model in which a triadic female–male–female relationship is replaced by a female dyad in the course of the narrative. Terry Castle (1990) has identified this pattern in an early British novel, *Summer Will Show* (1987) by Sylvia Townsend Warner, and argues that it is characteristic of lesbian plotting. Indeed, since the 1970s the plots of lesbian romances have tended to follow a formulaic pattern: girl meets girl and, after overcoming misunderstandings and obstacles – in the form of family, male rivals and forms of patriarchal authority – the lovers recognize their true feelings and embark on a life together.

Lesbian romance therefore tends to follow the opposite trajectory to that of heterosexual romance. Whereas the latter is concerned with the heroine's *integration* into patriarchal society, lesbian romance enacts the lovers' *separation* from it and their retreat into their own idyllic space. The majority of lesbian romances are 'conversion' narratives which, following the pattern of the lesbian novel of development, or *Bildungsroman*, portray the protagonist's journey to lesbian identification. In the heterosexual genre the central problematic hinges on sexual power relations between men and women, and on women's anxieties concerning their desires for man, the 'oppressor' (Modleski 1982). This is not at issue in the lesbian genre, where men feature not as objects of desire but as obstacles to women's love for each other. Independence rather than class status is the key factor in the lesbian genre, and represents the prerequisite for self-determination and sexual fulfilment. Female dependency is frequently used as a device to increase the romantic tension. Like the heterosexual romance, the lesbian genre functions partly as a wish-fulfilment fantasy, articulating emotional and libidinal desires, and offering fantasy resolutions. Both operate as fantasies which apparently explore, but frequently repress, real power relations between and among men and women. Whereas the heterosexual romance tends to transform the potential rapist into the loving husband (Modleski 1982) or insist that men, beneath a tough exterior, are really sensitive and nurturing (Radway 1984), the lesbian romance implies that women really can find love and happiness outside male-dominated and homophobic society, frequently placing the idealized lesbian couple beyond social reality. It tends to erase differences between women and offer a utopian depiction of lesbian love. The representation of the lovers in lesbian romance fiction owes much to the lesbian-feminist redefinition of lesbian relationships as egalitarian and non-hierarchical, assuming, idealistically, that lesbian identification transcends barriers of class and finance. However, in practice this has resulted in a narrow focus on young, white, childless, middle-class women.[4] On the whole, the lesbian romance genre has flourished since the emergence of Second Wave feminism, and this is undoubtedly because it marginalizes institutional heterosexuality and privileges the bonds between women.

From *Oranges* onwards, Winterson clearly writes in the wake of and contributes to the important semantic and ideological shift brought about by Second Wave feminism, and her work shares many features of the lesbian novel outlined above. As in the lesbian romance, Winterson's work may be seen to enact the characteristic separation from patriarchal ties and heterosexual marriage, by which lesbian desire is accorded a privileged narrative space. Her protagonists, whatever their gender, appear to be 'always already' lovers of women: from *Oranges* to *Lighthousekeeping*, the narrator's sexuality is presented as 'naturally' woman-oriented. In so far as most of the love objects in Winterson's fiction are previously heterosexual women, she retains an element of the 'conversion' narrative. From Melanie in *Oranges* to Louise in *Written on the Body*, the beloved is seduced from the path of normative hetero-sexuality by the narrator's passionate overtures. The emphasis on independence from men is also echoed in Winterson's work in which the beloved seems trapped by her comfortable, bourgeois life; although in *Written*, Louise's relationship with Elgin is characterized by her dependence on him not so much as a wife but as a cancer patient. And while Winterson shares the lesbian genre's predilection for young, sexy lovers, her characters are not idealized in the manner of lesbian romance. Moreover, Winterson's texts invariably eschew any straight-forward 'happy-ever-after' resolution; the obligatory wish-fulfilment fantasy of the romance genre is largely absent. Her endings are ambiguous and occluded, if not in fact anti-romantic, and this, I will argue, becomes a key issue in her relationship both to the romantic tradition and to lesbian-feminism.

Reconfiguring the lesbian romance: *Oranges Are Not the Only Fruit*

Despite being read most commonly as an original and charming first novel, treating universal themes of family, adolescent love and the conflict between the individual and the community, *Oranges* is also 'an avowedly lesbian novel' (Hinds 1992: 153), which shares many features with the lesbian romance and *Bildungsroman* genres. In the latter genre especially, the female protagonist's unusual upbringing produces a sense of difference, specialness and indeed of election, typified by Hall's character Stephen Gordon. Early in *Oranges*, the young Jeanette encounters a gypsy who predicts: 'You'll never marry ... not you, and you'll never be still' (1985: 7). And, later on, Jeanette justifies her love for Melanie by setting it apart from the everyday world: 'Melanie and I were special' (106). As Hinds (1992) observes, Winterson's portrayal of young lesbian love in *Oranges* was generally approved by both her mainstream and her lesbian readers, even as they interpreted it in dif-ferent ways, and all the more remarkable given Winterson's radical subversion of the mainstream genre. Just as in the lesbian genre, Winterson's characters are more or less equally matched in social terms, and it is precisely the issue of economic independence as a precondition for their insertion into the romance genre that is foregrounded in Winterson's depiction of the workaday context in which Jeanette and Melanie as two working-class girls doing Saturday jobs meet and fall in love. The juxtaposition between their mundane environment and Jeanette's romantic feelings is drawn to striking comic effect:

> She was boning kippers on a big marble slab.
> ...
> 'I'd like to do that,' I said.
> She smiled and carried on.
> ...
> 'Can I have some fish-bait?' I asked.
> She looked up and I noticed her eyes were a lovely grey, like the cat Next Door.
>
> (1985: 80)

While Winterson's inscription of lesbian desire in *Oranges* is explicit and incontrovertible, she does not depict lesbian sex in a graphic manner. Approximating the feelings and language of a young woman who is sexually inexperienced but knows what she wants, Winterson presents an understated account: 'She stroked my head ... it felt like drowning. I was frightened but couldn't stop' (88–9). And, in the tender yet matter-of-fact depiction of Jeanette's relationship with Katy, Winterson seems to write both within and beyond the conventions of romance to record: 'We weren't cold, not that night nor any of the others we spent together over the years that followed. She was my most uncomplicated love affair, and I loved her because of it' (123). Winterson utilizes a model of sexual attraction based on sameness rather than difference, which is common to forms of lesbian representation including the romance (Zimmerman 1990). The lesbian lovers are not, as in Hall's canonical text, presented as either troubled inverts or as acting out exaggerated butch-femme roles. Indeed, it is the heterosexual relationships which appear by contrast strange, dysfunctional and in the case of the woman who 'married a pig' downright grotesque (1985: 71). As Laura Doan points out, Winterson's 'reconceptualization of the normal makes lesbian existence possible by, in effect, reversing the dominant culture's definition of natural and unnatural' and thus rendering 'heterosexuality as unintelligible' for many of her characters (1994: 138).

The undeniable girlishness and, in the TV adaptation, the extreme slenderness of the lovers could be seen as a way of infantilizing lesbianism by representing it as 'innocent', immature and therefore non-threatening (Hinds 1992). But this view is hardly justified given the threat Jeanette's desire represents to the patriarchal values of the Church. This is made clear when the Church council's judgement on Jeanette's behaviour is delivered:

> The real problem it seemed was going against the teachings of St Paul, and allowing women power in the church. [My mother] ended by saying that having taken on a man's world in other ways I had flouted God's law and tried to do it sexually.
>
> (1985: 133–4)

The novel explicitly challenges patriarchal and religious views of lesbianism, aligning it clearly with feminism. It explores and rejects a series of explanations of lesbian sexuality including traditional religious views that homosexuality represents a form of demon possession and/ or a sin: 'It all seemed to hinge around the fact that I loved the wrong sort of people. Right sort of people in every respect except this one; romantic love for another woman was a sin' (127). While the pastor carries out an exorcism on the basis of the first interpretation, seeing Jeanette herself as an innocent victim of the fiend, her mother inclines to the more blameworthy view that Jeanette acting on free will has chosen her 'sin': 'My mother saw it as a wilful act on my part to sell my soul' (128). The more liberal view derived from sexology that homosexuality is an inborn, natural condition and therefore 'I couldn't help it' (128) is also expressed by some members of the church, and sits alongside the more feminist account voiced by Jeanette herself. In the scene in which Pastor Finch accuses her in church and demands, 'do you deny that you love this woman with a love reserved for man and wife?', Jeanette bravely replies, 'No, yes, I mean of course I love her', thereby refusing the terms of his question and affirming the rightness of her love despite her confusion. In *Oranges*, as Doan avers, Jeanette's strength 'emerges from a profound and unshakable conviction that her lesbianism is right and that any attempt to condemn or despise her – a celebrant of that most natural of passions – constitutes perversion' (1994: 137).

When her mother accuses her of 'aping men', thus colluding with a narrow patriarchal model of gender-appropriate behaviour, Jeanette's sense of betrayal is complete: 'Until this moment my life had made some kind of sense. Now it was making no sense at all' (1985: 133). Winterson's distancing of lesbianism from male homosexuality accords with the radical feminist theory of Adrienne Rich (1996) in which lesbianism is seen not as a movement away from womanhood, towards male behaviour, gay or straight, but as an enrichment of femaleness. 'Now if I was aping men she'd have reason to be disgusted ... At that point I had no idea of sexual politics, but I knew that a homosexual is further away from a woman than a rhinoceros (1985: 128). Although Winterson's later work adopts queer models of sexuality that challenge this binary view, the notion of lesbianism as enhanced femaleness persists as a strand in her work. Moreover, *Oranges* appears to endorse Rich's near contemporaneous theory of 'lesbian continuum' (Rich 1996) which sought to detach lesbianism from the clinical, sexological and generally negative meanings which had accrued to it in post-Freudian discourses, and to redefine it in terms of positive, nurturing relationships between women. In an influential passage Rich writes:

> I mean the term *lesbian continuum* to include a range – through each woman's life and throughout history – of woman-identified experience, not simply the fact that a woman has had or consciously desired genital sexual experience with another woman. If we expand it to embrace many more forms of primary intensity between and among women, including the sharing of a rich inner life, the bonding against male tyranny, the giving and receiving of practical and political support ... we begin to grasp breadths of female history and psychology which have lain out of reach as a consequence of limited, mostly clinical definitions of 'lesbianism'.
>
> (1996: 26)

The novel introduces a range of female characters which may be seen as existing on a lesbian continuum. It includes the two women in the sweetshop which her mother forbids her to visit: 'She said they dealt in unnatural passions. I thought she meant they put chemicals in the sweets' (1985: 7). It encompasses Miss Jewsbury who, when Jeanette's affair with Melanie is discovered, provides sanctuary and, briefly, sexual solace, telling Jeanette 'It's my problem too' (106). It includes the daughter of a minor character of whom it is said, 'she spends all her time at that Susan's doing her homework' (76). Elsie Norris, too, Jeanette's much older friend, provides non-judgemental friendship and love when she is cast out by the church. Even Jeanette's mother is revealed to have had a close relationship with another woman and briefly finds a place on the continuum. Jeanette sees a picture of a young woman in the photo album to whom she refers mysteriously as 'Eddy's sister' (36). But when Jeanette looks at the album again the picture has disappeared.

To a greater extent than in either the lesbian romance genre or radical feminist theory, however, Winterson acknowledges ambivalence about as well as pleasure in lesbian identity and desire. Indeed the aspect of sexual ambivalence is interpolated into the text through the magic realist device of the orange demon. Puncturing the realist narrative at the moment of maximum trauma following her 'exorcism', the orange demon appears to Jeanette as a representation of her (sexual) difference and an expression of her ambivalence about her new-found sexuality: 'If I let them take away my demons, I'll have to give up what I've found' (108). Later, when she asks what will happen if she elects to keep it, the demon tells her, 'You will have a difficult, different time' (109). In the course of the novel Jeanette perceives that oranges, contrary to her mother's belief, and once comforting and sufficient, are no longer the only fruit. The titular metaphor works to suggest that there are different ways of living life and different forms of sexual desire and expression. However, while binary oppositions are challenged through inversion in *Oranges*, they are never ultimately erased, as Laura Doan persuasively argues:

> Winterson's lesbian subject, though imbued with a voice and granted a threatening masculine power, still cannot transcend the condition of binarism, a predicament that interferes with the complete overthrow of heterosexual hegemony ... For the lesbian writer, the task, the political agenda if you will, is to displace and explode the binary.
>
> (1994: 147)

Queer loves and losses: *The Passion*

In the novels that followed, Winterson appeared to make this agenda her own. The 'specialness' discourse that pervades *Oranges*, and characterizes the lesbian novel, gives way in subsequent texts to a wider notion of a 'polymorphous' sexual continuum in which different varieties of love and desire, across the lines of gender and sexuality, are depicted and explored. In *The Passion* and *Sexing the Cherry* (1990) Winterson mirrors – and indeed anticipates – the queer turn of lesbian politics in the 1980s and early 1990s. Just as political groups such as ActUp and Queer Nation took to the streets, challenging the narrow 'hetero versus homo' binary of conventional sexual politics, Winterson provided a wealth of queer subjects which mirrored the theoretical and political voices reinventing lesbian and gay identities. Judith Butler rejected the view that sexual identity was the outward expression of a core self, which could be seen as essentially 'masculine' (Hall's invert) or 'female' (Rich's lesbian subject). She argued rather that all gender is a kind of 'drag', 'an imitation' or 'performance' that 'produces the illusion of an inner sex' through 'that array of corporal theatrics understood as gender presentation' (2004: 134). In contrast to the relatively stable and transparent models of sexuality posited by sexology and radical feminism, Butler emphasized the fluidity, mobility and indeed opacity of desire:

> There are no direct expressive or causal lines between sex, gender, gender presentation, sexual practice, fantasy and sexuality. None of those terms captures or determines the rest. Part of what constitutes sexuality is precisely that which does not appear and that which, to some degree, can never appear.
>
> (2004: 131)

For Eve Kosofsky Sedgwick, the term 'queer' signified both the overdetermined sexual identity of certain texts by homosexual writers and the deconstructive practice of critics engaged in reading them. Tracing the etymological roots of the term 'queer', from '*torquere*, to twist', she emphasizes its indeterminate qualities, 'crossing genders, sexualities, genres and perversions' (1994: xii) and the:

> [O]pen mesh of possibilities, gaps, overlaps, dissonances and resonances, lapses and excesses of meaning when the constituent elements of anyone's gender, of anyone's sexuality aren't made (or can't be made) to signify monolithically.
>
> (1994: 8)

Indeed, Sedgwick's delineation of queer perfectly captures both Winterson's narrative strategy from this point in her career and the extraordinarily diverse forms of sexual identity and desire that appear in *The Passion* and *Sexing*.

If the title of *The Passion* clearly signifies its subject matter of love and intense emotion in the widest sense, this may be seen to take a variety of forms including religious connotations of the suffering of Christ (see Chapter 7), and secular, romantic and platonic forms of love on the part of its characters Henri and Villanelle. Henri, the Napoleonic foot-soldier, like the rest of the French people, hero-worships his commanding officer; he also feels an unrequited passion for the marvellous and elusive Villanelle, who in turn has a brief but passionate affair with the Queen of Spades, apparently literally 'losing her heart' for love. The section concerning Villanelle, 'The Queen of Spades', presents a magical world of indeterminate sex, in which the predominant motifs are those of masquerade and gaming. Venice is 'the city of disguises' (1988: 56) in which people's identities, like lives, are 'uncertain and temporary' (57). A carnival atmosphere reigns in which 'all things seem possible'; 'the laws of the real world are suspended' (76); and 'there are women of every kind and not all of them are women' (58). Playfully invoking literary and historical traditions of cross-dressed women as well as referencing Butlerian theories of gender as drag, Winterson has Villanelle dress as a boy while working in a casino: 'It was part of the game, trying to decide which sex was hidden behind the tight breeches and extravagant face-paint' (54). In describing the practice and pleasures of disguise, Winterson employs what was a common eighteenth-century notion of sexual identity as masquerade, encapsulated in the masked ball:

> I made up my lips with vermilion and overlaid my face with white powder … I wore my yellow Casino breeches with the stripe down each side of the leg and a pirate's shirt that concealed my breasts.
>
> (55)

The dominant refrains of this section of the novel – 'You play, you win. You play, you lose. You play' (66) and 'In between fear and sex, passion is' (76) – suggest respectively that love, like life, is an uncertain game of chance and that to love is far from the comfortable emotion depicted in mainstream romance. On first encountering the Queen of Spades who comes 'with a mask over her face', Villanelle wonders, 'Will she try the cards?' (59). Admitting to a polymorphous bisexuality, she states 'I am pragmatic about love and have taken my pleasure with both men and women, but I have never needed a guard for my heart' (60). The 'Queen', or so Villanelle supposes, thinks she is a boy, raising the specifically lesbian fear of whether the beloved will want her as a woman: 'My heart shrivelled at this thought. To lose her again so soon' (65). But as she goes on to ask, highlighting the ambiguity of sexual identity and desire:

> And what was myself? Was this breeches and boots any less real than my garters? What was it about me that interested her?
> You play, you win. You play, you lose. You play.
>
> (66)

These scenes are also intermittently and characteristically comic: Villanelle can't take off her shirt and reveal her breasts and can't take off her boots because that would reveal her webbed feet. The moment when Villanelle reveals her femaleness is simultaneously humorous and poignant:

> 'I'm a woman,' I said, lifting up my shirt and risking the catarrh.
> She smiled. 'I know'.
> I didn't go home. I stayed.
>
> (71)

The episodes concerning Villanelle and the Queen of Spades treat the fears of queer lovers throughout history and express the lengths to which women who love women have sometimes gone – as cross-dressed women or female husbands – to keep the beloved. Indeed, after their first, awkward kiss she wonders: 'Could a woman love a woman for more than a night?' (69), acknowledging that it 'is not the usual thing' (94). The affair ends, however, on the husband's return and Villanelle realizes that 'they did not live in the fiery furnace she and I inhabited, but they had a calm and a way that put a knife to my heart' (75). Thereafter Villanelle leaves the city only to return with Henri to search for her heart. As with the heterosexual narrative, represented by Henri's unfulfilled love for Villanelle (see Chapter 8), the representation of lesbian love in this novel is bitter-sweet, tinged with sadness and longing, and ultimately unrequited. With *The Passion* Winterson acknowledges the universal effect of loss that is an integral part of sexual love regardless of sexual orientation. Yet, while clearly no longer inhabiting the genre of lesbian romance, with its focus on a single lesbian dyad, to the same extent, Winterson's women, as Laura Doan points out, 'still discover ecstacy with one another rather than with the male companion a conventional telos demands' (1994: 54). However, some lesbian-feminist critics register more ambivalence about Winterson's queer turn: Lynne Pearce has worried that her work after *Oranges* serves 'to subsume the homoeroticism of the texts in their apparent humanism' (1995: 163). In her re-reading of Winterson, she foregrounds the places in Winterson's work, as in *The Passion*, where there is an acknowledgement of the difference that lesbian object choice makes:

> This acknowledgement that love between two women is 'not the usual thing' offers an important corrective to what I do see as a universalizing tendency in Winterson's work ... which does tend to detract from the political significance of homosexual relationships.
>
> (1995: 163)

While concurring with Pearce that there is certainly a 'universalizing tendency' in Winterson's work I disagree with her assessment, for while Winterson's project is not, as Pearce would like it to be, to represent 'the political significance of homosexual relationships', neither does her work 'universalize' by effacing sexual difference. On the contrary, it uses the particular and the specific experience, whether that be a passionate same-sex relation (as it so frequently is in Winterson's work), an intense mother–son bond, or a soldier's hero-worship, to express something universal about what it is to love.

Anti-romance: *Written on the Body*

Throughout the 1980s, and the so-called 'lesbian sex wars' (Stein 1993), critics voiced a concern that the emphasis in radical feminism on the positive aspects of lesbian identification made difficult the exploration of (sexual) power relations *between* women and the acknowledgment of negative emotions and desires *within* lesbianism. Elizabeth Wilson commented that,

> The power of positive thinking will never help us to understand the darker and more poignant elements of sexual desire, the many ambiguities of sexual attraction, the mixture of the masculine and the feminine in each of us.
>
> (1983: 194)

The subgenre of lesbian anti-romance writing developed out of and as a deliberate critique of the romance.[5] It consciously eschews both the wish-fulfilment fantasies and romantic clichés of the genre and, more controversially, the positive image discourse of lesbian-feminism. The anti-romance mode, notwithstanding the emergence of the women's and gay movements, is sceptical about the feminist ideals of community and sisterhood, and voices a doubt that lesbian identity can resolve our problems or fulfil our desires.

It is precisely this terrain of the 'ambiguities of sexual attraction' and 'the mixture of masculine and feminine in each of us' that Winterson's work, especially her work from the 1990s on, explores. Moreover, the deconstruction of the romance – and specifically the *lesbian* romance – genre is seen most clearly in *Written on the Body*. The novel expresses a cynicism about sexual love almost entirely absent in the romance genre. It explores the roguish narrator's quest for sexual love and highlights power relations as an integral part of sexual relationships, rather than focusing on reciprocity as the lesbian romance does. In common with writers such as Sarah Schulman (1990), Winterson treats themes largely absent from lesbian-feminist discourses including promiscuity, the lack of mutuality in relationships and objectification of the love object. In this respect, she is explicitly writing against the feminist tradition of positive images.

The novel's central conceit is its use of a sexually indeterminate narrator. Depending on whether the narrator is read as female or male, their relationship with Louise is either lesbian or heterosexual; as is their relationship with Inge, Jacqueline and Gail Right. Either reading is, however, complicated by the revelation of the narrator's previous sexual relationships with Carlo and Bruno, which renders them demonstrably bisexual. Critics have debated exhaustively the implications of sexing the narrator, with some deciding on a lesbian narrator and others on an unfixed subject position (Lindenmeyer 1999). As Nunn demonstrates, the narrator can certainly be read through textual codes as lesbian: 'the still-present fluidity of desire, the movement from a phallocentric to post-genital erotic economy and subversive celebration of a (sick) female body sustain a reading of the text as an affirmation of lesbian love, pleasure and desire (1996: 17). However, it is also clear that Winterson is reaching beyond gender identity to explore love without the restrictive conventions imposed by either heterosexual or lesbian romantic discourse.[6] Whichever template of gender/sexual orientation is brought to bear, the novel is significantly more anti-romantic than her earlier work. It continues the theme of loss from *The Passion* and *Sexing*, but also highlights to a greater degree the commodification, commercialization and impoverishment of love as romance.

Articulating, in particularly savage form, Winterson's staple critique of heterosexual marriage and domesticity, the novel uncompromisingly dissects the ideological and delusional aspects of romance. The narrator is a romantic 'trapped in cliché', 'looking for the perfect coupling', 'the never-sleep non-stop mighty orgasm' and 'ecstacy without end' (1992: 21). Romance, and the domestic bliss it celebrates, is a defence against the terror of love. In fear of the real thing, which is shoved 'under a dump bin of cuddly toys' (10), the narrator takes refuge in 'the diluted version, the sloppy language, the insignificant gestures' (10). Presenting romance as that 'saggy armchair of clichés', she continues:

> It's all right, millions of bottoms have sat here before me. The springs are well worn, the fabric smelly and familiar. I don't have to be frightened, look, my grandma and grandad did it, he in a stiff collar and club tie, she in white muslin straining a little at the life beneath. They did it, my parents did it, now I will do it, won't I, arms outstretched, not to hold you, just to keep my balance, sleepwalking to that armchair. How happy we will be. How happy everyone will be. And they all lived happily ever after.
>
> (10)

As this diatribe suggests, Winterson's target is heterosexual marriage, but her critique applies to the generic clichés of both the heterosexual and the lesbian romance genres. Her defamiliarizing use of language is striking: whereas the romance is a euphoric mode which always speaks in a heightened, poetic language, the anti-romance uses vernacular language to describe sexual experience and reveal the gap between fantasy and reality. As the novel's refrain puts it: 'It's the clichés that cause the trouble' (10, 21, 26, 71, 155, 180). According to Marianne Børch, *Written* refers back to 'the medieval tradition of self-conscious love romance' exemplified by Chaucer and Dante and finds in it 'a resource for filling the verbal gaps in today's lexicon which show that love has lost its cognitive credibility' (1999: 43). Børch maintains that Winterson problematizes 'romance's characteristic idiom', showing 'how the clichés destroy the love they are often invoked to express', and identifying the cause: 'cliché is prior to individual usage, repetition and iterability being the conditions of its recognisability and use; love, however, is unique' (45). Moreover, Børch argues, through an exploration of 'the enigma that this tritest of generic clichés still seems ideal for authentic and innovative expression', Winterson protests 'the need for a new, serious discourse of love' (42–3).

In my reading, Winterson uses a variety of literary devices in her attempt to find new non-clichéd ways of writing about sexual desire including lesbian desire, which comprise of register switching; defamiliarization; lesbian intertextuality; and reclaiming the 'abject'. Two passages from the novel will suffice to illustrate these techniques: the first employs and reworks a conventional sexual discourse, drawing a familiar equation between natural and animal imagery and the female body:

> She arches her body like a cat on a stretch. She nuzzles her cunt into my face like a filly at the gate. She smells of the sea. She smells of rock pools when I was a child. She keeps a starfish in there. I crouch down to taste the salt, to

run my fingers around the rim. She opens and shuts like a sea anemone. She's refilled each day with fresh tides of longing.

(1992: 73)

Despite the conventional oceanic imagery, there is an audacity to the language; the techniques of register switching and juxtaposition – cats, fillies, starfish – work to defamiliarize or 'make strange' what have become clichéd images of female sexuality. In the second passage, Winterson pushes the limits of sexual imagery and 'good taste' much further to astonishing effect:

The smells of my lover's body are still strong in my nostrils. The yeast smell of her sex. The rich fermenting undertow of rising bread. My lover is a kitchen cooking partridge. I shall visit her gamey low-roofed den and feed from her. Three days without washing and she is well-hung and high. Her skirts reel back from her body, her scent is a hoop about her thighs.

(136)

For readers familiar with Djuna Barnes' *Nightwood* (1987), this passage references intertextually a specifically lesbian set of sexual practices and cultural meanings by connoting oral rather than penetrative sex; using the register of smell rather than sight (connected in Freudian theory with a female rather than a male economy); and reversing, eroticizing and reclaiming the usually abject connotations of the unwashed female genitalia of misogynist scatology. Whether the narrator – that trans-spatial figure constructed through the text as precisely a kind of fiction – is finally fixed as 'lesbian' or not is ultimately irrelevant. The *text* retains sexual and linguistic specificity even as it explodes the binaries and boundaries of the romance genre. What Winterson achieves in *Written* is a critique of the clichés of the discourse of romantic love including those of lesbian romance.

What's left for romance? *Lighthousekeeping* and beyond

In *Lighthousekeeping*, a novel that focuses on the close, platonic rela-tionship between a young woman and an older, seemingly ageless man, the lesbian narrative has been reduced to an almost incidental subplot. Towards its end, the protagonist Silver falls in love with a woman whom she meets in Athens and thereafter spends the night with her lover in a hut on the edge of a forest. While this kind of decentring of the lesbian plot may be seen as a positive development, demonstrating that lesbian characters and relationships can exist happily alongside other stories without need for justification, it could also be argued, as several critics did (Briscoe 2004; Crumley 2004), that the love affair and scenes of an adult Silver in Capri and Athens feel 'tacked on', sitting awkwardly with the central narrative concerning Silver and Pew the lighthousekeeper.[7] For other critics, such as Armitt in this volume, this development signals a further movement away from her earlier woman-centred perspective. Lynne Pearce (1998) has carefully charted her own 'romance' with Winterson's work and her growing disillusionment with her treatment of specifically lesbian and feminist themes. In response to such 'disenamoured' views, I would maintain that while it is undoubtedly true that Winterson's work mirrors the queer turn in lesbian theory and politics, it is not the case that her work from *Written* onwards either effaces or ignores feminist, lesbian and woman-oriented themes, subjectivities and narratives. They are present among the multiplicity of other queer subjects, from the lesbian subtexts and intertexts of *Written* to the explicitly lesbian characters of her later work: Sappho, whose mythical lesbianism is rendered legible in *Art & Lies* (1995); Alice and Stella, whose relationship in *Gut Symmetries* (1998) displaces their respective affairs with the phallocentric Jove; the mercurial and woman-loving Ali in *The PowerBook*; as well as Silver in *Lighthousekeeping*, whose Greek love affair seems to have no narrative point other than to anchor her lesbian desire.

Where, therefore, does this leave Winterson's relationship to the lesbian romantic tradition today? While most of her novels depict love between women and utilize many features of the lesbian genre, her decentred, ambivalent lesbian narratives distance her work from that subcultural tradition. In contrast to the lesbian romance, Winterson emphasizes the perilousness of the quest rather than its certain completion, restless desire rather than its fulfilment. As psychoanalysis shows us, Winterson posits desire as that which cannot be satisfied, contrary to the romantic myth of plenitude. But, one may ask, what could be more romantic – and Romantic – than unsatisfied, unreciprocated desire? As Roland Barthes (1990) reminds us, *pace* Goethe's Werther, this is the condition of the modern lover *tout court*. Winterson's work is about desire itself, that of woman for woman being just one kind, the kind she often privileges as the means to meditate on what it is to be human and love. Undoubtedly, one of the major themes of her work is the importance of sexual love, between women, certainly, but more generally as a human imperative. Throughout her work, Winterson emphasizes the difference between real love and the ideology or discourse of romance, stating in *Oranges*: 'Romantic love has been diluted into paperback form and has sold thousands and millions of copies. Somewhere it is still in the original, written on tablets of stone' (170); and writing ten years on in *Art and Lies*, she castigates romance in the media as the 'daily doses of world malaise that poison the heart and mind to such a degree that a strong antidote is required to save what humanness we have left in us' (1995: 13). Nevertheless, in *Lighthousekeeping*, she still wants to retain the concept in all its paradoxical character as something necessary to human life:

I used to be a hopeless romantic. I am still a hopeless romantic. I used to believe that love was the highest value. I still believe that love is the highest value. I don't expect to be happy. I don't imagine that I will find love, whatever that means, or that if I do find it, it will make me happy. I don't think of love as the answer or the solution. I think of love as a force of nature – as strong as the sun, as necessary, as impersonal, as gigantic, as impossible, as scorching as it is warming, as drought-making as it is life-giving. And when it burns out, the planet dies.

(2004: 199)

If in this view, romantic love *just is*, romantic *discourse* which gives it a voice represents, as feminist critics have pointed out, a form of utopianism, expressing a desire *for something else*, for change and transformation, albeit personal, individual change rather than the social, collective change of political utopianism (Modleski 1982; Radway 1984). It is precisely this aspect that Winterson privileges and celebrates. Her work offers the reader narratives of desire full of fabulous sexual and linguistic transformations. Her project, in my view, has been the creation of a new language for the expression of sexual love, drawing on, as Børch shows, the long tradition of Western quest romances and more recently and humbly the specific genre of lesbian romance. In the process she has contributed to the reinvigoration and reinvention of the genre as a whole in both its popular, subcultural and its canonical, 'universal' forms. Jeanette Winterson's particular contribution to contemporary fiction is therefore the inscription of same-sex desire and specificity into a universal story about love.

Notes

1. In *Gut Symmetries* Winterson both exemplifies and comments on her characteristic erasure of the lesbian signifier in the context of homophobic reactions to lesbian love: 'Whoever saw us would say, "There's a couple of …", and this kiss, tentative, ambivalent, would become a lock and key' (1998: 118).
2. As Bonnie Zimmerman asks, 'When is a text a "lesbian text" or its writer a "lesbian writer"?' (1986), indicating that the term 'lesbian writer' is fraught with theoretical difficulty. While it is one that Winterson herself would certainly challenge, she is, however, happy to acknowledge that she is a lesbian and treats lesbian themes in her work.
3. Examples of lesbian romances from the period of Second Wave feminism include Isabel Miller's *Patience and Sarah* (1973), Sarah Aldridge's *All True Lovers* (1978) and Katherine V. Forrest's *Curious Wine* (1983).
4. Some lesbian novels do, however, question the romantic myth from a lesbian perspective; examples include Jane Rule's *Desert of the Heart* (1986) and June Arnold's *Sister Gin* (1979).
5. Examples of the lesbian anti-romance mode include *Don Juan in the Village* by Jane de Lynn (1991) and *After Delores* by Sarah Schulman (1990).
6. A Wittig-influenced reading may well designate the narrator as lesbian on the basis that 'Lesbian is the only concept I know of which is beyond the categories of sex (woman and man), because the designated subject (lesbian) is not a woman, either economically, or politically, or ideologically' (Wittig 1992: 20).
7. My own view is that Winterson's authorial identification with Silver led her to include a

lesbian trajectory for her character in an extended semi-autobiographical narrative that transcends individual novels.

Works cited

Aldridge, Sarah (1978), *All True Lovers*. Tallahassee: The Naiad Press.

Arnold, June (1979), *Sister Gin*. London: The Women's Press.

Barnes, Djuna (1987) [1936], *Nightwood*. London: Faber and Faber.

Børch, Marianne (1999), 'Love's ontology and the problem of cliché', in H. Bengston, M. Børch and C. Maagard (eds), *Sponsored by Demons: The Art of Jeanette Winterson*. Odense, Denmark: Scholars' Press, pp. 41–54.

Briscoe, Joanna (2004), 'Full beam ahead', *Guardian*, Saturday 8 May http://books.guardian.co.uk/reviews/general fiction (accessed 13 July 2005).

Butler, Judith (2004), 'Imitation and gender insubordination', in Sarah Salih (ed.), *The Judith Butler Reader*. Oxford: Blackwell, pp. 119–37.

Castle, Terry (1990), 'Sylvia Townsend Warner and the counterplot of lesbian fiction', *Textual Practice*, 4, (2), Summer, 213–35.

Crumley, Andrew (2004), 'Delight at the end of the tunnel', *Scotland on Sunday*, 2 May http://news.scotsman.com/print (accessed 13 July 2005).

De Lynn, Jane (1991), *Don Juan in the Village*. London: Serpent's Tail.

Doan, Laura (1994), 'Jeanette Winterson's sexing the postmodern', in Laura Doan (ed.), *The Lesbian Postmodern*. New York: Columbia University Press, pp. 137–55.

Forrest, Katherine V. (1983), *Curious Wine*. Tallahassee: The Naiad Press.

Hall, Radclyffe (1983) [1928], *The Well of Loneliness*. London: Virago.

Hinds, H. (1992), 'Oranges are not the only fruit: Reaching audiences that other lesbian texts cannot reach', in S. Munt (ed.), *New Lesbian Criticism: Literary and Cultural Readings*. Hemel Hempstead: Harvester Wheatsheaf, pp. 153–72.

Lindenmeyer, Antje (1999), 'Postmodern concepts of the body in Jeanette Winterson's *Written on the Body*', *Feminist Review*, 63, Autumn, 48–63.

Miller, I. (1973), *Patience and Sarah*. New York: Fawcett Crest.

Modleski, Tania (1982), *Loving with a Vengeance: Mass-Produced Fantasies for Women*. London: Methuen.

Nunn, Heather (1996), '*Written on the Body*: An anatomy of horror, melancholy and love', *Women: A Cultural Review* 7, (1), 16–27.

Pearce, Lynne (1995), ' "Written on tablets of stone"?: Jeanette Winterson, Roland Barthes, and the discourse of romantic love', in Suzanne Raitt (ed.), *Volcanoes and Pearl Divers: Essays in Lesbian Feminist Studies*. London: Onlywomen Press, pp. 147–68.

—— (1998), 'The emotional politics of reading Winterson', in Helena Grice and Tim Woods (eds), *'I'm Telling You Stories': Jeanette Winterson and the Politics of Reading*. London: Whittaker, pp. 29–39.

Radicalesbians (1970), 'The woman identified woman', in Anne Koedt, Sarah Lucia Hoagland and Julia Penelope (eds), *For Lesbians Only: A Separatist Anthology* London: Onlywomen Press, pp. 17–22.

Radway, Janice (1984), *Reading the Romance: Women, Patriarchy, and Popular Literature*. Chapel Hill and London: The Univerisity of North Carolina.

Rich, Adrienne (1996) [1980], 'Compulsory heterosexuality and lesbian existence', in Mary Eagleton (ed.), *Feminist Literary Theory: A Reader*. Oxford: Blackwell, pp. 24–9.

Rule, Jane (1986), *Desert of the Heart*. London: Pandora Press.

Schulman, Sarah (1990), *After Delores*. London: Sheba.

Sedgwick, Eve Kosofsky (1994), *Tendencies*. Hemel Hempstead: Harvester Wheatsheaf.

Stein, Arlene (ed.) (1993), *Sisters, Sexperts, Queers: Beyond the Lesbian Nation*. New York and London: Plume.

Townsend Warner, Sylvia (1987) [1936], *Summer Will Show*. London: Virago.

Wilson, Elizabeth (1983), 'I'll climb the stairway to heaven: Lesbianism in the seventies', in Sue Cartledge and Joanna Ryan (eds), *Sex and Love: New Thoughts on Old Contradictions*. London: The Women's Press, pp. 180–95.

Winterson, Jeanette (1985), *Oranges Are Not the Only Fruit*. London: Pandora.

—— (1988) [1987], *The Passion*. London: Penguin.

—— (1990) [1989], *Sexing the Cherry*. London: Vintage.

—— (1992), *Written on the Body*. London: Jonathan Cape.

—— (1995) [1994], *Art and Lies*. London: Vintage.

—— (1998) [1997], *Gut Symmetries*. London: Granta.

—— (2000), *The PowerBook*. London: Jonathan Cape.

—— (2004), *Lighthousekeeping*. London: Fourth Estate.

Wittig, Monique (1992), 'One is not born a woman', in *The Straight Mind and Other Essays*. Boston: Beacon Press, pp. 9–20.

Zimmerman, (1986), 'What has never been: Lesbian literary criticism in the 1980s', in Elaine Showalter (ed.), *The New Feminist Criticism*. London: Virago, pp. 200–24.

—— Bonnie (1990), *The Safe Sea of Women: Lesbian Fiction 1969–1989*. Boston, MA: Beacon Press.

CHAPTER SEVEN

Religion and Spirituality

MICHELLE DENBY

Chapter summary: This chapter explores the importance of religion and spirituality in Winterson's work. Beginnning with her well-known challenge to Church authority in *Oranges*, it shows how in later works Winterson develops her critique of Christian fundamentalism into an acknowledgement of the significance of a more diffuse notion of spiritual experience and discourse in human life.

Key texts: *Oranges Are Not the Only Fruit; The Passion; Gut Symmetries*

Key words: religion, spirituality, fundamentalism, mysticism, selfhood, artistic expression

---

This chapter examines Winterson's treatment of religion and spirituality, focusing on three novels which represent the opposition developed in her work between organized religion and spiritual experience. *Oranges Are Not the Only Fruit* (1985) presents a critique of evangelicalism, targeting the fundamentalist discourses and capitalist consumer methods of manipulation that limit subjectivity and imagination. Two later novels, *The Passion* (1987) and *Gut Symmetries* (1997), turn towards the converse intuitive world of Art, love and non-institutionalized spirituality represented by mysticism and alchemy. Winterson's adoption into a family committed to the Pentecostal evangelical Church is well known, and the novels draw on Winterson's experience as a preacher and missionary protégée, expelled from the Church as a young adult for her homosexuality. If the fundamentalist practices of Pentecostal evangelicalism inform the novels' critique of institutionalized religion, its belief in divinely bestowed charismatic gifts is reworked in their valorization of subjective, spiritual reality, the divinity of romantic love and the sacred power of language. 'I started writing', Winterson tells us, 'because I wanted to write sermons, because I was driven to preach to people and convert them ... now I do it for art's sake, and then I did it for God's' (in Reynolds 2003: 11).

Winterson's emphasis on the spiritual role of language and literature in the reinvention of reality is developed in *Art Objects* (1996), a manifesto for Romantic, aesthetic and modernist writing published as a critical compendium to her literary production. Art reveals a new and timeless world; confronts us with other dimensions of emotional and spiritual experience; provides a guiding vision; and elevates us above the mundane. Winterson's criticism maintains the Romantics' notion of the 'imagination [as] spiritual sensation' (Blake 2006a: 241), capable of effecting revolutionary change in the outside world. The 'true effort [of art]', says Winterson, 'is to open to us dimensions of the spirit and of the self that normally lie smothered under the weight of living' (1996: 137). The artist is a 'prophet', endowed with a 'prescience' and 'an immanence that allows him or her to recognize and make articulate the emotional complexities of his age' (39–40). Winterson's sources are both the biblical and Blakean prophets, encapsulated by the latter's distinction between the 'Priesthood', who enslave others through the creation of dogmatic systems, and the 'Prophets', who embody 'Poetic Genius' (Blake 2006b: 210–11). *Oranges*, *The Passion* and *Gut Symmetries* similarly invoke the spiritual dimension of art to counter the effects of institutionalized religion and the consumer culture that 'deadens our sensibilities' (1996: 15–16). Structured on the archetypal spiral, biblical books, alchemical correspondences and mystical Tarot, the novels chart the intellectual, spiritual and emotional maturation of the protagonists from 'Priesthood' to 'Prophet'.

Oranges Are Not the Only Fruit

In the decade that saw the growth of evangelicalism in the USA, the 'Rushdie Affair'[1] in the UK, and the rise of all forms of religious fundamentalism globally, the intellectual climate of the 1980s was marked by intense conflict around fundamentalist religion and artistic censorship. While all Winterson's novels reject dogmatic thinking, *Oranges* both contributed towards and capitalized on these cultural debates (Hinds 1995). The novel parodically rewrites biblical themes, events and styles in ways that highlight evangelicalism's production of universalizing, dogmatic stories. *Oranges* is characteristic, therefore, of the 1980s literary trend towards 'postmodern parody', 'a value-problematizing, de-naturalizing form of acknowledging the history (and through irony, the politics) of representations' (Hutcheon 1991: 94). By equating the Bible with fiction and fable, the novel directly challenges religious fundamentalism's central tenet: 'the [factual] authority of scripture' (Harris 1998: 4). Its adoption of biblical styles equally reminds us, however, of the Bible's own status as 'a work of great literary force and authority' (Alter and Kermode 2002: 2), whose 'Poetic Genius' encompasses myth, poetry and history. In this sense, *Oranges* is illustrative of contemporary 'narrative' and 'poetical' theology's re-evaluation of the Bible as both 'epic narrative' and 'sacred poetry' (Cupitt 1998: 228).

A semi-autobiographical *Künstlerroman*,[2] *Oranges* relates the adoption of Jeanette into a working-class, Pentecostal evangelical family in Lancashire, mapping her maturation from loyal child through turbulent teenage years, catalysed by her burgeoning creativity and homosexuality, towards her status as an independent adult and writer. Realistic episodes are interrupted by sections of fantasy, which embody the character's endeavour to shape imaginatively her emotional and spiritual dilemmas and hence mark her alignment with Blakean 'prophet'. *Oranges* is interwoven with numerous literary and biblical intertexts, which underpin the religious themes and allow Jeanette, as young protagonist and adult narrator, to explore creatively a world apart from biblical doctrine. Chapters are structured around the opening eight books of the Old Testament, loosely linking key events and themes with Jeanette's maturation process. Genesis parodically compares God's creation story with Jeanette's adoption story. In her nonprocreative production of Jeanette, her mother Louie is a runner up to the Virgin Mary, who '[got] there first' (1991: 3); Jeanette herself is the product of an intellectual and visionary project to 'get a child, train it, build it, dedicate it to the Lord':

> a missionary child
> a servant of God
> a blessing.
>
> And so it was....
> She took the child away and for seven days and seven nights the child cried out. ... The mother sang to the child, and stabbed the demons.
>
> (10)

Louie's orphanage visit finds a similar conclusion to God's completion of the universe within seven days, punctuated by the proclamation 'and it was so'.[3] Although the parodic references to the Bible undercut the authority of her mother's evangelicalism, the poetic and declamatory narrative voice marks it as a formative scene. Its literary style recalls the biblical book of Genesis, which draws its effect from the 'polarity between prose and poetry ... the prose function[ing] as a setting in which, repeatedly, the gem of a poem sparkles' (Fokkelman 2002: 36). If her mother is compared with God, Jeanette's own story parallels that of Christ, beginning with her birth in the orphanage crib and preparation for the messianic role of preacher and missionary.

In Exodus, Jeanette, following the Israelites, departs the family home and, unlike the Israelites, loses her way in the 'pillar of cloud', or fog of unfamiliar school rules, attracting, like Christ (1991: 44), the scorn of teachers and peers. 'Testifying Elsie', an eccentric who 'liked the prophets' (38), oversees Jeanette's induction to the mystic poets, highlighting the central role of 'creative imagination' in the production of external reality. The school's failure to recognize her creative projects on account of their religious themes provides Jeanette with an under-standing of 'relative value' (44). Indeed, the following biblical books, Leviticus, Numbers and Deuteronomy, focus on the compilation of Christian laws and, in the corresponding chapters, Jeanette increasingly questions the singular authority of Church rules. The Church's doctrine of 'perfection' generates her 'first theological disagreement' (58), explored in the fable of the prince seeking a 'perfect' wife and 'A perfect race' (60). Deuteronomy, 'The Last Book of the Law', concludes with the proclamation of an alternative law by a newly distanced narrative voice that parodies the 'anonymous narrator' (Polzin 2002: 92) of the original biblical book: 'If you want to keep your own teeth, make your own sandwiches' (93).

Chapter Six, 'Joshua', focusing on the exposure of Jeanette's homo-sexuality, opens with the analogous recollection of the discovery of her adoption: 'It was Easter time and the cross on the hill loomed big and black. "Why didn't you tell me," I screamed at the painted wood' (1991: 99).[4] Casting herself and Louie as Christ and God, Jeanette's anecdote anticipates her pending suffering and rejection, temptation by demons and betrayal by family and Church. In her battle with the Church, like Joshua's Battle of Jericho (Onega 2006), the comparison with Christ supports her claim for the 'genuinely spiritual dimension' (120) of her love for Melanie, 'to the pure all things are pure' (103), reversing the ideal of physical purity in St Paul's epistles.[5] Jeanette's 'orange demon' is the product of the ensuing exorcism and 36-hour-long confinement that recalls, again, the biblical siege of Jericho (Rusk 2002). *Oranges* subverts evangelical demonism by recasting the demon as a Blakean manifestation of 'Poetic Genius',[6] whose function is to accommodate those aspects of self – creativity and lesbianism – outlawed by the Church. The episode represents an integration of 'id' and 'ego', 'unconscious' and 'conscious', 'comparable to the mythical hero's ritual death and rebirth' (Onega 2006: 25): 'We're here to keep you in one piece', says the demon to Jeanette, 'if you ignore us, you're quite likely to end up in two' (1991: 106). Invoking the spiritual symbolism of the tower (Chevalier and Gheerbrant 1996) and the anti-linearity of the original book of Joshua, two dream-fables, 'the city of Lost Chances' (1991: 109) and 'The Forbidden City' (110), allegorize the attempts of her unconscious to escape the ego's self-imposed limitations. The chapter culminates in a second lesbian relationship and a further fable of the pilgrim's arrival at and departure from an Edenic 'secret garden' (120), representing the assimilation of her homosexuality and the progression of her maturation process.

Like the Queen of Spades' ruling in *Alice in Wonderland*, 'Either you or your head must be off' (125), that comprises the chapter's epigraph, in Judges, the teenage Jeanette is judged for her lesbianism and expelled from Church and home. The root of her offence lies in her usurpation of the masculine role of preacher: 'I had flouted God's law and had tried to do it sexually' (131). By supporting the Church's fundamentalist reading of Paul's injunction against female priests, Louie not only betrays Jeanette but the congregation's other female members, including herself, for whom evangelicalism provided an outlet for a range of suppressed strengths. Once again, the chapter's fusion of realism and fable reflects the original Judges' 'randomly assembled anthology of tales' while, at the same time, since Jeanette refuses to repent her demon, reversing the biblical book's 'cyclical pattern of sin, oppression, repentance, and salvation' (Gunn 2002: 103).

The final chapter sees the protagonist's journey reach full circle as the adult Jeanette returns to visit her mother, mirroring the key theme of family and female ties that underlies the biblical book of Ruth (Bollinger 1994). This theme is reworked in two extended fables, Perceval's quest for the Holy Grail and Winnet's quest for the 'sacred city' (1991: 154). Winnet Stonejar, an anagram of Jeanette Winterson, remains bound to the magician, a version of Louie, who adopts and trains her in the magic arts. Winnet's 'powers' (148) derive from the magician, reminding us that Jeanette's own prophetic power with words originates from her mother. For Jeanette, 'The priest has a book with the words set out. Old words, known words, words of power. ... They do what they're supposed to do; comfort and discipline. The prophet has no book. The prophet is a voice that cries in the wilderness.[7] The prophets cry out because they are troubled by demons' (156). Winnet's arrival at the 'ancient city' (156), achieved by a symbolic descent to the inner self via the brow chakra and an archetypal journey across water (155), allegorizes Jeanette's own completed maturation and accession to the status of Blakean prophet.

The Passion

Winterson's third novel, *The Passion*, departs from the autobiographical towards the historical and the magical, combining historical narrative with myth, fantasy and romance. Recalling *Oranges*, the novel is representative of the rise of 'historiographic metafiction' and 'magical realism' in the 1980s, which revalorize unempirical 'modes of knowledge production generally rejected within the dominant Western paradigm' (Hegerfeldt 2005: 3). Set in France and Venice during the Napoleonic Wars, *The Passion* follows the fortunes of Henri, a cook in Napoleon's army, and Villanelle, a Venetian croupier, pursuing their quest for passion through the Wintersonian paradigms of spirituality, romance and creativity. Drawing on her childhood Pentecostal evangelicalism as well as a range of literary and spiritual traditions, passion is conveyed, thematically, through the motifs of physical temperature, light and darkness, risk and gambling, suffering and madness and, formally, through the villanelle[8] structure of the protagonists' narratives.

Presented in the form of Henri's journal, *The Passion*, like *Oranges*, is a *Künstlerroman*, structuring its four chapters on spiritual models of self-development embodied by the Tarot and Eliot's *Four Quartets*.[9] With its pastiche of biblical intertexts, in particular the evangelical Gospels, the novel, recalling *Oranges* once more, celebrates the visionary power of the Bible while undercutting its dogmatic authority. The narrative (re)construction of (biblical) truth is reinforced by the novel's metafictional references to the role of oral and narrative storytelling in the production of reality; 'I'm telling you stories. Trust me' (1988: 5, 13, 39, 69, 160), say Henri and Villanelle in one of the novel's key refrains. *The Passion*'s title with its central allusion to the 'Passion narratives', the account in the canonical Gospels of Christ's mental and physical suffering prior to and during crucifixion, introduces its key definition of passion as both suffering and pleasure. Christ's 'Agony', counterbalanced by the pleasure of offering eternal life, which reappears in the symbiosis of suffering and freedom in mystical writing, mirrors the protagonists' own experience of passion.

In the first chapter, 'The Emperor', Henri recounts his passion for Emperor Napoleon, evoking key motifs – fire, burning, light and darkness – from the fifteenth-century mystic St John of the Cross (Harvey 1998). Henri's desire to transcend the confines of peasant life is first manifest at the winter bonfires. 'I wish I were a holy man', he says, 'with an angel to protect me so I could jump inside the fire and see my sins burned away' (1988: 7). Henri embodies the aspirations of the French people whose 'lukewarm' lives long for the extraordinary: 'We lie awake at night willing the darkness to part and show us a vision' (7). In a reversal of St Paul's epistle 'it is better to marry than to burn' (9),[10] Henri's mother, Georgette, ardent Catholic and unrealized nun, teaches Henri that 'it is better to burn than to marry' (9). Albeit educated by the priest, Henri's own experience of God fails to 'meet passion with passion' (10). His guiding vision appears in the guise of Napoleon, the 'new Messiah' (16) according to the priest, who nets Henri and the French peasants like Christ did with his disciples. As a repository for romantic passion, Napoleon ignites the peasants' hearts in 'an explosion of dreams and desires that can find no outlet in everyday life' (13). However, Napoleon is also an embodiment of his Tarot archetype, The Emperor, disillusioning Henri with his rational disregard for human life. Alluding to the Christian Passion, the army prostitute 'lost consciousness at twenty nine'[11] men (38) while 2,000 men are sacrificed at noon to Napoleon's unrealistic drill (24).[12] Henri's own analogy with Christ appears in his 'stigmata' (42) from the communion chalice, marking not only his displaced guilt but also his remove from religious solace. Drawing on the literary motif of life as a lottery, it is passion, Henri reflects in a key refrain, that keeps us in the game: 'You play, you win, you play, you lose. You play. It's the playing that's irresistible. Dicing from one year to the next with the things you love, what you risk reveals what you value' (43).

The Queen of Spades chapter relates Villanelle's job as a cross-dressing croupier and her passion for a married woman, the Queen of Spades, the literary and archetypal figure of 'a mature woman with an independent mind' (Gwain 1994: 147), who represents Villanelle's 'ideal-I' (Onega 2006). Like Henri, Villanelle expounds a belief in creative imagination as a prerequisite to shaping one's own life. In a reversal of gender paradigms, Villanelle inherits the legendary webbed feet of Venetian boatmen, and, like Christ, is able to walk on water, demonstrating that 'With faith all things are possible' (1988: 49). Her passion for the Queen of Spades is also couched in the terms of religious calling: 'Memories of a single touch. How could anything so passing be so pervasive? But Christ said, "Follow me," and it was done' (64). Similarly, the expression of her passion draws, like Henri, on Eliotean refrains: 'In between freezing and melting. In between love and despair. In between fear and sex, passion is' (76).[13] Although Villanelle seeks to assuage her suffering in the Venetian churches, as for Henri, the Church provides scant compensation for romantic passion. Albeit analogous, religious passion is diluted by the comfort and certainties offered by the Church: 'Where else could you indulge without fear the exquisite masochism of the victim? ... Where else could you be so in control? Not in love, certainly' (73). The Church constructs, furthermore, a series of 'man-made' (74) fictions between humanity and God, recalling Patrick's revision of the canonical story of the Virgin Mary in Henri's narrative.

In 'The Zero Winter', the alternating character-narrators, Henri and Villanelle, desert the French army across a frozen Europe, recalling the barren, war-ridden lands of the Book of Isaiah and the 'unimaginable/Zero summer' of *Four Quartets*. Henri's desertion symbolizes his integration of and freedom from the father figure, 'superego' or Emperor archetype, 'embodiment of the Logos, or rational principle' (Nichols 1980: 103), represented by Napoleon. Villanelle's Poe-like tale of the gambler's forfeit of 'dismemberment piece by piece beginning with the hands' (1988: 93), alluding to religious dismemberment and resurrection, presages the deconstruction of the characters' own egos in the process of maturation (Onega 2006). The novel draws on the symbolic association of gambling with divination, imagination and self-development (Chevalier and Gheerbrant 1996); for Bataille, gambling is analogous not only to passion but also to 'sovereign existence' in which our encounter with fear and chance ultimately leads to self-awareness (Bényei 1997). This (de)(re)construction takes place in the topos of Venice, a 'sacred site of initiatory transformation' (Onega 2006: 67), able to resist the rationalism of the Emperor archetype. While Villanelle's wager and forfeit of her 'valuable, fabulous thing', her heart, is redeemed from its imprisonment by the Queen of Spades, Henri's murder of their mutual enemy, Napoleon's cook, who represents his own suppressed sexuality, liberates Henri even further from his Oedipal passion for Napoleon (Onega 2006).

Echoing Eliot's 'Choruses from "The Rock"', the final chapter, 'The Rock', concludes with the protagonists' abandonment of idealistic, infantile passion. If Villanelle relinquishes cross-dressing and the Queen of Spades, like Napoleon's exile to Elba, Henri selects an ascetic confinement on 'the rock', the Venetian madhouse, where his love for Villanelle completes his understanding of passion: 'being free is not being powerful or rich ... but being able to love. To love someone else enough to forget about yourself even for one moment is to be free. ... [T]hrough the flesh we are set free ... our desire for one another will lift us out of ourselves more cleanly than anything divine' (1988: 154). The esoteric dimension of sexual passion offers one route to the transcendental and provides the basis for mystical poetry's representation of our relationship with God. Freedom is not achieved through war but through the spiritual dimension of love, embodied by the 'gentle giant' (154) Perceval, who discovers the Holy Grail, and Henri's rose garden, literary and spiritual symbol of universal love. 'If we had the courage to love we would not so value these acts of war' (154), says Henri, alluding to the similarly prison-based writings of St John of the Cross: 'And if you love, if you really love, our guns will wilt' (Ladinsky 2002: 317). While for some critics, such as Fahy (2000) and Müller (2001), the novel's ending signifies the failure of religious or romantic passion to unify the fragmented subject, it is equally through the self-fragmentation wrought by passion that the protagonists achieve their quest for the self.

Gut Symmetries

Appearing a decade after *The Passion*, Winterson's seventh novel, *Gut Symmetries*, synthesizes and develops her characteristic Romantic themes and magic realist techniques. The divine imagination associated with art, spirituality and love in the earlier novels is here extended to science – twentieth-century New Physics and Renaissance alchemy. *Gut Symmetries* challenges purely rational modes of knowledge embodied by eighteenth-century mechanistic science, which constituted a 'denial of divine immanence in nature and [of] any natural immanence of God in the human mind' (Griffin 1988: 4). Like other contemporary texts, the novel utilizes new science to highlight the 'postmodern sense of the instability and perpetual flux of the universe' (Grice and Woods 1998: 118) and individual identity. By emphasizing the role of 'human consciousness in determining physical reality' (Keutzer 1984: 88), New Physics supports Winterson's long-standing belief in the power of the imagination and non-material reality.

The novel alternates the narratives of Alice, Jove and Stella, respectively a postgraduate in New Physics, a professor of Superstring Theory and a poet. The characters' parallel life-stories, extending from their ancestors to their own love triangle, interweaves the reality of contemporary New York and Liverpool with the magical experiences derived from astrology, Tarot, Kabbalah and quantum mechanics. The Prologue, based on Alice's lecture on 'Paracelsus and the new physics' (1998: 15), parodies Paracelsus's unconventional blend of poetic, scientific and mystical practices, which resulted in his mythologization as magus, Faust and charlatan (Ball 2006): 'Paracelsus, physician, magician, alchemist, urge, demiurge, *deus et omnia* was born under the sign of the occult, ruled by Mars and driven by a mountain in his soul' (1998: 1). Alchemy charts the correspondence between the human body, the microcosm, and the universe, or macrocosm: 'heaven ... lies in each of us in its entire plenitude, undivided and corresponding to each man's specificity ... split into our diversities by the various moments at which we are born' (Paracelsus 1951: 113–14). As Alice tells us, Paracelsus 'was a student of Correspondences, "As above, so below". The zodiac in the sky is imprinted in the body. "The galaxa goes through the belly"' (1998: 2). For Alice, alchemy is realized in 'the infant theory of hyperspace, where all the seeming dislocations and separations of the atomic and sub-atomic worlds are unified into a co-operating whole' (2). This correspondence between Renaissance and New Physics is highlighted by the title, *Gut Symmetries*, referring simultaneously to intuitive 'gut feelings' and modern science's GUTs (grand unified theories), which seek to encompass all modes of knowledge in a single explanation of the world. 'This story', therefore, says Alice, 'is a journey through the thinking gut' (13).

The novel is structured according to Jungian 'Synchronicity ... a modern differentiation of ... correspondences' (Jung 1998: 101), often triggered by an activated archetype that has a role to play in the protagonists' individuation process.[14] Each character's life-story is predicted by their name and astrological co-ordinates. While Stella's astrology links her to Paracelsus, Alluvia, or Alice, 'born ... under an exacting star' (1998: 74), 'Sun in Gemini' (51), dreams of 'correspondences' (72) and 'join[s] that band of pilgrims ... who, call it art, call it alchemy, call it science, call it god, are driven by a light that will not stay' (73). The protagonists' lives are similarly linked by a series of coincidences contiguous with their individuation, such as Alice's research at Princeton, where Jove is professor, and their encounter and subsequent liaison on the *QE2*. Alice's physical relationship with Stella, Jove's wife, ensues from their meeting at the Algonquin Hotel, where, previously, their parents had conducted an affair. As Alice concludes, 'the distance we imagine separates one event from another had folded up, leaving the two clock faces to slide together ... synchronous' (199). Like the 'creative imagination' in the Jungian and alchemical systems,

'Energy precedes matter' (19, 83), rendering New Physics a modern version of the Blakean divine imagination (Keutzer 1984).

'Imitat[ing] the Celtic Cross Spread' (Onega 2006: 163), the novel's 11 chapters are structured on the Tarot, 'a silent picture text representing the typical experiences encountered along the age-old path to self-realization' (Nichols 1980: 3). For Jung, astrology and Tarot 'presuppose ... a synchronistic correspondence between the psychic state of the questioner and the answering hexagram' (1998: 98). Like other contemporary texts, *Gut Symmetries'* use of the Tarot supports its exploration of the characters' intellectual, spiritual and emotional experience. The 'Tarot [like] post-modernist art and literature' self-consciously mixes 'distinct genres and symbolic systems', 'blur[s] the categorical boundaries between fiction and non-fiction' and operates within 'a heterotopian space where memories of the past, present realities, and future possibilities exist simultaneously' (Auger 2004: 57). The Fool signifies the beginning of Alice's voyage of self-discovery and reflects the symbolism of travel, new potential and uncertainty represented by the archetype (Nichols 1980). Alice's journey to America, the commencement of her affair with Jove and reflections on science are interwoven with childhood memories: 'I know I am a fool, trying to make connections out of scraps but how else is there to proceed?' (1998: 24).

Like its corresponding Tarot, the following chapter, 'The Tower', focuses on destruction, expulsion and, also, liberation, following Jove's thunderbolt – his affair with Alice. We witness Stella's mental disintegration, her physical assault on the marital home, Jove's departure and the commencement of her self-reconstruction. Mirroring Alice, Stella considers the role of her unconscious in catalysing Jove's affair: 'I built a tower. ... Now it has been struck down. Did the lightning come like an indifferent God or did I draw it in?' (38). As the dream of the well indicates (48), however, Stella, poet and mystic, is liberated, like the Tarot figures, from the constraints of rationality embodied by Jove's materialism. Her namesake, The Star, recounts Stella's birth under the auspices of intuitive Scorpio and her Kabbalistic father, Ishmael,[15] prophet and social outsider, as well as her embodiment, by ingesting the diamond, of the 'stellated brightness' (92) of intuition. The emotional cul-de-sac and ensuing change predicted by the 'Ten of Swords' chapter materializes in the commencement of Alice and Stella's affair in the following chapter, 'Page of Cups', harbinger of emotional, creative and spiritual renewal (Gwain 1994). The Page, 'Young hopeful of the Tarot deck. My identity card' (1998: 118), captures Alice's propensity towards the inner world and, through its link with Narcissus, the mirror equality of her love for Stella.

In 'Death', Alice recounts the physical and emotional death of her father, working-class boy made businessman, named David after the biblical king, who learned to 'shroud' his 'bright self' in 'dead men's clothes' (144) only to be haunted by his own 'shadow'. The archetype signifies the release of David's unconscious self and his rebirth in the form of a quantum movement to 'an alternative point of his wave function' (161). The theme of death continues in the next chapter in which Stella, lost at sea with Jove, confronts the physical and mental dissolution symbolized by the Moon card and fights for 'victory over the devouring aspects of the unconscious, which would otherwise engulf [the] ego, resulting in psychosis' (Nichols 1980: 314). Stella recalls her father, Ishmael, student of Kabbalah and New Physics, whose death, recalling David's, is presented as a successful experiment involving the use of the body as 'its own gateway' to 'transcend the illusion of matter' (1998: 168). Jove's character is brought to light in his singularly narrated chapter, 'Knave of Coins', where his practical realism not only threatens Stella's mystical sense of self but also her material body, which he cannibalizes in a pursuit for self-survival. The novel's central proposition, that 'Mathematics and physics, as religion used to do, form a gateway into higher alternatives' (208), is realized in the form of 'a temporary imprint' (209) of Ishmael, who materializes to Alice in order to aid his daughter's rescue.

While for many critics *Gut Symmetries'* numerous 'competing cosmological, irrational, literary and philosophical interpretations' fail to 'achieve resolution' (Grice and Woods 1998: 119), others counter that the discourses of hermeticism, Kabbalah and New Physics produce 'a multi-dimensional and yet unitary textual world' (Onega 2004: 98). The final chapter, 'Judgement', represents rebirth into the present through confronting and integrating the past (Nichols 1980). Having encountered a series of archetypes, including the Jungian shadow and scientific materialism represented by Jove, we witness the successful completion of Alice and Stella's personal, artistic and spiritual maturation (Onega 2004, 2005). The novel concludes synchronistically on '10 November' (1998: 1, 219) with Alice and Stella's relationship fulfilling their parents' uncompleted love affair (218).

Collectively, *Oranges*, *The Passion* and *Gut Symmetries* chart a progression away from organized religion towards spiritual experience. In their critique of fundamentalist and institutionalized religion and, conversely, their valorization of subjective spirituality, the novels draw on Winterson's formative Pentecostal evangelicalism and critical investment in the visionary arts. This division between religion and spirituality equally reflects the shift towards spirituality within the wider cultural context of the late twentieth century. Interested in revalidating those identities marginalized by the rational focus of Enlightenment modernity, many postmodern writers and critics, like Winterson, have sought to revalorize spiritual experience, pointing to the origins of postmodernism in Romantic thinking (Maagaard 2004). Within this context, spiritual experience takes on a counter-cultural aspect in its ability to present alternatives to the dominant materialistic discourses and capitalist-consumer ethos of Western society (Heelas 2005). For some social commentators (Heelas *et al.* 2005), the rise of alternative spiritualities is ascribable to the 'subjective turn' within late-twentieth-century culture, whose valorization of subjective experience over external authority has led to the decline of traditional religion. From Jeanette's reinterpretation of Christianity to Alice and Stella's belief in alchemy, the novels valorize subjective spirituality in ways that counter a variety of rationalistic, dogmatic discourses. We 'can't take back the Old Testament', says Winterson, 'There's too much in there which is oppressive. What we can do is claim spirituality' (in Stroh 2005: 2). Winterson was raised within a branch of Christianity in which 'fundamentalism commonly remains the ideological standard' (Barr in Harris 1998: 1). What she retains is a continuing faith in 'a highly personal, experiential' (11) spirituality and the transformative power of the Word.

Notes

1. The fatwa issued by Muslim fundamentalists against the publication of Salman Rushdie's *The Satanic Verses* (1988).
2. Novels focusing on the development of an artist.
3. See Genesis 1.7, 9, 11, 15, 24, 30.
4. See Matthew 27.46 and Mark 15.34.
5. See 1 Corinthians 7 and Ephesians 5.
6. 'Poetic Genius' also goes by the name of 'Angel and Spirit and Demon' (Blake 2006c: 174).
7. See Mark 1.3; Luke 3.4; John 1.23 and Blake (2006c: 174).
8. A verse form based on rhyme, repetition and rhymed refrains.
9. Eliot's four-part poem based on Christian and Eastern mysticism.
10. 1 Corinthians 7.1.
11. Christ's 29 lashes prior to crucifixion.
12. The time of Christ's crucifixion (Gospel of St John).
13. See 'Litttle Gidding', line 11, in *Four Quartets.*
14. 'Individuation' seeks 'to redeem and liberate those aspects rightfully belonging to ourselves which have been held hostage in the unconscious' (Nichols 1980: 344).
15. See the Islamic prophet and the protagonist of Melville's *Moby Dick* (1851).

Works cited

Alter, R. and Kermode, F. (eds) (2002) [1987], *The Literary Guide to the Bible.* Cambridge: Belknap Harvard.

Auger, E. E. (2004), *Tarot and Other Meditation Decks: History, Theory, Aesthetics, Typology.* Jefferson and London: McFarland and Co.

Ball, P. (2006), *The Devil's Doctor: Paracelsus and the World of Renaissance Magic and Science.* London: Heinemann.

Benson Brown, A. (1997), 'Inverted conversions: Reading the Bible and writing the lesbian subject in *Oranges Are Not the Only Fruit*', in R-J. Frontain (ed.) (1997), *Reclaiming the Sacred: The Bible in Gay and Lesbian Literature.* London: Haworth Press, pp. 233–52.

Bényei, T. (1997), 'Risking the text: Stories of love in Jeanette Winterson's *The Passion*', *Hungarian Journal of English and American Studies*, 3, (2), 199–209.

Blake, W. (2006a) [1799], 'Letter from William Blake to the Revd Dr Trusler, 23 August 1799', in D. Wu (ed.), *Romanticism: An Anthology*. Oxford: Blackwell, pp. 240–1.

—— (2006b) [1790], 'The marriage of heaven and hell', in D. Wu (ed.), *Romanticism: An Anthology*. Oxford: Blackwell, pp. 206–17.

—— (2006c) [1788], 'All religions are one', in D. Wu (ed.), *Romanticism: An Anthology*. Oxford: Blackwell, pp. 174–5.

Bollinger, L. (1994), 'Models for female loyalty: the biblical Ruth in Jeanette Winterson's *Oranges Are Not the Only Fruit*', *Tulsa Studies in Women's Literature*, 13, (2), 363–80.

Chevalier, J and Gheerbrant, A. (1996), *Dictionary of Symbols*. London: Penguin.

Cosslett, T. (1998), 'Intertextuality in *Oranges Are Not the Only Fruit*: the Bible, Malory and *Jane Eyre*', in H. Grice and T. Woods (eds), *'I'm telling you stories': Jeanette Winterson and the Politics of Reading*. Amsterdam: Rodopi, pp. 15–28.

Cupitt, D. (1998), 'Post-Christianity', in P. Heelas (ed.), *Religion, Modernity and Postmodernity*. Oxford: Blackwell, pp. 218–32.

Eliot, T. S. (1974) [1963], *Collected Poems 1909–1962*. London: Faber and Faber.

Fahy, T. (2000), 'Fractured bodies: Privileging the incomplete in Jeanette Winterson's *The Passion*', *Mosaic*, 33, (3), 95–106.

Fokkelman, J. P. (2002) [1987], 'Genesis', in R. Alter and F. Kermode (eds), *The Literary Guide to the Bible*. Cambridge: Belknap Harvard, pp. 36–55.

Grice, H. and Woods, T. (eds) (1998), 'Grand (dis)unified theories? Dislocated discourses in *Gut Symmetries*', in H. Grice and T. Woods (eds), *'I'm telling you stories': Jeanette Winterson and the Politics of Reading*. Amsterdam: Rodopi, pp. 117–26.

Griffin, D. R. (1988), *Spirituality and Society: Postmodern Visions*. New York: State University of New York Press.

Gunn, D. M. (2002) [1987], 'Joshua and Judges', in R. Alter and F. Kermode (eds), *The Literary Guide to the Bible*. Cambridge: Belknap Harvard, pp. 202–21.

Gwain, R. (1994), *Discovering Your Self Through the Tarot: A Jungian Guide to Archetypes and Personality*. Vermont: Destiny.

Harris, H. A. (1998), *Fundamentalism and Evangelicals*. Oxford: Clarendon Press.

Harvey, A. (ed.) (1998), *Teachings of the Christian Mystics*. Boston, MA: Shambhala.

Heelas, P. (2005), *The New Age Movement: The Celebration of the Self and the Sacralization of Modernity*. Oxford: Blackwell.

Heelas, P., Woodhead, L., Seel, B. and Tusting, K. (2005), *The Spiritual Revolution: Why Religion is Giving Way to Spirituality*. Oxford: Blackwell.

Hegerfeldt, A. C. (2005), *Lies that Tell the Truth: Magic Realism Seen Through Contemporary Fiction from Britain*. Amsterdam: Rodopi.

Hinds, H. (1995), '*Oranges Are Not the Only Fruit*: Reaching audiences that other lesbian texts cannot reach', in T. Wilton (ed.), *Immortal Invisible: Lesbians and the Moving Image*. London: Routledge, pp. 52–69.

Hutcheon, L. (1991) [1989], *The Politics of Postmodernism*. London: Routledge.

Jung, C. G. (1998) [1951], 'On synchronicity', in R. Main (ed. and introd.), *Jung on Synchronicity and the Paranormal*. Princeton, NJ: Princeton University Press, pp. 93–102.

Keutzer, C. S. (1984), 'The power of meaning: From quantum mechanics to synchronicity', *Journal of Humanistic Psychology*, 24, (1), 80–94.

Ladinsky, D. (ed. and trans.) (2002), *Love Poems from God: Twelve Sacred Voices from the East and West*. New York and London: Penguin Compass.

Maagaard, C. A. (2004), 'Postmodern prophet of the word', in E. Borgman, B. Philipsen and L. Verstricht (eds), *Literary Canons and Religious Identity*, Hants: Ashgate, pp. 151–61.

Müller, M. (2001), 'Love and other dismemberments in Jeanette Winterson's novels', in N. Beaute (ed. and introd.), *Contemporary Writers in Britain*. Amsterdam: Rodopi, pp. 41–51.

Nichols, S. (1980), *Jung and Tarot: An Archetypal Journey*. York Beach, ME: Weiser.

Onega, S. (2004), 'Science, myth and the quest for unity in Jeanette Winterson's *Gut Symmetries*', *Anglistik*, 15, (1), 93–104.

—— (2006), *Jeanette Winterson*. Manchester: Manchester University Press.

Paracelsus (1951) [1530–1534], 'Man and the created world', in J. Jacobi (ed. and introd.), *Paracelsus: Selected Writings* (trans. by N. Guterman). New York: Pantheon.

Polzin, R. (2002) [1987], 'Deuteronomy', in R. Alter and F. Kermode (eds), *The Literary Guide to the Bible*. Cambridge: Belknap Harvard, pp. 92–101.

Reynolds, M. (2003) [2002], 'Interview with Jeanette Winterson', in J. Noakes and M. Reynolds (2003), *Jeanette Winterson: The Essential Guide*. London: Vintage.

Rusk, L. (2002), *The Life Writing of Otherness: Woolf, Baldwin, Kingston, and Winterson*. London: Routledge.

Sinkinson, D. L. (1999), ' "Shadows, signs, wonders": Paracelsus, synchronicity and the New Age of *Gut Symmetries*', in H. Bengston, M. Børch and C. Maagaard (eds), *Sponsored by Demons: The Art of Jeanette Winterson*. Denmark: Scholars' Press, pp. 81–91.

Stroh, S. (2005), 'Winterson's way', *Advocate*, 940, 58–9.

Winterson, J. (1988) [1987], *The Passion*. London: Penguin.

—— (1991) [1985], *Oranges Are Not the Only Fruit*. London: Vintage.

—— (1996) [1995], *Art Objects: Essays on Ecstasy and Effrontery*. London: Vintage.

—— (1998) [1997], *Gut Symmetries*. London: Granta.

CHAPTER EIGHT

Wintersonian Masculinities

PHILIP TEW

Chapter summary: Philip Tew's chapter points out that while criticism of Winterson's work invariably foregrounds gender, it tends to focus on women or gender blurring. The chapter sets out to fill a critical gap by making visible Winterson's depiction of men, and argues that far from reproducing stereotypes of masculinity, her early novels represent a complex, nuanced meditation on forms of male identity.

Key texts: *Oranges Are Not the Only Fruit; The Passion; Sexing the Cherry*

Key words: men, masculinity, gender, heroism, power, desire, ambivalence

Non-linearity, Winterson and masculinity

From *Oranges Are Not the Only Fruit* (1985) onward, Jeanette Winterson's novels have been dissected largely in terms of a certain cluster of interrelated issues: gender and sexuality; and 'Queer Theory' and its specific readings of aesthetics. However, Carolyn Allen contends that '*Oranges* is Winterson's only explicit lesbian text' and Allen regards the two subsequent novels, *The Passion* (1987) and *Sexing the Cherry* (1989), as concerned with 'liminal sexuality rather than lesbian identity ...' (1996: 49). In all three I suggest there exists a particular economy of male identity, not simply what Christine Di Stefano identifies as the 'instability of gender' (1991: xiv), rather, male identities grounded in a narrative recognition of what Di Stefano describes as a Nietzschean admission of the ubiquity of power (1991: 195). Moreover Winterson characterizes men as elements of a series of contending and complex life experiences prone to a universal and yet undermining order of passion.

Curiously, in terms of specifically re-reading the Wintersonian male, there is little current criticism concerned primarily with such masculinities, scant interpretation focused upon her plurality of masculine characters and contexts. Any such new interpretations must first heed R. W. Connell's warning about naturalizing 'pattern masculinity' and its apparent cultural normativities (1995: 69); second, they cannot be literalist about Winterson's male characters, since as Celia Shiffer specifies, Winterson's novels incorporate impossible quests within the context of a legendary narrative, and utilize the dynamics of the epic, hardly a realm ordered by either solely mimetic or realist principles (2004: 33).

In addressing the critical deficiencies cited above, this essay insists that masculinity – suitably interrogated, troubled, subverted and tampered with, to adopt Doan's terms (1994: 154) – is a vital component of Winterson's ensemble of central themes, a crucial part of the matrix of sexuality, identity and passion so central to all of her early work. I consider variously *Oranges*, *The Passion* and *Sexing* (published in a five-year period), which share one consistent, interconnecting structural element, as Winterson makes evident in her introduction to a reissued version of *Oranges*:

> Its interests are anti-linear. It offers a complicated narrative structure disguised as a simple one, it employs a very large vocabulary and a beguilingly straight-forward syntax. ... A spiral narrative suits me very well and I have continued to use it and to improve upon it in *The Passion* and *Sexing the Cherry*. I really don't see the point of reading in straight lines. We don't think like that and we don't live like that.
>
> (1991: xiii)

Certainly these novels seem, at least superficially, strongly interrelated; although in terms of form and plot her later work is not strictly 'spiral', subsequent novels abjure linear reading and interpretation. Merja Makinen says of *Passion* and *Sexing*, 'Both sport dual narrators, a "feminine" male narrator alongside a woman narrator singled out by her fantastic or grotesque features (Villanelle has webbed feet, the Dog Woman is a giant), to deconstruct the concepts of gender identity and the fluidity of sexual desire' (2005: 1). I suggest other equally important emphases in Winterson's early aesthetic, characterized, like all her work, by indirection, detours and a sense of narrative discovery. She extols an underlying sense of fantasy and romance, utilizing from them codes of both the imagination and the possibilities of spirit. Winterson deploys recurrently a dialectic of the familiar and unfamiliar, as we shall see below. Her male characters are variously perverse, uncertain, enigmatic, heroic, anti-heroic, noble and vicious by turns, but impelled by the ambivalence of their natures. In portraying them Winterson charts firstly, in R. W. Connell's terms, the significant understanding that 'gender is a way in which social practice is ordered' (1995: 71), and secondly incorporates what Laura Doan describes as an exploration of 'possible essences (hidden, secretive, delicious, and juicy) and appearances (which may or may not be a true indication of what resides beneath the surface)' (1994: 148).

Oranges: Ambivalent males?

Oranges is a gendered *Bildungsroman*; as Paulina Palmer indicates, a form more characteristic of early 1970s feminist writers (1990: 43). Winterson inverts the traditional *Bildungsroman*'s predisposition toward young men's emergence and maturation, creating a world chiefly peopled, articulated and imagined by women, although as its beginning indicates, men inhabit the interstices of these female lives, apparently patriarchal, yet peripheral and weak. Winterson's narrator implies a parody of narrative expectations, and indicates the peculiarities of her protagonist's world. 'Like most people I lived for a long time with my mother and father. My father liked to watch the wrestling, my mother liked to wrestle; it didn't matter what. She was in the white corner and that was that' (1991: 3). As Rusk says, there is a refusal of otherness in *Oranges* (2002: 105) and 'Jeanette, as she grows, disputes other people's assumptions and resists fitting into pigeonholes: missionary, heterosexual, virgin, demon. Accordingly, her narrative also defies categorization' (110). As Rusk comments, Jeanette certainly likes her father; however, his presence and specificity remain residual, indistinct (114). Certainly Winterson deals with the issue of masculinity very specifically in *Oranges*. Rusk concludes, arguably unfairly, that Winterson's men appear essentialized (113) and that her stereotyping, especially of men, comes across more vividly than her qualifications, something Rusk finds 'injudicious, to say the least, in a work that insists on the uniqueness and the inclusive humanity of its speaker, and that addresses itself ... to the unspecified individual reader, one on one' (114). Perhaps correctly, Rusk assumes that Jeanette's church is a woman-centred community where women have power (115); nevertheless the pastors retain significant authority, and Pastor Spratt with his missionary work in Africa has a charismatic influence over the narrator's mother, who relates her own romantic conversion by him. 'Pastor Spratt spoke of the fate of the damned. My mother said he looked like Errol Flynn, but holy. A lot of women found the Lord that week' (1991: 8).

Despite the subjugation of Jeanette's father, a reformed gambler according to her mother's account of their courtship, man's authority persists silently in the interstices of the text, much like the assumption of the infallibility of the prince in the recurrent fairy tale, whose advisers insist he cannot apologize, ' "Because you are a prince, and as a prince you cannot be seen to be wrong" ' (63). The men's enigmatic silence sets them apart from the 'collective self' and communitarian orality identified by Rusk (2002: 3–4). As Rusk indicates, the women articulate a sense of their presence or self-conception and thereby Rusk concludes they experience a *'communal* selfhood' (115), and within this scheme men are either demonized or idealized. Pastor Spratt serves a similar function to a fairytale prince or knight in her mother's life, his distant otherness contrasting with the mundane realities, among which Jeanette identifies the repulsive ugliness of Pastor Roy Finch. Another dimension is found in the seducer of Mrs Butler, owner of the Morecambe guest house:

> She had got herself a job as a matron of a local old folk's home. While there she had taken up with a strange charismatic man who had once been the official exorcist to the Bishop of Bermuda. He had been dismissed under mysterious circumstances for some kind of unmentionable offence with the curate's wife. Back in England and safe within the besotted arms of Mrs Butler, he had persuaded her to let him practice voodoo on some of the more senile patients. They had been caught by a night nurse.
>
> (1991: 170–1)

This offstage vignette serves to emphasize the otherness and perverse authority and power of men; they draw women either into (Spratt) or away from (the exorcist) any equilibrium. As Rusk indicates, significantly 'in "Judges," Louie, the pastor, and the religious council judge Jeanette to have unlawfully assumed male power in the church' (2002: 107). Although for the men the perversity of Mrs Butler's passion might equate with Jeanette's feelings for Melanie, interestingly the latter is interpreted and disapproved of differently. Jeanette fears betrayal and requires a profound sense of romantic possibility, something she cannot perceive in most men. For her men retain a controlling emphasis, a destructive urge:

> Romantic love has been diluted into paperback form and has sold thousands and millions of copies. Somewhere it is still in the original, written on tablets of stone. I would cross seas and suffer sunstroke and give away all I have, but not for a man, because they want to be the destroyer and never be destroyed. That is why they are unfit for romantic love. There are exceptions and I hope they are happy.
>
> (1991: 165)

Men other than her father are either seductively (almost devilishly) handsome or grotesque. Her dismissal of them ironically appears to bring her closer to her mother's perspective, although unlike the mother, Winterson sustains a potentially conciliatory and yet tortured sense of love in the world, love between beings rather than the divine kind.

In 'A Voyage to the Houyhnhnms,' an introduction to an edition of Jonathan Swift's *Gulliver's Travels*, Winterson retrieves a universal value that is found in the common fear, whatever one's sexual orientation or identity, of being out of control: 'We all of us, when we fall in love, explain it to ourselves, explain it away, try to offer sensible rational strategies of behaviour. It is not that we lie, only that the truth is too painful. Our ordered world of self-control has been broken up for ever. We are no longer what we were' (1999: ix). Winterson returns to the breaking of the apparent ordered mechanisms of self-control, of social expectations and of recurrences. She returns to romantic structures and possibilities, despite reaching, as Reynier indicates, more of an ironic than a miraculous revelation in her first novel (2004: 71). Moreover, despite the theme of men's ambivalence, as Rusk concludes, Jeanette in *Oranges* possesses two alter egos in the fairy tales dealing with the notion of the noble and heroic, Winnet and Sir Perceval, one male and the other female. It seems as if she intuits a sexual and larger identity that includes her lesbianism, but the enigmatic quality Rusk identifies is at the heart of every encounter with otherness (2002: 110), and as Rusk reminds us, the orange demon refuses to name its sexuality or gender (111).

The Passion: A fervent masculinity

The protagonist of *The Passion*, Henri, is apparently defined by a militaristic location and identity, a typical expression of an idealizing masculine context. George L. Mosse comments that the rise of gymnastics fostered the ideal of manly courage, bodily development, and introduced a perversion of the Christian ideal that culminated in a militaristic framing of the masculine: 'A messianic element was introduced into the formation of the male body, never to leave it entirely. The notion that a true man must serve a higher ideal became in the end an integral part of what could be called the militarization of masculinity' (1996: 44). Such passion both constrains and defines the masculine, and Henri finally admits the passion of soldiery evades him. 'I was a bad soldier because I cared too much about what happened next. I could never lose myself in the cannonfire, in the moments of combat and hate' (1987: 122–3). The potential freedom of excess and abandon eludes him.

Throughout, Henri remains unfulfilled, uncertain about an overwhelming sense of passion that has permeated and shaped his life first in response to Napoleon Bonaparte and, after approaching Moscow and deserting the Grand Army, for Villanelle. Both figures, as the 'other' of his projections, promise to satisfy different kinds of desire. For Bényei: 'His choice of the objects of desire is typical of the paradoxical nature of what he wants, since both Napoleon and Villanelle become destructive forces in his life and are narrative agents that threaten to put an end to Henri's quest and his narrative ... Villanelle, the archetypal object of desire (an allegory of desire, a written agent with the name of a poetic structure), is aware of the link between holy desire and violence that Henri denies' (1997: 205–6). Henri seeks to transform himself; but although he sees in Villanelle a catalysing effect, Villanelle sees in him an underlying nature shared with other men. As Henri says of Napoleon:

> Why would a people who love the grape and the sun die in the zero of winter for one man?
> Why did I? Because I loved him. He was my passion and when we go to war we feel we are not lukewarm people any more.
> What did Villanelle think?
> Men are violent. That's all there is to it.
>
> (1987: 108–9)

Even thinking over the first occasion that he made love to Villanelle, Henri admits 'I lose all sense of day or night, I lose all sense of my work, writing this story, trying to convey to you what really happened. Trying not to make up too much' (103). He cannot confront headlong the pain of the loss of the potential of the moment, or happily admit the loss of control.

Arguably, these two different kinds of passion are configured stereotypically as masculine and feminine, and yet most importantly neither figure is finally comforting for Henri. Winterson in this sense neither prioritizes nor favours either sex in any essentialist fashion. Napoleon, who deludes Henri (the latter equally deludes himself), offers a temporary respite from Henri's gnawing discomfort. Despite the latter's lack of religiosity and belief, he moves from the company of priests, with their relationship to a self-sacrificing violence, to that of the putative emperor. As he reflects retrospectively:

> When I started working for Napoleon directly I thought he spoke in aphorisms, he never said a sentence like you or I would, it was put like a great thought. I wrote them down and only later realized how bizarre most of them were. ... Even when I hated him, he could still make me cry. And not through fear. He was great.
>
> (30)

The retrospective and quasi-scholarly quality of a narrator apparently re-reading his old journals at such points of reflection distances the account from an economy of immediacy and the unknowingness of the present, and also bifurcates Henri's already confused identity into two selves, the current and the past. At other points he seems to merge with the past and its compulsions. Villanelle's vitality (a characteristic she shares with Napoleon) contrasts with Henri's penchant for stillness.

> I think about her body a lot; not possessing it but watching it twist in sleep. She is never still; whether it be in boats or running full tilt with an armful of cabbages. She's not nervous, it's unnnatural for her to be still.'
>
> (123–4)

Significantly, her men are less concerned with her sexual ambiguity, that Allen so emphasizes, than her mercurial refusal of their economy of passion, of love. Love troubles her in terms of both sexes. Villanelle confounds Henri, with her very independence, and he confesses 'I will always be afraid of her body because of the power it has' (123). His sense of Napoleon diminishes, while that of Villanelle expands. Allen concludes 'The first brings disillusion, the second disappointment' (1996: 53).

Winterson's novel conjures an overarching frame from the very paradoxes of passion and its intersubjective trajectory, which both reveals and destabilizes the conflicted identities of those so enthralled. Moreover it is by comprehending the very mercurial intensity of Winterson's concept of passion that one can understand Winterson's fiction correctly, a concept which offers the exegetical codes within which Winterson's treatment of gender and of masculinity ought to be situated. Of Villanelle Henri adds in confessional mode:

> Infatuation. First love. Lust.
>   My passion can be explained away. But this is sure: whatever she touches, she reveals.
>
> (1987: 123)

The enigmatic style conveys a sense of the profound, the universal, the revelatory. Significantly the feminine ideal offers revelation; the masculine ideal appears to do so, but finally delivers disillusionment. Nevertheless, despite this antinomy, throughout the novel Winterson's portrayal of masculinity remains complex and intriguing, and from the outset it is rendered ambivalent by its initial, largely bellicose setting, following as the narrative does the campaigns of Napoleon, initially in attempting to invade England and continuing up to the approach to Moscow. This remains a largely masculine world, one oriented toward imperial gains, honour and heroism, and in part the sexual drives of men that displace their fears, as does their drunkenness. After Moscow Henri rejects any vestiges of an active allegiance, turning himself into a deserter, abandoning his hero, Napoleon, for another figure and thus as well as opting for survival, engaging a different sense of passion.

Educated among the largely illiterate, Henri, the narrator and protagonist, has volunteered as an act of personal signification, his attempt to find some consequence in himself. His ultimate quest is for purpose, meaning and love, none of which God can satisfy, but all of this is challenged by the vicissitudes of the Russian campaign. 'There was nothing we wouldn't believe to get us through ... And the heaviest lie? That we could go home and pick up where we had left off. That our hearts would be waiting behind the door with the dog' (83). Nevertheless, there are many conventional romance elements in Winterson's novel, ones delineated by Ganteau, from the episodic, the use of archetypes, to a preference for excess (2003: 226), but it is his notion of the text's ethical dimensions that is most intriguing in terms of masculinity (227). In Winterson's novel the romance involves a refusal of closure, an openness, and its whimsicalities not only allow the author the opportunity to exploit a thoroughgoing rejection of mimesis (237), but it may also represent a contemporized genre deriving from a Woolfian mode of writing found in *Orlando*, which as Ganteau argues, is capable of 'relaying the ethical imperative formerly voiced in critical and philosophical discourse, on the one hand, and in the realistic idiom, on the other' (238). Although androgyny, as Ganteau suggests, is an important theme, it is the lack of fixity, the irrationality, the mystery of things that finally defeats Henri, his refusal to live among the contingent magnitude and eventfulness of the historical present. Hence in his cell he considers what Venice signifies across the bay:

> Over the water in that city of madmen they are preparing for Christmas and New Year. ... I stay up the whole night, listening to the dead moan round the rock and watching the stars move across the sky.
> At midnight the bells ring out from every one of their churches ..., but it is a living city and no one really knows what buildings are there from one day to the next.
>
> (1987: 158)

On one level this sense of fear responds to the underlying threat to a masculine order. For Bényei the text, like Venice, is uncanny, 'mercurial and volatile' (1997: 200), and finally excessive. And yet such layers of excess stand in contrast to the excesses of the campaigns, of the related deaths with their logic of despair. As Bényei points out, Henri's nature is paradoxical, incorporating the contradictions of passion and masculinity.

> What Henri does is divide passion into two distinct realms or two opposing kinds of desire. One is a desire for life, for finding oneself, for safety in stillness. The other is a base, violent emotion, a passionate rage for absolute loss, a desire whose principle is the desire for death as the ultimate risk to sovereign existence.
>
> (205)

Henri fails to mediate between these apparently opposing polarities; they co-exist within him.

For Judith Seaboyer the 'soldier protagonist is a type of quester' (1997: 484) and deeply imbued with a romantic sensibility. Despite Henri's apparent reflective passivity, clearly many of the men are more aggressive and oppress others, particularly women. Examples of such violence punctuate the text. In an early episode that defines the different categories of male in terms of their treatment of women, Henri appears

not only dismayed at the cook's violence toward a prostitute in Boulogne, but also quietly enraged.

> 'Fine man your friend,' said my woman. . . .
> He came towards her with his fist raised but it never fell. My woman
> stepped forward and coshed him on the back of the head with a wine jar. She
> held her companion for a moment and kissed her swiftly on the forehead.
> She would never do that to me.
>
> (1987: 14–15)

Henri's final comment is suggestive. Despite his masculine identities, he
feels both excluded and marginalized, since he cannot adopt entirely
stereotypical roles, cannot incorporate many of the required tenets.
Moreover, Henri requires commitment and purpose in a random and
seemingly purposeless world. Violence is an irrepressible response.
Either sexual jealously or inadequacy (or both) tinges his view of the
embrace. Villanelle adapts more resourcefully to the contingencies and
intensities of life and love. She has been sold into prostitution, and
sleeps with Russians to obtain food for their survival. Henri recognizes
at their first meeting that she would never love him even though they
are physically intimate and she bears his child. The very cook who
Henri encounters in Boulogne turns out in a twist of fate to be the
pernicious trader who rapes and marries Villanelle. The cook enacts and
epitomizes many potentially monstrous qualities of masculinity.
Although Villanelle concludes he is heartless, curiously he proves
physically to possess a heart, in macabre circumstances refuting his
wife's expectations. Villanelle's story of cross-dressing in Venice, and
her fondness for lovers of both sexes, fictionally stress a fact of orientation that is outlined by Connell, 'gender ambiguity can be an object of
fascination and desire, as well as disgust' (2002: 5).

After the long and arduous journey by Henri and Villanelle to reach
freedom in the city of her birth, their stay in Venice soon becomes
uneasy. Emerging from both of their pasts, the cook pursues them
relentlessly in his final appearance, recognizing Henri's status as a
deserter. As a figure, the cook remains grotesque and craven, as we see
in his final moments recollected by Henri before he kills him after the
cook reaches for his throat. 'I remember his mouth opening and coming
towards her, his hand loosed from the boat side, his body bent. His
hand scraped her breast. His mouth is the clearest image I have. A pale
pink mouth, a cavern of flesh and then his tongue, just visible like a
worm from its hole' (1987: 128). And yet curiously the extracted heart
serves to emphasize the cook's common humanity, his literally visceral
presence that Henri revisits as a source of his nightmarish guilt.

Napoleon shares something of the intensity of the cook, representing
yet another dimension of an exaggerated and grotesque masculine
image, both being pre-emptive and reductively sexual. Winterson's

depiction of the emperor in the comic mode is stereotypical not only in terms of one's prior knowledge of the historical counterpart, but also of men in such positions of power. This is purposeful and can be read in terms of certain aspects of masculinity and its ideological meaning historically. However, he is not a fixed or stable personality in Winterson's text; he is by turns ambitious, charismatic, heroic, compulsive, and finally self-deluding, for as Henri comments of Bonaparte's final campaign and subsequent incarceration on Elba where he puts on weight, 'Odd that a man should come to believe in myths of his own making' (151).

Henri admits his complicity in the relationship with Bonaparte, something that might be regarded as omnipresent in all extremes of love and passion. Despite this, Henri rejects any such possibility regarding his feelings for Villanelle. One suspects his protestations are inflected by a recognition that in fact he suffers from a profound inner doubt:

> I am in love with her; not a fantasy or a myth or a creature of my own making. Her. A person who is not me. I invented Bonaparte as much as he invented himself. My passion for her, even though she could never return it, showed me the difference between inventing a lover and falling in love.
>
> (157–8)

Bonaparte represents a raw, almost unmediated masculine self-avowal, a naturalizing of the self as if nature requires such energy, contrasting the passivity and patience of 'Perceval, the gentle knight, who came to a ruined chapel and found what the others had overlooked, simply by sitting still' (154). Both Bonaparte and the cook do not simply represent symbolically, but actively articulate and purvey a number of different, easily identifiable codes of masculine behaviour. The cook avows vulgar sexuality and drunkenness; Bonaparte is compulsive and demanding. Finally for Henri both of these grotesques remain very definite models of masculinity, offering paradigmatic behaviour, constituting a broad concept of masculinity that contributes to France's warlike, masculinist culture, of the kind Mosse regards as the distinct and pervasive Western masculine ideals characteristic of 'the self-definition of modern society' (1996: 3). In contrast, Henri remains attuned to both the dead whose presence haunts him, and over his eight years in military service he kills nothing but the numerous chickens for Napoleon.

Towards the end of *The Passion* Henri reflects on the meaning of his love for Villanelle. 'It means I review my future and my past in the light of this feeling. It is as though I wrote in a foreign language that I am suddenly able to read. Wordlessly she explains me to myself. Like genius, she is ignorant of what she does' (1987: 122). Previously he has resisted the intuitive, but this epiphany highlights the reductive male rationality that has subtended his experience until he reaches Venice, an environment that confounds both himself and his idealized male,

Napoleon; and even though it allows Henri to cast off his old self, he also loses himself both symbolically and literally.

> I got lost from the first. Where Bonaparte goes, straight roads follow, buildings are rationalised, street signs may change to celebrate a battle but they are always clearly marked. Here, if they bother with street signs at all, they are happy to use the same ones over again. Not even Bonaparte could rationalise Venice.
>
> (112)

Venice is iterative, and as intuitive as Villanelle, its web-footed offspring. Henri remains tied to a masculine rationalism, cautious and resistant to the intuitive. Toward the end when Villanelle attempts to rescue Henri from his prison, she sees in him an image that reflects the dying moments of the cook. He insists that they are married. ' "I'm your husband," and he came leaning towards me, his eyes round and glassy and his tongue so pink' (148). It seems as if Henri is condemned in his masculinity to being a chameleon; he cannot retrieve a sense of himself, given that his past has been effaced and he has no viable other upon which he can project to obtain a sense of self. As Shiffer explains, the novel 'works continually to express loss so total and profound that it cannot be spoken; it resides below the surface, within the silences' (2004: 35).

Sexing the Cherry: Unrequited passions

The fantastical element of *The Passion* is strongest in the episode where Henri appears to steal a jar from the house of Villanelle's lover, the Queen of Spades, that contains her heart. Although promised a miracle by his lover, she fails to return his passion. A far more consistently fantastical element is central to the historiographic account of *Sexing*, the tale of Dog Woman, an ugly and rumbustious breeder of dogs at the time of the English Civil War, and her adopted son, Jordan. As with *The Passion*, one-sided love appears to lie at the heart of the narrative, and both of these central characters narrate different episodes, epitomizing the extremes of storytelling. As Angela Marie Smith explains, Jordan becomes a traveller of 'exotic lands' whereas his adoptive mother is the 'archetypal storytelling figure' who stays at home and comprehends 'the local tales and traditions' (2005: 26). Dog Woman retains and represents a sense of both traditions, a centring. Even though her sexual persona is ambiguous, she is an extremely masculine presence, and heterosexual, although as Marilyn R. Farwell points out, 'only in a technical sense because her fantastical size defeats her few attempted sexual liaisons' (1996: 177).

Bente Gade comments on Jordan's decision to look in the interstices and imagine that which remains undone as part of his 'ambition to record his secret inner life [which] opens the novel and unleashes the question of identity and adequate ways of representing it' (1999: 27). In accounting for themselves, both Jordan and his mother attempt to specify the nature of their love for a significant other but, as Shiffer notes, to articulate or narrate is to inscribe something lost and to suppress the intuitive and pre-linguistic self (2004: 36). Although he tells stories, Jordan attempts to deploy them in a becoming, desiring other than the worldly, as if he were divided. 'To escape from the weight of the world, I leave my body where it is, in conversation or at dinner, and walk through a series of winding streets to a house standing back from the road' (2001: 17). Seeking the woman he admires he dresses like a woman, just like many others he meets 'anxious to be free of the burdens of gender' (31), so that he might enter 'a pen of prostitutes kept by a rich man for his friends' (30). When continuing life as a woman, Jordan recognizes a silent language, a conspiracy among women, and he recounts 12 of the many rules propounded by the owner of a fish stall where he worked. Men generically appear controlling, insensitive, easily duped (32–3), although 'Your greatest strength is that every man believes he knows the sum and possibility of every woman' (33). Nevertheless, as Mary Bratton points out, Jordan's heroic desire can be 'seen as a form of blindness to women' (2002: 210).

Such truths appear proverbial, potentially universal, relevant to the literal world, although that world's qualities contrast with those of Jordan's utopian, typically Wintersonian weightless and hallucinatory imaginary, its qualities like the literal mercurial effect that impacts upon the contemporary counterpart of the Dog Woman, poisoned by nuclear waste (Winterson 2001: 123). As Palmer observes, 'Jacobean London is squalid rather than glorious' (1990: 184); and yet in London itself the inhabitants seem both unconcerned with and unsurprised by the condition of the city. The river of the past, unlike that of the contemporary addenda, offers an image of purity, not in the city, but beyond. Together Jordan and the Dog Woman escape briefly this 'foul place, full of pestilence and rot' (Winterson 2001: 13). Jordan rows his mother along the Thames until it merges with the sea, where she reveals the profundity of her love for him, not so much in articulate language as in the unfamiliar world she briefly shares.

> We were out at sea. Grey waves with white heads. A thin line in the distance got louder and louder until we were shouting to make ourselves heard, and I saw the sun on Jordan's face, the last glimmers of lanterns, and against the final trace of the moon a flight of seagulls that came from nowhere and seemed to be born of the sun itself.
>
> (16)

Such love, much like the quotidian processes of nature described above, is epiphanic and miraculous. Palmer finds in Dog Woman's strengths the archetypal masculine, 'whereas Jordan displays a feminine sensibility' (1990: 185).

Until the end, other than this single shared rowing trip out to sea, the pair remain in polar opposition. Jordan abandons his mother to explore ephemerality, tied as she is to a 'flat earth' view of the world, prosaic and engaged. Jordan's restlessness is in part expressive of a masculine ideal found in Tradescant, but he transforms its nature, voyaging as much, if not more, in the realm of imagination as in the physical, empirical world. Gade points out the difference in Tradescant and Jordan's journeys undertaken together: whereas the former categorizes and maps meticulously, the latter achieves a different mode of truth; and unlike the natural heroism of Tradescant, 'Jordan's style undermines traditional heroism' (1999: 31).

Women are drawn into desire with its concomitant violence, although like the princesses in Jordan's tales the Dog Woman seeks to direct such violence back toward repressive men. The power of narrative is an undoubted theme, and as Smith points out, in an almost Whitmanesque manner, both protagonists contain a host of contradictions, neither is bound by gender or sexual proclivities. Both are hampered by the subversive quality of passion, something that, as Jordan says, can be shaken off, but 'When I have shaken off my passion, somewhat as a dog shakes off an unexpected plunge into a canal, I find myself without any understanding of what it was that ravaged me' (Winterson 2001: 74). As Smith points out, following Walter Benjamin's dictum in 'The Storyteller', *Sexing* grafts 'auratic stories and dominant histories' (2005: 38) and the contemporary scenes in *Sexing* affirm the germinative power in radical narratives that hybridize those of the past (38).

Jeffrey Roessner sees *Sexing* as a project designed to 'historicize the larger patriarchal forces that shaped the lives of ... characters, and [which] expose[s] the contingency of universal values, including the naturalness of heterosexuality and the father's authority in a partrilineal culture' (2002: 102–3). He sees a revision of the role of the puritans that 'presents passion as an instinctual and uncontrollable force that cannot be repressed without harsh consequences' (105). According to this view, certain (but not all) men are therefore cast as primordially complicit in reframing patriarchy and the case of the puritans demonstrates the underlying hypocrisy of masculine control, founded upon a synthesis of self-avowal, self-belief and rationalizing one's own hegemony. The choice of period is doubly significant because it allows Winterson to revisit the extremes of religiosity and its predisposition for a patriarchal order, and explore a time when gender roles were not as bifurcated as subsequently. As Connell says, not only was the early modern period the time of emergent empire and capitalism producing an ideological belief 'in individual difference and personal agency' (1995: 68), but also before the eighteenth century '[w]omen were certainly regarded as different from men, but different in the sense of being incomplete or inferior examples of the same character (for instance, having less of the faculty of reason)' (68). Roessner's critique of the novel is both complex and perhaps over-nuanced, its subtleties tending to obscure the original literary text; he describes a 'third wave' feminism designed 'to remedy the first wave's identification with male power and the second wave's reification of a female counter society' (2002: 104), and identifies *Sexing* as characterized by a tension between the second- and third-wave thinking, although 'Ultimately, however, Winterson rejects linear temporality and endorses an apocalyptic urge to escape history and the power structures of a male-dominated society' (104). Winterson perhaps intends to bridge all three, and through a mythopoeic sense maintains an almost paradoxical equilibrium. This is part of her subtlety and virtuosity as a novelist, one who breaches ideological positioning *per se*.

Almost contradictorily with regard to Roessner's idea of a feminist shift toward 'historicizing the patriarchal values' (103), so as to challenge constructed oppressions, one central positive male character is the King, Charles I, who according to the royalist Dog Woman's account renders a dignified paradigm of masculine authority, and for whom she engages in a campaign of apparent savage and grotesque revenge against the puritans. Roessner attempts to situate Winterson as part of an innate 'instinctualism' which 'celebrates an excessive and ungovernable passion' (109), and he concludes that, 'By presenting Charles I's execution as a wrong turn in history, Winterson supports a longing for a prelapsarian age when the sins of excess were tolerated' (110).

In terms of the internal logic of the text, the Dog Woman's vengeful actions can be positioned as an inversion of the oppressive and constricting tenets of a new masculinist order. For Smith the Dog Woman's monarchism is 'anachronistic' (2005: 34), her narratives inadequate given their suspicion of complexity (34) and given their 'idealization of monarchy ... [which] suggest[s] her inability to encompass fully the implications of gendered power structures', although Smith admits that a vision of the character certainly inspires her modern counterpart (33). She concludes that the King is both symbolic and literal, with Winterson 'all the while straining to illuminate the spiritual transcendence of which the sacred-secular body of the King is but a profane spark' (42). Arguably there is an appropriate balance in the Dog Woman's responses, for as Roessner comments concerning the 'counter-history' of Charles, a perverse, often bestial and always threatening sexuality defines his opponents' because 'Despite their chaste public manner, the Puritans, especially men, unleash their frustrated sexual desires in grotesque form' (2002: 107). There is an underlying malevolence in this puritanical libidinous economy. Roessner assesses the critical attempt to understand Dog Woman's grotesque size as a resistance to normativity and control (110), implying that it contrasts with the many characters who seek 'to transcend the limitations of the physical self' (110), culminating in Fortunata's dance, a character who becomes 'a metaphorical object of Jordan's spiritual rather than simply physical desire' (111). Smith reads Jordan's narratives as counter-histories depicting the archetypal and inverting power structures (2005: 27–8); for Roessner Jordan's quest is Dantesque, finally presenting 'Fortunata as a symbol of an irrational, ungovernable passion, the novel actually perpetuates the mythic use of the desirable woman as an Other to masculine rationality' (2002: 111). Roessner conflates Jordan's quest for a transcendent identity or inner meaning with 'his essential self – a self again clearly distinct from his body' (112), imagining that it is dealt with as if it were a solely ideological function. He adds, 'Although the reader sees the pain endured by the characters, the novel does not suggest that it could be lessened by better, more forthright communication between them' (112). And yet this particular bonding of Jordan and the Dog Woman ensures the validity of both the economy of the text and its enigmatic and contradictory masculinities. If they fail fully to communicate, this curiously renders their mutual love more profound, more resistant to the vicissitudes of the material aspects of power, less constructed by gendered cultural expectations. Their failures are profound and moving, and the power of the novel, its poignancy and sense of longing, derives from the very enigmatic qualities that are the basis of Roessner's objection. Fortunata appears fleetingly toward the novel's end, glimpsed by Dog Woman as they voyage away from the burning city. As Jordan says, ending the novel, 'Even the most solid of things and the most real, the best-loved and the well-known, are only handshadows on the wall. Empty space and points of light' (Winterson 2001: 144). Bratton would situate this within 'carnival time' (2002: 212) and certainly, as Farwell says, this emphasizes ambiguity (1996: 181), but rather than simply merging with the female subject as Farwell suggests (182–3), Jordan re-enters that poignant spacelessness of the ocean, not the isolation of a voyage shared within Tradescant, but rediscovering that momentarily epiphanic space described earlier by the Dog Woman, merging with the vast ambiguities of nature, outside of history. Finally, the 'proto-new man' is absorbed into the universal passion that is nature.

Works cited

Allen, Carolyn (1996), *Following Djuna: Women Lovers and the Erotics of Loss*. Bloomington and Indianapolis: Indiana University Press.

Bényei, Tamás (1997), 'Risking the text: Stories of love in Jeanette Winterson's *The Passion*', *Hungarian Journal of English and American Studies*, 3, (2), 199–209.

Bratton, Mary (2002), 'Winterson, Bakhtin, and the chronotope of a lesbian hero', *Journal of Narrative Theory*, 32, (2), Summer, 207–26.

Connell, R. W. (1995), *Masculinities*. Cambridge: Polity Press.

—— (2002), *Gender*. Cambridge: Polity Press.

Di Stefano, Christine (1991), *Configurations of Masculinity: A Feminist Perspective on Modern Political Theory*. Ithaca and London: Cornell University Press.

Doan, Laura (1994), 'Jeanette Winterson's sexing the postmodern,' in Laura Doan (ed.), *The Lesbian Postmodern*. New York: Columbia University Press, pp. 137–55.

Farwell, Marilyn R. (1996), *Heterosexual Plots and Lesbian Narratives*. New York and London: New York University Press.

Gade, Bente (1999), 'Multiple selves and grafted agents: a postmodernist reading of *Sexing the Cherry*', in Helene Bengtson, Marianne Børch and Cindie Maagaard (eds), *Sponsored by Demons: The Art of Jeanette Winterson*. Odense, Denmark: Scholars' Press, pp. 27–39.

Ganteau, Jean-Michel (2003), 'Fantastic, but truthful: the ethics of romance', *Cambridge Quarterly*, 32, (3), 225–38.

Makinen, Merja (2005), *The Novels of Jeanette Winterson*. Basingstoke and New York: Palgrave Macmillan.

Mosse, George L. (1996), *The Image of Man: The Creation of Modern Masculinity*. New York and Oxford: Oxford University Press.

Palmer, Paulina (1990), 'Contemporary lesbian feminist fiction: Texts for everywoman', in Linda Anderson (ed.), *Plotting Change: Contemporary Women's Fiction*. London and Melbourne: Edward Arnold, pp. 43–62.

Reynier, Christine (2004), *Jeanette Winterson: Le Miracle Ordinaire*. Bourdeaux: Presses Universitaires de Bourdeaux.

Roessner, Jeffrey (2002), 'Writing a history of difference: Jeanettte Winterson's *Sexing the Cherry* and Angela Carter's *Wise Children*', *College Literature*, 29, (1), Winter, 102–22.

Rusk, Lauren (2002), *The Life Writing of Otherness: Woolf, Baldwin, Kingston, and Winterson*. New York and London: Routledge.

Seaboyer, Judith (1997), 'Second death in Venice: Romanticism and the compulsion to repeat in Jeanette Winterson's *The Passion*', *Contemporary Literature*, 38, 483–509.

Shiffer, Celia (2004), ' "You see, I am no stranger to love: Jeanette Winterson and the extasy of the word', *Critique*, 46, (1), Fall, 31–52.

Smith, Angela Marie (2005), 'Fiery constellations: Winterson's *Sexing the Cherry* and Benjamin's materialist historiography', *College Literature*, 32, (3), Summer, 21–50.

Winterson, Jeanette (1987), *The Passion*. London: Bloomsbury.

—— (1991), [1985], *Oranges Are Not the Only Fruit*. London: Vintage.

—— (1999), 'Introduction: Gulliver's Wound', in Jonathan Swift, *Gulliver's Travels*. Oxford and New York: Oxford University Press, pp. v–xii.

—— (2001), [1989], *Sexing the Cherry*. London: Vintage.

CHAPTER NINE

Winterson's Adaptations for the Stage and the Screen

SONIA MARIA MELCHIORRE

Chapter summary: Melchiorre's chapter examines Winterson's writing for the stage and screen. Discussing the adaptation of *Oranges* for BBC television, her original screenplays and scripts for film and radio, and the stage adaptation of *The PowerBook*, it demonstrates that Winterson, despite her highly literary reputation, has always been willing to 'go beyond the book', and engage with different media to reach a wider audience.

Key texts: *Oranges Are Not the Only Fruit; Great Moments in Aviation; Shades of Fear; The PowerBook*

Key words: adaptation, the literary text, theatre, television, film, radio

Jeanette Winterson's reputation as a 'serious' author was consolidated between the late 1980s and the beginning of the 1990s, when she received the first prizes for her fictions – *Oranges Are Not the Only Fruit* (1985), *The Passion* (1987), *Sexing The Cherry* (1989) and *Written On The Body* (1992)[1] – and her work started to be anthologized along with that of the best British young writers. At the same time, the first adaptations of her work appeared: when the first episode of *Oranges* was shown, on BBC television on 10 January 1990, Winterson's books had already been moved from the 'cookery' shelves to the 'gay and lesbian' section, finally finding a 'proper' place in the 'A to Z authors' section in bookshops around Britain.[2]

As is well known, Jeanette Winterson was brought up by a family of evangelists to become a missionary and she started writing sermons – 'a good exercise for writing precise prose' – when still a child (Cooper 1986). 'Being brought up by Pentecostal Evangelists meant that there was tremendous drive', Winterson explains, 'to go out there and make a difference ... It's a natural progression which seems bizarre perhaps – from those days of preaching the word to these days of trying to make people see things imaginatively, transformatively' (*Windrush* 2002). It seems that Winterson found new ways of 'spreading the Word' in the media; she had already realized, with great insight, when still very young and at the very beginning of her literary career, that the 'mass' media could help her to reach a wider audience.[3] In the introduction to the script of *Oranges Are Not the Only Fruit* she states: '[m]y interest in working for film and television is inevitably evangelical ... I have a mission and it is this: to restore to the image the power of the word' (Winterson 1994: viii). There are, according to the writer, close parallels between the activity of the preacher and the work of the artist: the most successful preachers, and artists, 'are able to convince their audience that the audience themselves got it wrong and the preacher's got it right' (Wachtel 1994). And she adds, 'I was driven by a need to preach to people and convert them which possibly I still am, except that now I do it for art's sake, and then I did it for God's sake'(*Windrush* 2002). In *Boating For Beginners* (1985), an exhilarating parodic rewriting of the story of the 'Flood' – Winterson's comic book too often overlooked by critics – Noah's preaching activity is inextricably linked to the use of the 'mass' media on which he relies for the success of the broadcast he's prepared in collaboration with God, 'the Unpronounceable'. Indeed, Jeanette Winterson's works for television, cinema and theatre have always been inspired by her original passion for preaching – also evident in her most recent activity as a journalist and in the monthly columns she writes for her website.[4]

When in 1988 Winterson presented her first radio play called *Static*, on BBC Radio 3, she was convinced that radio drama represented an excellent training for scriptwriters and radio itself was a useful means to gain a wider audience interested in listening to 'the Word' (Winterson 1994: 75).[5] The radio, as both an object and a symbol, subsequently became a central feature in the television adaptation of *Oranges Are Not The Only Fruit*: 'It's time for my broadcast', Mother says in the final scene of the TV series. In the late 1980s Winterson turned to film, scriptwriting *Great Moments in Aviation* (1988) in addition to the script for the TV version of *Oranges Are Not the Only Fruit* (1990).

The experimental writings of the 1990s – *Art and Lies* (1994), *Art Objects* (1995), *Gut Symmetries* (1997) – were not as successful as Winterson expected them to be. 'It's no secret', she said in an interview, 'that the 90s weren't a great decade for me, so maybe that's why I'm glad they're gone' (Brooks 2000).[6] Winterson returned to her work as a radio playwright in 2001 when in November BBC Radio 3 presented her new play, *Text Message*, in which she showed a continuing interest in the relationship between technology and writing practices in the twenty-first century – a subject already treated in *The PowerBook* (2000), and later expanded in that book's adaptation for the stage (2002-3). In 2002 Winterson wrote a new script for a screen version of *The Passion* (2002).[7] Unfortunately Miramax was not happy with the script and the film, not yet distributed, will be made using a script by someone else. Apparently it calls for 'explicit sex scenes between the two women' – Villanelle and the unnamed mysterious woman – and Gwyneth Paltrow, who is bound to play the part of Villanelle, observed that 'the love scene is great, and it will be quite a challenge' (*Advocate* 2002).

In the 'Column' section of her website for September 2006, Winterson also announced that she intended to start a theatre piece, her first original dramatic text, in January 2007. In the same note she reveals that she has just finished 'the first episode of *Tanglewreck*' (2006) for the BBC and that she is 'looking forward to starting the second part' (www.jeanettewinterson.com). The rest of this chapter will focus on the adaptation of *Oranges* for BBC television; look briefly at Winterson's work for the cinema, *Shades of Fear/Great Moments in Aviation*; and finally discuss *The PowerBook*, Winterson's first adaptation for the stage.

The adaptation of *Oranges Are Not the Only Fruit*

Given the emphasis on literariness and fictional experiment in Winterson's works, it is extremely interesting to see how they have translated into the mediums of screen and stage. The screen version of *Oranges Are Not the Only Fruit* (1990)[8] was the first of Winterson's adaptations, and a great success, seen by more than six million people. It was the winner of the BAFTA Award in Britain and the Prix Italia, for 'Best TV Drama', in 1991.[9] Its skilful promotion resulted in increased sales of Winterson's previous fictions and in a new edition of the novel, with a cover featuring Geraldine McEwan and Charlotte Coleman in a scene from the film.

The adaptation was expertly analysed in two important essays published in the 1990s. In '*Oranges Are Not the Only Fruit*. Reaching audiences other lesbian texts cannot reach', Hilary Hinds examined the 'ambiguous cultural status' of Winterson's text, one which crosses the divide between high and popular culture and is, according to her interpretation, capable of breaking through many barriers. Hinds reads the TV adaptation in its historical and political context – the passing of Section 28 of the Local Government Act and the death threat made against Salman Rushdie – and in the context of British TV drama series since the 1960s. She gives a detailed account of the possible reasons for the work's success, its positive reception by both critics and viewers and even the widespread public acceptance of the lesbianism in *Oranges*, arguing that not only did the adaptation's 'quality' status mitigate its treatment of lesbianism, and viewers were able to see it in relation to other issues – religion, family and growing up – but that its very status as a lesbian text also worked to defy conventional categorizations. As she concludes, the adaptation of *Oranges* really represents 'the infiltration of that bastion of television high cultural respectability by a programme directed and produced by women, scripted by a lesbian and one whose main theme was lesbianism' (Hinds 1995: 66).

The same point is made by Margaret Marshment and Julia Hallam in their essay entitled ' "From string of knots to orangebox": lesbianism on prime time'. The authors 'assume that this all-female team were aware of the sexual politics of their project' (Marshment and Hallam 1994: 144) and describe the television version of *Oranges Are Not the Only Fruit* as a 'realist text', one 'that works within the conventions of mainstream film and television fictions' and is aimed at changing people's mind about a particular social issue (146). Lesbianism is analysed in opposition to religious fanaticism as 'a strategy that uses one unpopular minority in order to present another unpopular minority in a favourable light' (150). As for the controversial sex scene, Marshment and Hallam point out how it is 'couched within the culture's conventional representations of "young love" ' (150), producing what they term a 'naturalization of lesbianism' (151).

Jeanette Winterson declared, one week before the screening of *Oranges*, that while she was not keen on writing for television, she was very pleased with the final product (Dunn 1990). She said she wanted the adaptation to be bolder than the book and, most importantly, anticipated what was to be the main theme of the version for the screen, namely the clash between love and power. Her definition of the Church as a symbol of power rather than of love was significant as the conflict between self and society became a central theme in Winterson's work (Dunn 1990). However, while this conflict is evident in the novel, where the many stories interspersed throughout the narration accompany the young protagonist in her journey to self-determination, in the adaptation the theme becomes obvious only in the part concerning the protagonist's sexuality.

In the screen version, the protagonist of *Oranges Are Not the Only Fruit*, Jeanette – significantly Winterson's first name – is renamed Jess (her part is played by Charlotte Coleman), as if the writer meant to distance herself from the role. Like Jeanette in the novel, Jess is adopted, and brought up to become a missionary, by a family of religious fanatics – a tough mother (played by the actress Geraldine McEwan) and a marginal, silenced father, who, like Joseph in the 'Holy Family', is reduced to a mere spectator of events in Winterson's parodic version of this figure. Even though Geraldine McEwan's performance remains one of the highlights of the series – along with that of Charlotte Coleman – the character of the mother loses, in the adaptation, the 'comic' touch used by Winterson in the original text, a clever device aimed at tempering the autobiographical references.

The relationship between mother and daughter, as Rachel Blau du Plessis points out in her study of the *Künstlerroman*, is the central one in the female novel of development, in which the romance plot is replaced by the story of a daughter becoming an artist 'to extend, reveal and elaborate her mother's thwarted talent' (Blau du Plessis 1985: 93). Jeanette, and more explicitly Jess in the adaptation of *Oranges*, becomes the expression of Mother's skills – she plays the piano, she speaks French and is the Secretary of the 'Society for the Lost' – that the world around her forces her to repress. The mother–daughter relationship is threatened when Jess, as a teenager, falls in love with another girl. Mother's reaction is extreme, as this love story is a denial of all her principles and the failure of her educational and moral teachings. The girl who had been chosen to embody her moral crusade proves a sinful creature and, what is worse, betrays Mother's principles and expectations.[10] Mother has chosen Jess to be a 'creature' of her own making and decides that if the girl can't be hers and hers alone, she won't be anybody else's. The betrayed person betrays in turn. Mother takes her revenge by organizing her daughter's terrible punishment for her unfaithfulness and she publicly exposes Jess's 'unnatural passion' in the church during the Mass. This is followed by a more physical attack in the private space of the parlour – which, in the adaptation, is represented as Mother's privileged space. Jess/Jesus must be punished for her disobedience. She refused to be what Mother/Creator intended her to be: the saviour of the sinful world. But Mother has not the necessary power to do it by herself and needs the help of the pastor, the only male character of the religious sect and official representative of the supreme authority.

Once separated from her mother, Jess starts a personal quest for her identity. Jeanette Winterson's works are always concerned with journeys, 'the space travelled, physical and metaphysical, between two points of beginning' because all the stories continue, according to the writer, even when people are convinced that 'the only important thing is to get from A to B' (Winterson 1994: vii). In my view, the element of formal experiment and subversion of narrative models, which made *Oranges Are Not the Only Fruit* such an innovative novel, seems to be to a great extent lost in the adaptation for the screen, partly due to the greater importance given to the moving image over the spoken word.

Great Moments in Aviation/Shades of Fear

The journey or quest is one of the most important *leitmotifs* in all Winterson's literary and extra-literary productions, from *Oranges Are Not The Only Fruit* (1985) to the more recent *Tanglewreck* (2006). *Great Moments in Aviation/Shades of Fear* is the tale of another journey, which seems to have emerged from a series of conversations between Winterson and her friend, the black actress Vicky Licorish (Winterson 1994: vii). Originally a short film on 16 mm made in 1988, directed by Paul Shearer and edited by Melanie Adams, the very different final movie-length version was written in the company of the same crew responsible for the BBC version of *Oranges*, the film director Beeban Kidron and the producer Philippa Giles, and presented at the 1993 Cannes Film Festival as *Shades of Fear*, starring Vanessa Redgrave and Jonathan Pryce.

As rightly pointed out by a commentator, '*Great Moments in Aviation* must have meant a new set of problems to overcome, since it was written from scratch without any novel to lean back on' (Troberg, jeanettewinterson.net). 'I do not feel, as I did with the TV version of *Oranges Are Not the Only Fruit*', Winterson wrote in the introduction to the script, 'that *Great Moments in Aviation* is the definitive film. I could not see how we could have done *Oranges* better, I do see how we could have done *Great Moments* better' (Winterson 1994: xii). Winterson also had to rework the end of the script to get Miramax to put up the money to finish the shooting, but concluded that 'the new ending is satisfying'. She adds: 'I think that the film has lost some of the dimensions that were important to me but it has gained a pacey and well balanced very filmic sense (Winterson 1994: xiv).

In *Shades of Fear*, finally shown on BBC television in November 1995, we find all the main issues at the heart of Winterson's work: love, in its many forms; betrayal and disguise, in different people and situations; religious imagery reworked in several ways; and the discussion of various political issues concerning race, class and gender. Set in the early 1950s, Gabriel Angel, a young black woman from the Caribbean, embarks on a solitary journey on an ocean liner – from Grenada to England where she wants to become an aviator – but we never see her disembark once they get to England: what matters is not, according to the author, where people come from or where they're heading to, but how they are changed by the experience of the journey, which is at the same time factual and metaphysical. Nobody on board is what they seem to be: Duncan Stewart (alias Alistair Birch) is an art forger hunted by Professor Goodyear, an art expert, who turns out to be Birch's last lover's husband; two eccentric missionary women, returning to Britain after 30 years of life together in another continent, suddenly realize that they are lesbians and have sex together for the first time in their lives; Michael Angel is a black girl, apparently married to a man who's waiting for her in England, who pretends she is Mr Stewart's wife in order to justify the fact that they're sharing the same cabin as a consequence of a bureaucratic mistake.

Shades of Fear has been defined as 'a film about transcending mundane racial and sexual thinking' (Toombs 1995). Alan Toombs has also observed that its being 'drenched in sepia tones achieved through adherence to the brown décor and clothing of the period' and its 'succession of brown veneered cabins and deeply sensuous effect is created so that we become aware of the skin colour' (Toombs 1995). Toombs also points out a similarity between *Shades of Fear* and Derek Jarman's *Caravaggio* (1986), 'another film seeking to create a mode of seeing rather than tell an absolute story' (Toombs 1995). The final result is a film which, notwithstanding its obvious ambitions, never really takes off and doesn't develop all the main themes – religious, sexual and racial – which represent the basis of the script. By the end of the film the story remains suspended in the air, as in the case of Gabriel Angel shown in the final scene piloting a plane over the Caribbean Sea.

The PowerBook

The PowerBook (2000) was, according to Jeanette Winterson, the last 'chapter' of her first cycle of works begun with *Oranges* in 1985 (Rérolle 2002) although in my view *The PowerBook* already shows, as both literary text and stage play, signs of a new course in Winterson's artistic life. As I shall show in the last part of the chapter, Winterson's novel – and her stage adaptation – is built on an intertextual engagement with the Western literary canon in order to renew her experiment in language and form, more in line with *Sexing the Cherry* (1989) and *Written on the Body* (1992) than *Art and Lies* (1994) or *Gut Symmetries* (1997), to which *The PowerBook* bears only a slight resemblance. Indeed, *The PowerBook* has been described by Winterson as the product of a multimedia time where the exhausted 'master' narratives of the Western canon are no longer acceptable and need to be redefined (Winterson 2003).

Winterson responds positively to the challenge offered by the internet, convinced that, in a time of fast communication, it is the duty of the artist to use all the means of expression offered by the modern world and create art through them. In *The PowerBook* Winterson parallels the activity of web surfers, and on-line chatters, to the artist's creative experience and imagines the space of the internet as 'a masked ball', 'a place of disguise and possibility' where everyone, for the first time in history, has the chance to do what artists have always done, that is, to reinvent themselves as other people, as different selves. In the world of the internet more flexible concepts of time, space and gender are possible (Winterson 2003). 'One of the exciting and dangerous things about e-mails', Winterson observes, 'is that we have no way of discerning gender and that upsets a lot of our notions about innate masculine or feminine traits' (Winterson 2003). Furthermore, the internet offers everyone the chance of transforming a one-to-one dialogue into a public communication. And it is a very particular public communication Winterson has always wanted to achieve, both as a human being and as an artist. She sees it as a kind of relationship resembling the one between a preacher and her audience. Such a relationship, in the case of *The PowerBook*, takes place in a non-physical space – the World Wide Web – where her 'salvational' message can be delivered globally.

Winterson announced in February 2002 that '*The PowerBook* starts workshops this month at the National Theatre London, for a limited season in May and June' (jeanettewinterson.com). Previews of the show ran from 9 May and press night was eventually on 18 May. Again, on 1

September 2003, a note by Winterson read: 'Today, is the first day of the new rehearsals for *The PowerBook* ... I am very tired, but can't rest until October 5th – the day *The PowerBook* finishes in Rome' (jeanette-winterson.com). The première was staged in London on 18 May 2002 as part of the Lyttelton *Transformation* Project – a project of £1.5 million aimed at creating 'a more intimate relationship between actor and audience and to introduce a younger generation to London theatre' (Schifferes 2002) and which included a number of contemporary experimental works. It was later performed in Paris, from 17 to 27 September 2003, and at the RomaEuropa Festival in Rome, from 3 to 5 October in the same year.

Although *The PowerBook* was a decidedly literary experiment not meant for the stage, Winterson took on the challenge of adaptation in concert with the talented 'terrible twins' of the British contemporary theatre, actress Fiona Shaw and director Deborah Warner, for a co-production by the National Theatre of London and the Theatre National de Chaillôt of Paris.[11] Shaw and Warner had worked together for 15 years before the staging of *The PowerBook* and had adapted many classics, from Greek and Shakespearean theatre to T. S. Eliot's *The Waste Land*, performed in London and New York in 1995. Shaw, an actress with a wide experience of Elizabethan drama, was reportedly impressed by the complexity of Winterson's text and commented that *The Power-Book* was 'a beautiful work with a perfect structure' (Winterson 2003). For Shaw, *The PowerBook* represented 'a very exciting experiment' because both Winterson and Warner abandoned the worlds they normally inhabit to explore new territories (Winterson 2003). For her part, Warner saw it as a chance to move away from the kind of theatre in which the text dominates: 'Let's take Shakespeare or let's take the Greeks', Warner observed. 'One is completely a servant to that text' (Tusa 2005).

When the director asked Winterson to rework the novel, the latter accepted only on the condition that it was not to become a 'mere' stage adaptation. For Winterson, in fact, the text remains 'the prism through which the light of invention must be filtered', the light being given by direction, acting and music (Winterson 2003). Warner, defined by an interviewer on BBC radio as a 'revolutionary even if not an ideologue' (Tusa 2005), interpreted *The PowerBook* as a musical composition because of the complexity of the text and because, like a musical performance, it rests on a solid structure. Mel Mercier, the composer, and Jean Kalman, the light designer – who had already worked in a team with Warner on Mozart's *Don Giovanni*, performed in London in 1995 – made a significant contribution to the staging of Winterson's essentially non-dramatic text. Mel Mercier's 'exquisite trance music ... conveys a melancholy sense of rapture and loss, [which] helps speed the lovers to a last encounter at Paddington Station' (De Jongh 2002). Moreover, to the recurring themes and interweaving elements of the soundtrack, there corresponded in the performance an appropriate use of lights – particularly evident in the sections of the lovers of the past.

Tom Pye, the set and video designer of *The PowerBook*, created special visual effects which turned the theatre into the inside of a computer so that, as a commentator observed, 'through projected images, the stage becomes a site of passage from the second to the third dimension' (Schifferes 2002). Like the original text, the stage adaptation

> employ[s] a strategy of hyperrealism [in which] spatial narrative, and technological design exaggerates the cyborgian dimension of postmodern reality by suggesting that realities, subjectivities, and bodies are merely doubles – projected ghost images – already diffracted into the media and no longer distinguishable from their simulation by the media.
>
> (Birringer 1997: 135)

The stage play was organized into eight scenes with no interval between them, introduced by a pre-recorded voice, which represents the omniscient narrator of the novel. The voice repeats the refrain, tells the stories of the ruinous lovers of the past, and is mixed up with the voices of the two women lovers at Paddington Station in the final scene. Some sections of the story are presented in the original order while others are cut entirely, as the following summary shows:

I: CHAPTER: 'Open Hard Drive';
II: CHAPTER: 'Terrible things to do to a flower';
III: CHAPTERS: 'New Document', 'Virtual World';
IV: CHAPTERS : 'Search', 'great ruinous lovers', 'open it';
V: CHAPTERS: 'View', 'Night Screen';
VI: CHAPTER: 'View as Icon' – CUTS: 'blame my parents', 'EMPTY TRASH';
VII: CHAPTER: 'Special' – CUTS: 'Show Balloons', 'own hero', 'Spitafields', 'meatspace';
VIII: CHAPTER: 'Chooser' – CUTS: 'strange', 'Quit', 'Really Quit', 'Restart', 'Save'.

In the play text the ending is anticipated and the last five chapters of the book are omitted. According to my reconstruction, the cuts were made mainly on the second part of Winterson's novel and concerned the more specific autobiographical references. This appears to mirror the process used for the adaptation for the screen of *Oranges*, in which fairytales and inset stories were left out, along with the most metafictional parts – such as 'Deuteronomy' – of the narrative, similarly distancing the text from Winterson's own (literary) persona. The scene representing the story of George Mallory's explorations – told by Fiona Shaw who plays the part of a man standing up on a bed reading from the explorer's journal – suddenly changes the rhythm of the piece which then slowly progresses towards the final scene, where two women exit the stage holding hands and proposing two different endings. Yet, notwithstanding the heavy cuts and the reworked ending, Winterson and her co-adaptors have arguably succeeded in keeping intact the 'perfect' structure of *The PowerBook*.

According to Julia Kristeva, 'every text is constructed as a mosaic of quotations' (1969: 46). Each fragment from other texts 'can be easily distinguished from each other just like the parts which form a mosaic in visual art' (46). The idea of 'the mosaic of references' as intertextual play takes, in *The PowerBook*, what Paul Fisher has called an 'interesting episodic form' (Fisher 2002). The influence of specific canonical writers is particularly evident in the stage version: in section II, we find obvious references and allusions to Ludovico Ariosto's *Orlando Furioso* (1591) – for instance, the sixteenth-century girl in *The PowerBook* resembles Marfisa and Bradamante – and to Virginia Woolf's elaboration of the hero in *Orlando* (1928), certainly one of the most reworked texts in *The PowerBook*. Other references are, in section IV, to Thomas Malory's *Morte D'Arthur*, and to Dante's *Divina Commedia* in section VI. Some other allusions in the text are to medieval legends concerning the Paladin Orlando, as told in Matteo Maria Boiardo's *Orlando Innamorato* (1476).

In *The PowerBook*, 'Jeanette Winterson replays her fascinations with myth and fable, gender ambiguity and romance' (Anshaw 2000). The protagonist of *The PowerBook*, Ali, is presented as an ungendered 'language costumier' who makes up stories, mainly and significantly romances, for her/his online customers. 'This is a world where sex is common', actress Fiona Shaw pointed out, 'but love is taboo, and love "pierces the hands and the feet" not to mention the hearts and marrows' (Nightingale 2002). Ali's genderlessness – partially lost in the adaptation for the stage where we always recognize the actress, Fiona Shaw, playing the part of the storyteller – makes her/him a 'nomad' of the web, 'a figuration [that] expresses the desire of an identity made of transitions, successive shifts and coordinated changes, without and against an essential unity', according to the definition given by the feminist scholar Rosi Braidotti (1994: 22). Ali's very name is a reference to her/his multiple identity – ali(as) in Latin stands for 'the same by another name' – and to the many literary, and extra-literary, sources reworked in the text, from the *Arabian Nights* to *Ali(ce) in Wonderland*. Through the character of Ali, 'the Orlando of cyberspace' (Dickon 2000: 32), Winterson represents a figure embodying the possible reconciliation of all the oppositions between the characters related with the legend and the character of Orlando, a process that becomes particularly evident in the stage version.

The very name of the protagonist, Ali/Alix, is particularly significant. The X is symbolic, and, besides marking the spot for the web surfer/reader, is used from the first page of the fiction as the chromosomic indicator of a female narrator. Critical responses to the fascinating ambiguity of this complex character were, however, mixed: Shaw's performance, according to De Jongh, 'disappoints by its strangeness and overpitched flippancy' and 'surrenders to her character's obsession' (De Jongh 2002). Paul Taylor thought that 'Shaw struggles, like the production, to find the right tone' (2002). According to his view of the performance, it is 'the spectacle of an actress stuck in a theatre-piece whose cyberspace metaphor is quickly exposed as being more of an embarrassing encumbrance than a genuine organising principle' and that 'the addictiveness of being on line is never communicated' (2002). However, Shaw's 'boyish' physical presence and her history of playing male roles (*King Lear, The Waste Land*) arguably make her an ideal choice for the ambiguous Ali/Alix.

The stories of the 'great and ruinous lovers' of the past are treated as side-stories in the novel but become central in the stage performance, where they are represented as ghostly figures suddenly appearing in the middle of the scene set in Capri. This scene is divided into two parts: one takes place before the story of Lancelot and Guinevere; the other occurs before the story of Francesca da Rimini – the ghost of Francesca (Shaw) stands near a big bed and wears a long black dress and a bandage over her eyes, while the whole story of the tragic love between Paolo and Francesca is narrated by a recorded female voice.

A major theme in the stage adaptation of *The PowerBook* is the juxtaposition between the faithful, 'eternal' love of older times and contemporary love represented as devoid of commitment and always on the run – 'I stay on the run' repeatedly appears not only in the novel but also in the adaptation, where it becomes the main refrain played by the recorded voice in several scenes. In the adaptation, moreover, the stories concerning the lovers, including the contemporary ones, are all played in a nocturnal setting: the night is always, in the Romantic imagination, the time of love and truth, in contrast with the falseness of daylight. Again, past and present are juxtaposed with the same oppositional implications. But, arguably, as Paul Taylor comments, 'there's no eroticism in the risibly staged inset stories of legendary couples, nor in the contemporary love scenes where the decision to express things by opposites ... ends up looking coy and keeps the temperature too cool' (Taylor 2002).

In the third section of the performance we are told a story of two lovers meeting in Paris, in which both Lover and Beloved are women, a theme Winterson carries over from her previous novels *Written on the Body* (1992) and *Gut Symmetries* (1997), which centre on an affair between a lover and a married woman. Another significant example of Winterson's re-elaboration of her own previous works is the scene in section five set in a lively, modern-day Capri. The director created a crowded scene with actors dancing and singing and moving across the stage. This scene, the only one entirely performed in broad daylight, is set in a Capri which also significantly recalls Venice during the mundane event of the International Film Festival. A catwalk – where the Beloved woman (Saffron Burrows) elegantly runs away from the paparazzi – is, accordingly, positioned in the background. Kasia Boddy points out that 'like the American modernist Gertrude Stein Winterson is repeating things', quoting from her own previous works, 'in order to explore the potential for different variations within the similar' (Boddy 2000). Winterson's intertextual references in *The PowerBook* seem, though, to be more in the line of postmodernist authors who 'tend to compose their "echo chambers" (Barthes 1975: 78) from widely diverging texts, ranging from the classics to pop' (Pfister 1991). Furthermore, 'self-reflection', as argued by Linda Hutcheon, 'is inextricably bound up with a critique of power and domination' (1989: 61), two key concepts present in all the sources reworked by Winterson and particularly evident in the dramatized version of *The PowerBook*.

One of the key props used in many scenes of the performance is a double bed, which could be considered as a character in its own right. The bed on the stage, although it initially appears of no consequence, actually represents an important reference to the theatrical tradition concerned with stories of love, disguise and betrayal, starting in the Middle Ages. The so-called 'bed-trick' became a well-established convention of the Elizabethan and the Jacobean stage in the sixteenth and seventeenth centuries, where it represented a break with the courtly past by shifting the attention from romantic love to lust. One of the basic situations in the theatre – common since the Middle Ages in popular literature and also present in more erudite narratives, such as Boccaccio's *Decameron* – was 'the sexual substitution of at least one partner without the other partner's knowledge', in which the bed played an important role (Desens 1994: 31). In the episode of the Princess and the sixteenth-century girl, the director of *The PowerBook*, following the written text, alluded to one particular aspect implied in the bed-trick convention, namely the power imbalance between kings and princes and the women, generally of a lower social class, but also belonging to their world, who they force into a sexual relationship, or who they actually rape. The device of the substituted bride/groom allows the male characters to maintain a split between the idealized and non-sexualized wife and the woman they desire sexually.

The convention of the substituted bride or bridegroom is implied, with a special twist, in the story of the Italian lovers Francesca and Paolo. On her wedding day, Francesca is accompanied to the altar by Paolo and as a consequence she wrongly assumes that she will be married to him – whereas her bridegroom is Paolo's brother Gianciotto. Francesca's adulterous love with Paolo, who betrays his own brother, is originated in a deceit in the form of 'substitution'. Francesca, like Guinevere – in the play the ghost of the Queen is represented standing near a bed inside a transparent cube – is an upper-class and aristocratic woman, but she is not free in the choice of a husband and like Guinevere she is not allowed to feel sexual desire. They are confined to the roles of non-sexual wives. Their adulteries represent the assertion of female sexuality and are, therefore, particularly transgressive of the old order and of the double standard which has extended well into the twentieth century, and to a great extent into contemporary life. That the issue of sexuality, and female sexuality in particular, has been deeply felt in all its contradictions throughout history, is evident from the constant presence of the bed-trick convention in all the narrative sources reworked in the *The PowerBook*. The use of this convention 'depicts betrayal on the most intimate level' (Desens 1994: 142), and is strongly connected with one of the *leitmotifs* in Winterson's works, from *Oranges* to *The PowerBook*: the repression of women's sexuality.

Although Paul Taylor, in his review of the play, observed unenthusiastically that 'the project pushes further down the road that the director and actress explored in their staging of *The Waste Land*: to make theatre out of non-theatrical texts' (2002), Nicholas De Jongh acclaimed *The PowerBook* as a 'faithful adaptation' which 'captures Winterson's rare, strange, lyric eloquence' (2002) and Michael Billington attested that Winterson's fiction 'gains from the tangible physicality of the theatre and gleefully combines eroticism and wit' (2002). Winterson and her co-adaptors declared that what they wanted to do with *The PowerBook* was 'to keep the impression of the journey, that connection with the heart' (Winterson 2003). They accordingly tried to find a structure which, through that 'emotional journey' allowed them 'to find a range of theatrical inventions to play' and they came to see their adaptation as 'a massive celebration of love' (*ibid*). I concur with Winterson's view that 'in a new century we need new ways of looking at old things' (Winterson 2003) and while some of the negative criticism directed at her adaptations for stage and screen may be merited, I believe that 'a new way of looking' has indeed been offered by the adaptation of her novels into other media and that, as a result, her work has indeed reached the wider audiences so desired by Winterson the 'missionary'.

Notes

1. Whitbread First Novel Award for *Oranges Are Not the Only Fruit* in 1985; John Llewellyn Rhys Prize for *The Passion* in 1987; E. M. Forster Award for *Sexing the Cherry* in 1989 and Lambda Literary Award for *Written On The Body* in 1993.
2. 'In the old days, when it first came out, *Oranges Are Not the Only Fruit* used to appear on the cookery shelves of mainstream bookshops' (Winterson 1994: vii).
3. Winterson's name featured 72 times in the BBC broadcasting list from 31 December 1985 to 10 February 2006 (BBC.co.uk). It is interesting to note that she first featured as critic and journalist in 'Talking Tate' (17 July 1997) on BBC 2 television, in which she discussed Lucian Freud's *Girl with a White Dog*. Along with the running of her website she has recently been editing new editions of Virginia Woolf's novels published by Vintage. She has also become a regular contributor of reviews and articles to British newspapers and magazines.

4. In 2000 Winterson won a legal challenge concerning the right to use her own name on the internet. As reported by a journalist, an arbitrator of the World Intellectual Property Organisation (WIPO) established that Jeanette Winterson's name 'although never registered – effectively constituted a trademark and ordered that jeanettewinterson.com (and .org and .net variations) be taken away from Cambridge resident Mark Hogarth' (Bonisteel 2000).

5. 'Static' appeared in a collection called *Young Playwrights Festival* (1988), edited by Jeremy Mortimer and published by BBC Books. The broadcast was produced by Richard Wortley and starred Pat Heywood and Barbara Atkinson.

6. See also Maya Jaggi, 'Jeanette Winterson: Redemption Songs', *Guardian*, 29 May 2004.

7. According to an article published in *The Times* on 6 January 2001, entitled 'The Pride, The Passion and the problems of working with film Moguls', Winterson had also been working on a script based on *Sexing the Cherry* and 24 short pieces for the BBC and the internet.

8. It featured Kenneth Cranham as Pastor Finch; Freda Dowie as Mrs Green; Cathryn Bradshaw as Melanie; Charlotte Coleman as Jess; Peter Gordon as William, Jess's father; and Geraldine McEwan as Jess's mother.

9. The series was repeated in the three-episode form in January 1991 and April 1994, and in its full three-hour length on 1 May 2002, just a few weeks before the première of *The PowerBook* on stage at the National Theatre of London.

10. 'Unnatural passions' are no mystery to Mother, as is clearly stated in both the novel and the adaptation: she is aware of and strongly condemns the 'tender attachment' between the two sweetshop keepers of the village and knows Miss Jewsbury's reputation as a lover of 'the wrong people'. See Chapter 6 in this volume for a discussion of this episode.

11. Jeanette Winterson had worked for the theatre before the staging of *The PowerBook:* when she first arrived in London, after university, she found a job as assistant manager at the Round House, a small experimental theatre.

Works cited

Advocate, The (2002), 'Paltrow's lesbian sex scenes heat up the gossip mill', 16 August.

Anshaw, C. (2000), 'Power outage'. *The Advocate*, 21 November.

Barker, P. (2000), 'A dotcom. enterprise gone dotty', *Sunday Times*, 43, 27 August.

Barthes, R. (1975), *Roland Barthes par Roland Barthes*. Paris: Seuil.

Billington, M. (2002), Review, *Guardian*, 20 May.

Birringer, J. (1997), 'Postmodernism and theatrical performance', in H. Bertens and D. Fokkema (eds), *International Postmodernism. Theory and Literary Practice*. Amsterdam and Philadelphia: John Benjamins Publishing Company, pp. 129–40.

Blau du Plessis, R. (1985), *Writing Beyond The Ending: Narrative Strategies of Twentieth-Century Women Writers*. Bloomington: Indiana University Press.

Boddy, K. (2000), 'Love again', *TLS*, 9, 1 September.

Bonisteel, S. (2000), 'ICANN domain-name disputes getting personal', *Newsbytes PM*, 30 May.

Braidotti, R. (1994), *Nomadic Subjects: Embodiment and Sexual Difference in Contemporary Feminist Theory*. New York: Columbia University Press.

Brooks, L. (2000), 'Power surge'. www.jeanettewinterson.com

Cooper, D. (1986), *Meridian*. BBC Radio 4, 18 June.

De Jongh, N. (2002), Review, *Evening Standard*, 20 May.

Desens, M. C. (1994), *The Bed-Trick in English Renaissance Drama: Explorations in Gender, Sexuality and Power*. Newark: University of Delaware Press.

Dickon, E. J. (2000), 'Dot.com Dominiatrix'. *Independent on Sunday*, 32, 2 September.

Dunn, J. (1990), *John Dunn Show*. BBC Radio 2, 4 January.

Durling, R. M. (ed.) (1996), *The Divine Comedy by Dante Alighieri*. Vol. I, *Inferno*. New York and Oxford: Oxford University Press.

Fisher, P. (2002), 'The PowerBook'. www.britishtheatreguide.info/reviews/powerbook-rev.htm (accessed 16 August 2006).

Hinds, H. (1995), '*Oranges Are Not the Only Fruit*. Reaching audiences other lesbian texts cannot reach', in T. Wilton (ed.), *Immortal Invisible: Lesbians and The Moving Image*. London and New York: Routledge, pp. 52–65.

Hutcheon, L (1989), *The Politics of Postmodernism*. London and New York: Routledge.

Isaacs, J. (1994), *Face to Face*. BBC 2.

Kristeva, J. (1969), *Semeiotike: Recherches pour une Sémanalyse*. Paris: Edition du Seuil.

—— (1986), 'Word, dialogue and novel', in T. Moi (ed.), *The Kristeva Reader*. Oxford: Blackwell, pp. 35–61.

Makinen, M. (2005), *The Novels of Jeanette Winterson: A Reader's Guide to Essential Criticism*. Basingstoke: Palgrave.

Marshment, M. and Hallam, J. (1994), ' "From string of knots to orangebox": lesbianism on prime time', in D. Hamer and B. Budge (eds), *The Good, The Bad and The Gorgeous: Popular Culture's Romance with Lesbianism*. London: Pandora, pp. 142–65.

Nightingale, B. (2002), Review, *The Times*, 20 May.

Pfister, M. (1991), 'How postmodern is intertextuality?', in H. F. Plett (ed.), *Intertextuality: Research in Text Theory* 15. Berlin/New York: Walter de Gruyter, pp. 207–24.

Rérolle, R. (2002), 'The virus of love', *Le Monde*, April.

Schifferes, S. (2002), *BBC News Online*. 24 May (accessed 15 August 2006).

Taylor, P. (2002), '*The PowerBook* needs a new hard drive'. *Independent*, 21 May.

Toombs, A. (1995), 'Great moments in aviation'. www.imdb.com (accessed 25 August 2006).

Tusa, J. (2005), 'The John Tusa interviews', BBC Radio 3.

Wachtel, E. (1994), *Writers and Company*. Edmonton, Canada: CBC Radio.

Waugh, P. (1989), *Feminine Fictions: Revisiting the Postmodern*. London: Routledge.

Windrush (2002), www.randomhouse.co.uk/offthepage/guide.htm, 14 September (accessed 15 September 2006).

Winterson, J. (1985), *Oranges Are Not the Only Fruit*. London: Vintage.

—— (1985), *Boating for Beginners*. London: Methuen.

—— (1987), *The Passion*. London: Bloomsbury.

—— (1988), *Static*. Young Playwrights Festival. J. Mortimer (ed.). London: BBC Books.

—— (1988), *Static* (radio play). Produced by Richard Wortley. Cast: P. Heywood and B. Atkinson.

—— (1989), *Sexing the Cherry*. London: Bloomsbury.

—— (1990), *Oranges Are Not the Only Fruit*. Director: B. Kidron.

—— (1992), *Written on the Body*. London: Jonathan Cape.

—— (1993), *Shades of Fear*. Director: B. Kidron. Cast: V. Redgrave (Dr Angela Bead); J. Hurt (Rex Goodyear); J. Pryce (Duncan Stewart); D. Tutin (Gwendolyne Quim); R. Ayola (Gabriel Angel).

—— (1994), *Great Moments in Aviation and Oranges Are Not the Only Fruit*. London:Vintage Film Scripts.

—— (1994), *Art and Lies. A Piece for Three Voices and a Bawd*. London: Jonathan Cape.

—— (1995), *Art Objects. Essays on Ecstasy and Effrontery*. London: Jonathan Cape.

—— (1997), *Gut Symmetries*. London: Granta.

—— (2000), *The PowerBook*. London: Jonathan Cape.

—— (2001), 'The pride, the passion and the problems of working with film moguls', *The Times*, 6 January.

—— (2001), *Text Message*. BBC Radio 4, 24 November. www.bbc.co.uk/radio4/woman'shour/2001 (accessed 20 July 2006).

—— (2003), *The PowerBook*. Director: D. Warner. Cast: F. Shaw (Ali/Alix, Lover, Francesca); S. Burrows (Princess, Beloved Woman, Paolo Malatesta); P. Lynch (Sailor, Child in Capri).

—— (2003), 'Interview', Press Conference for *The PowerBook*. Rome: RomaEuropa Festival, 2 October.

—— (2006), *Tanglewreck*. London: Bloomsbury.

CHAPTER TEN

Winterson's Recent Work: Navigating Realism and Postmodernism

GAVIN KEULKS

Chapter summary: This chapter considers Winterson's most recent work in the light of the debate about her complex relation to postmodernism. It shows how since 2000 Winterson both stretches the postmodern aesthetic to its limits and appears to draw back from its more relativistic and ahistorical implications through a resuscitation of concepts such as history and love. The chapter concludes that it remains to be seen whether narrative realism will make a sustained return to Winterson's work in the twenty-first century.

Key texts: *The PowerBook; Lighthousekeeping; Weight*

Key words: postmodernism, realism, narrative technique, storytelling, history, myth

Labels seem especially attracted to Jeanette Winterson, eager to affix themselves to her varied personae, which range from distinguished author and cultural celebrity to web administrator and high-principled owner of a stylish Italian deli. Her writing has been similarly magnetic, although it is difficult to determine which – the author or her work – has been more notoriously maligned. Recent years have invigorated these debates, as literary scholars continue to reappraise such classifications as romanticism, feminism, modernism, and postmodernism. In numerous essays and editorials, as well as her website, Winterson has weighed in on these subjects herself, prognosticating about everything from literature and mythology to mass-market grocers and the shifting status of books. Her essay 'The Semiotics of Sex' admonishes anyone who might subordinate her writing to her status as a lesbian, and in *The PowerBook* section of her website she cautions that:

> We can't go on writing traditional nineteenth century fiction, we have to recognise that Modernism and Post Modernism have changed the map, and any writer worth their weight in floppy discs will want to go on changing

that map. I don't want to be a curator in the Museum of Literature, I want to be part of what happens next.[1]

That literary evolution – the 'part of what happens next' – necessarily involves postmodernism, and appropriately, given the writer under analysis, Winterson's relationship to postmodernism remains controversial and complex – a 'contested category' in the words of Monika Müller (2001: 42). On one hand, as Laura Doan (1994), Lisa Moore (1995) and Judith Roof (1994) have explained, postmodernism conflicts with the more materialist, lesbian-feminist matrix of Winterson's work.[2] On the other hand, her novels exemplify postmodern aesthetics, revealing high degrees of self-reflexivity, pastiche and intertextuality in addition to frequent mimetic and temporal dispersions. Her dominant themes and tropes – existential contingency and spectacle, the performative nature of gender and identity, the ontological burdens of love – are also quintessentially postmodern, as is her subversion of the liberal humanist 'master-narratives' that Jean-Francois Lyotard so famously critiqued: Knowledge, Truth, Meaning and History (1984: 30–60). In numerous essays Winterson has assailed the tenets of classical realism, and over the course of ten novels she has evolved a signature blend of postmodern prose, a mélange of Linda Hutcheon's 'historiographic metafiction', Diane Elam's 'postmodern romance' and Amy J. Elias's 'metahistorical romance'.[3]

Despite these elements – and their related quests for hybrid, polyphonic or indefinite space – Winterson's brand of postmodernism reveals a powerful yet decidedly problematic 'desire to reconstruct previously deconstructed categories of orientation and classification' (Müller 2001: 42). Paradoxically, these categories include the grandest 'grand narrative' of all – love, which assumes mythopoetic power in her work, functioning as both metaphysical summons and moral imperative. An emotion divided between spiritual faith and conscious will, love promises transcendence, however temporary, and its denial tends to terminate in exile – from others as well as the self. In this regard, Winterson's recent novels *The PowerBook* (2000), *Lighthousekeeping* (2004) and *Weight* (2005) can be read as artistic signposts – or core-samples – of her shifting relationship with both realism and postmodernism. These works position their author at a representational crossroads that has become predictably common in the twenty-first century – a transitional period that labours, for some, under the burdensome label the 'post-postmodern' age. For Winterson and other experimentalists – Martin Amis, Salman Rushdie and Don DeLillo chief among them – that crossroads is no longer the one between classical realism and postmodernism that David Lodge annotated in *The Novelist at the Crossroads* (1971). For these writers, the crossroads has instead seemed to take place as a bifurcation within postmodernism itself. Central to this internal schism are the categories of history and love, two transcendent absolutes that are more often circumvented than confirmed in traditional postmodern fiction. Winterson's recent fiction complicates such assertions, not only by resuscitating love from postmodern exhaustion but also – especially in *Lighthousekeeping* and *Weight* – compounding that dynamic with reconstituted versions of history and mythology, restabilizing, in other words, both the emotional present *and* the historical past.

This chapter will contextualize Winterson's recent novels (through 2005) as attempts to replenish postmodernism from within. Following the lead of feminist criticism, it will contend that such work might forecast the emergence of a late-phase (or second-phase) postmodernism that forswears the nihilism, ahistoricism and relativism of its earlier incarnation. On her website Winterson has written that *The PowerBook* concludes a 'cycle' of seven novels that commenced in 1985 with *Oranges Are Not the Only Fruit*.[4] It should therefore be seen as an artistic marker in her career, a culminating work whose subsequent texts might inaugurate her mature or 'Late' phase. Overweighed with references to electronic communication, performative identity and virtual reality, *The PowerBook* eludes even the most assimilative forms of realism that have recently been proposed.[5] It is her last full-fledged, first-phase postmodern novel, one that continues to thwart fixed conceptions of autonomy and agency – the dual crises of the postmodern self. By contrast, *Lighthousekeeping* and *Weight* try to refigure postmodernism for the inescapably historical, serious and decidedly *un*-ironic twenty-first century – what Winterson has memorably labelled the 'jerky amphetamine world' (2004: 135). These works broker an accord with select aspects of realism, especially historicism, linearity and motivation, yet they cannot comfortably be labelled realist texts, suffused as they are by self-reflexive or metafictional conflations of author and text, history and fiction. Themes of exile, selfhood and textuality are central to these artistic investigations, for it is through them that Winterson attempts the metaphorical mapping of the self that resides at the base of her fiction as well as postmodernism itself.

'What if my body is the disguise?' – mapping the margins of meaning and identity in *The PowerBook*

In an early section of *The PowerBook*, the narrator Ali debates the nature of reality with a character who is her client yet will soon become her lover. After defining the human heart as a 'Carbon-based primitive in a silicon world' (2000: 46), Ali is accused of being an 'absolutist'. 'What else is there?' she asks, receiving the response, 'The middle ground. Ever been there?' 'I've seen it on a map' (47), Ali concludes. This process of figurative mapping, or symbolic navigation, is crucial to the novel's portrait of reality, virtual reality, subjectivity, postmodernism and love.

Ali's stories-on-demand promise their purchaser 'freedom, just for one night' (29), but that freedom comes at a cost, and the price is textual immersion. Paulina Palmer has deftly analysed how this dualism between 'narrativity and subjectivity' (2001: 186) operates in Winterson's early novels, but in no other work has it been so openly exposed.

The PowerBook features numerous textual levels or 'tiers', ranging from its persistent privileging of textual transmission (Ali's emails and imagined stories) to its self-reflexivity: Winterson frequently alludes to her own life and work, as in the many references to Spitalfields (2000: 189, 191–9, 277) and Verde's (3, 190, 277) as well as *The Passion* (25; 'Never heard of it', the client playfully responds). Sonya Andermahr astutely observes that 'The novel itself works as a series of windows or vignettes, each adding a layer to the narrative so that reading it is analogous to surfing the web' (2005: 115), and indeed the narrative self confronts risk whenever these textual frames open or close. Open, they invite self-discovery and self-mapping; closed, they threaten self-cancellation or diminishment. 'The stories are maps' (63), Ali explains: 'When I sit at my computer, I ... disappear into a web of co-ordinates that we say will change the world. Which world?' (108).

The novel's opposition between the virtual and real worlds is crucial to this dialectic, of course, but one must remember that in this novel *both* worlds are invented, so the opposition ultimately implodes. Winterson interweaves discourses on narrative, subjectivity and reality with corresponding commentaries on emotional integrity and authenticity, trying to navigate the numerous 'boundaries' of 'desire' (40) that energize the novel. These discourses are not confined to their existential or ontological delineations, however; they also epitomize the rifts within postmodernism itself. The virtual world – performative, boundary-less, postmodern – would classify such abstractions as falsely ordered constructs, Lyotardian grand- or meta-narratives. By contrast, Winterson – and her authorial surrogate Ali – strive to revitalize transcendent emotion. For Jean-Michel Ganteau, this measure approximates the divine, as *The PowerBook* 'vindicates ... a human passion so absolute that it mixes up pleasure and pain and becomes at least the equivalent to (if not something more compelling than) divine love' (2004: 177). Fuelling the dynamic from the opposite direction, the novel aspires also to a hypertextual 'net-aesthetic' that theorist Jaishree K. Odin has charted – an '"environment" or a space that demands different mappings' (1997: 600), all inherently postmodern.[6] Similarly, as Ulf Cronquist and Sonya Andermahr have argued, the novel's virtual skylarking affiliates with post-humanism, prosthetics and 'netocracy' (Cronquist 2005: 47) as well as post-gendered, cyborg semiologies that appear in the work of Donna Haraway and Zoë Sofia (see Andermahr 2005: 111–13).[7] In relation to Odin and Sofia's ideas, Ali's 'web of co-ordinates' (Winterson 2000: 108) becomes heavily significant: like the earlier reference to mapping the middle ground (47), *The PowerBook* attempts to 'coordinate' the boundaries of postmodern desire. It is a tale of textual deletion and loss. It is also one of subjectivist navigation and emotional mooring, an embodying as well as a bodying forth.

In this regard, Ali's desire for her married lover wars with the novel's stylistic exhibitionism and excess. In theory, desire should collapse spatial boundaries and liberate human and textual relations; in practice, however, Ali's emotions seek to *discern* location, both spatial and emotional. At one point, reminiscent of her precursor in *Gut Symmetries*, she invokes quantum theory to validate postmodern relativism, claiming that 'It used to be that the real and the invented were parallel lines that never met. Then we discovered that space is curved, and in curved space parallel lines always meet' (108). But her desire evades such convenient containment. Similar comments about 'download[ing]' time and the absence of 'straight lines' in 'my universe' (108) equally fail to invalidate Ali's emotional integrity.

The most intriguing element of *The PowerBook* is arguably its internal bifurcation. The novel divides between a mediated 'net aesthetic' of competing narratives that collapse spatial and subjectivist relations, and an opposed inspirational moralism that is grounded in humanist pieties about desire, authenticity and integrity. As so often occurs in Winterson's work, this poetics of love becomes enmeshed with representation, hopelessly textualized and hypermediated. It becomes pure text or, as Catherine Belsey describes, 'another kind of fundamentalism' (1994: 685). At one point, perhaps sensing this problem, Ali relegates love to narrativity, concluding that it can culminate in only three possible endings: 'Revenge. Tragedy. Forgiveness' (Winterson 2000: 89). Of course, she neglects an additional one that Belsey foreshadows and that Winterson will revisit in *Weight*: mythology, expressed through iconography and/or allegory. This is implied through *The PowerBook*'s many intertextual references to Grail legends and later specified by Ali's remark that 'We are coming into a dark region. A single word might appear. An icon. This icon is a private Madonna, a guide, an understanding' (121). In true postmodern fashion, *The PowerBook* posits the body as a boundary-less 'disguise' (16), fictionalizing Judith Butler's lamentation that 'if everything is discourse, everything is a text, then what happens to the body? ... Does anything matter in or for post-structuralism?' (1993: 28). Ali certainly doesn't embrace relativism, but she also cannot enact her emotional transcendence in any form of reality, either virtual or human. As though abdicating her role in the dialectic, she proffers her readers two endings and invites them to choose, retreating to the 'blank spaces' which are her 'domain' (Winterson 2000: 279).

This ending is defeatist and decidedly postmodernist; it threatens to swamp Ali's desire for integrity in excessive signification. After constructing a primary narrative of passionate emotion, the novel thwarts both subjectivity and closure through its tiered textual frames. Despite

Ali's contention that 'There's only one reality. The rest is a way of escape' (122), the novel proves that escape can be at best transitory in a world of postmodern performativity, textuality and disconnection. *Lighthousekeeping* will eventually compound this quandary through an allusion to E. M. Forster, imploring its readers to *'Only connect'*, but even this famous modernist plea falters against the novel's residual postmodernism. The narrative immediately retorts, 'How can you do that when the connections are broken?' (2004: 107). In a novel such as *The PowerBook* – which features the question 'What happened to the omniscient author?' and the response 'Gone interactive' (2000: 31) – it is perhaps appropriate that Ali provides no lasting readerly consolations. An appropriate culminating text to Winterson's self-described septet, *The PowerBook* interrogates the standard crises of agency, subjectivity and authenticity in the postmodern age yet also suggests, through its divided rhetoric and abdicated closure, Winterson's need to move beyond such queries, or at least conceptualize them anew. Ali's narrative burdens, all unresolved, mirror Winterson's own, and emotional integrity fails to surmount the hypertextual boundaries it confronts. That is the quandary that *The PowerBook* cannot resolve but that *Lighthousekeeping* and *Weight* will attempt to remedy.

'Their watery map of the world' – shoring up meaning and history in *Lighthousekeeping*

Published four politically scarred years after *The PowerBook*, *Lighthousekeeping* exhibits a revitalized sense of realist historicism, emblematic of Winterson's efforts to rehabilitate postmodern relativism for the 'jerky amphetamine world' (2004: 135). Whereas *The PowerBook* extends her meditations on the metaphysics of love, *Lighthousekeeping* strives to restabilize linear history, topographical realism, and character motivation. Although Winterson never exempts these forces from postmodern harassment, their effects do distinguish *Lighthousekeeping* from her preceding books. The town of Salts and Cape Wrath – with its titular lighthouse – remain more impressionistic than real, but they are nowhere near as abstract as the conceptual spaces in *The PowerBook* or *Gut Symmetries*. In this novel, Winterson's prose intentionally balances fact and fabulation, history and invention, as her descriptions commence in the category of the presumptive factual, only to be assailed by romantic, anti-realist, suggestiveness:

Salts. My home town. A sea-flung, rock-bitten, sand-edged shell of a town. Oh, and a lighthouse.

(5)

Cape Wrath. Position on the nautical chart, 58°, 37.5° N, 5° W. Look at it – the headland is 368 feet high, wild, grand, impossible. Home to gulls and dreams.

(12)

This oscillation between the romantic and the realist fuels the novel's opposition between Darwin's *On the Origin of Species* and Wagner's *Tristan and Isolde*. 'Both', Winterson contends, 'are about the beginnings of the world' (169). Their significance as emblematic world-views cannot therefore be divorced from their literary representations. The former is 'objective, scientific, empirical, quantifiable' (169) – approximating realism, in other words. The opposed, Wagnerian, polarity – defined as 'subjective, poetic, intuitive, mysterious' (169) – begs to be grouped with postmodernism. Some caution, however, may be warranted, as Winterson voids this Wagnerian category of all specialized meaning, intentionally blurring categorical, generic and historical lines. Set in the novel's historical context, Darwin opposes obvious mid-nineteenth-century religious ideals as well as the narrator's own Dickensian upbringing. These forces coalesce in the novel's quests for stability, still-points and location – an extension of *The PowerBook*'s similar emphasis on 'a web of co-ordinates that we say will change the world' (2000: 108). Discussing metaphysics with Darwin, the character Babel Dark articulates the consequences of these duelling world-views:

> He [Babel] had always believed in a stable-system, made by God, and left alone afterwards. That things might be endlessly moving and shifting was not his wish. He didn't want a broken world. He wanted something splendid and glorious and constant.
> Darwin tried to console him. 'It is not less wonderful or beautiful or grand, this world you blame on me. Only, it is less comfortable'.
> Dark shrugged. Why would God make a world so imperfect that it must be continually righting itself?
> It made him feel seasick. ... 'There had to be a stable point somewhere'.
> (2004: 119–20)

Babel's desire for existential stability certainly represents a deliberate rejection of the fractured, disconnected, postmodern world of *The PowerBook*, but overall *Lighthousekeeping* does not assay any reassured return to realism, despite its solidified characters, topography and chronology. Instead, and reflective of Winterson's efforts to reshape postmodernism from within, it smuggles these realist characteristics across its postmodern borders, redrawing its metaphorical map.

Speaking about the lighthouse, the protagonist Silver subordinates contingency to coordination when she ruminates that 'for the first time the lighthouses were mapped. Safety and danger were charted. ... The lighthouse is a known point in the darkness' (38). Boundaries feature again as Winterson's chief theme, but for Silver, as opposed to Ali, this imaginative geography proves sustaining, culminates in self-affirmation rather than constriction or erasure. Whereas Ali seems to drown in dynamic, virtual formulations of identity, reality and textuality, Silver succeeds in reconstructing at least two, if not all three, of these forces. In other words, the 'virtual corporeality' (Sofia) and 'net aesthetic' (Odin) of *The PowerBook* find their corrective corollaries in *Lighthousekeeping*'s realist topographies, oral narratives, and old weathered books. The blatant allegorizing of the character's names also contributes to this structural re-stabilization. Babel's dual surnames are emblematic: in Salts, he is known as Babel Dark; in Bristol, married to Molly, he goes by Babel Lux. Far more telling, in one paragraph Winterson opposes the 'endless babble of narrative' with a desire to 'fit the template called language' (135), conjoining obvious biblical analogues with linguistic debates that lie at the heart of structuralism and post-structuralism. Silver herself navigates this spectrum of darkness and light, noting that her eponymous metal reflects 95 per cent of its own light (155), forecasting her ability – contra Ali – to enlighten the dualities of her world. In typical Winterson fashion, such epiphanies become entwined with love, which operates on three temporal levels in *Lighthousekeeping*: as 1) a timeless, ahistorical force; 2) a present condition, personified by Silver's relationship with her lover; and 3) a nagging admonishment from the past, crystallized by the doomed love between Molly O'Rourke and Babel Dark. This last pairing also clarifies Babel's allegorical correspondence with the lighthouse: he is described as Molly's 'navigation point. He was the coordinate of her position' (102).

Although it is tempting to label *Lighthousekeeping* a realist or at least anti-postmodernist text, the novel remains too tainted by metafiction and intertextuality to be so conveniently positioned. Its realism ultimately genuflects to the grander disorder of textuality. A plethora of narrative analogues and historical figures bracket the plot, ranging from Charles Darwin, Richard Wagner and Robert Louis Stevenson to Doris Lessing's *The Golden Notebook*, E. M. Forster's *Howard's End* and, most obviously, Virginia Woolf's *To the Lighthouse*. Such referentiality is not in itself a complicating issue, of course; rather, it becomes problematic when questions of genre, narrativity and subjectivity assume postmodern orientations. Similar to the fated ship *The McCloud*, which is 'fully equipped with the latest technology and a new crew, but with the old *McCloud* riding inside' (149), *Lighthousekeeping* contains numerous intertexts within itself as ballast, enacting nearly ten years later Winterson's comment in *Art Objects* that 'The novel form is finished. That does not mean we should give up reading nineteenth-century novels, we should read them avidly and often. What we must do is give up writing them' (1996: 191).

Whereas *The PowerBook*'s textuality was electronic in nature, in *Lighthousekeeping* that focus shifts to printed texts, especially manuscripts. Silver has a collection of 'silver notebooks' (2004: 160), invoking Doris Lessing. Literary precedents such as Tristan and Isolde, Jekyll and Hyde, and Lancelot and Guinevere complement (and at times overcrowd) the relationships between Silver and the lighthouse-keeper Pew, as well as Babel and Molly. Even Babel's own writings participate in the textual tiers, opposing the 'notebook' of his 'scholarly ... clergyman's life' with the polymorphous, polyphonic self that emerges from his 'wild and torn folder of scattered pages' that is exclusively postmodern: 'disordered, unnumbered, punctured where his nib had bitten the paper' (57). Finally, the novel's repetitive, choral, full-page epitaphs imploring Pew, then later Silver, to 'tell [us] a story' raise complicating issues of self-reflexivity. These requests shift subtly toward the end, as Pew ceases to tell such tales at Silver's invitation and as another character – Silver's lover – begins to request them. They also anticipate readerly demands, as when Silver's lover asks to hear 'The story of how we met' (189). In brief, the interpretive trajectory of these interludes is particularizing, not abstract: the allegorical becomes individualized, the metaphorical becomes personal.

In decidedly anti-realist ways, these aspects of the novel centralize the acts of storytelling and interpretation, of textual construction, transmission and reception. Like their precedents Henri and Villanelle in *The Passion*, Silver and Pew do not exist separate from their narrative creations. The stories they tell 'are complicated by the worlds their stories create' (Purinton 1998: 73) and 'their subjectivities and identities are produced through the process of storytelling' (Palmer 2001: 188). Such narrative filtration ultimately stands opposed to the novel's chief virtue of transcendent love, which exists in a jeopardized state, highly unstable and often linked to textual transmission, especially analogues of lost love. Silver is another orphan figure who extends the *flâneuse* tradition of female wanderers in Winterson's work, yet her 'transient' or 'nomadic subjectivity' (Geyh 1993: 104; Meyer 2003: 220) differs from that of other narrators. *The PowerBook* and *Lighthousekeeping* both dissipate traditional conceptions of space and identity, but whereas the former displaces the real and the gendered onto a hypermediated realm where narrative predominates, the latter reclaims space and identity *through* narrativity, including that ultimate spatial sign of patriarchy, the lighthouse. Writing about Marilynne Robinson's *Housekeeping* (1980) – another intertext for Winterson's novel – Paula E. Geyh contends that the act of housekeeping finds 'its corollary in the maintenance of the self' (1993: 110); after the automation of the Cape Wrath lighthouse, Silver must seek such maintenance in exile.

During her wanderings, or 'spatial mapping' (Geyh 1993: 115), Silver navigates between the polarities of realism and postmodernism embedded within the novel's textual tropes. 'The stories themselves make the meaning', she remarks; 'There is no continuous narrative' (Winterson 2004: 134). Her lament about the textuality of meaning changes only slightly – into grounding metaphors – when the narrative focuses on Molly and Babel. 'She had used her body as a grounding rod. She had tried to earth him', Winterson writes of Molly, 'Instead, she had split him' (101). In other words, although the novel embarks toward more realist, stable, *grounded* constructions of place, history and character, its emotional and ontological landscapes remain as fluid, contingent and boundless as ever – until the ending.

Significantly – and mirroring the end of *The PowerBook* – Winterson asserts a heavy authorial hand upon the finale of *Lighthousekeeping*, conflating the distance between character and author in a sermonizing, borderline confessional, passage:

> I used to be a hopeless romantic. I am still a hopeless romantic. I used to believe that love was the highest value. I still believe that love is the highest value. I don't expect to be happy. I don't imagine that I will find love, whatever that means, or that if I do find it, it will make me happy. I don't think of love as the answer or the solution. I think of love as a force of nature – as strong as the sun, as necessary, as impersonal, as gigantic, as impossible, as scorching as it is warming, as drought-making as it is life-giving. And when it burns out, the planet dies.
>
> (199)

These words could easily have been spoken by Ali in *The PowerBook*, whose conclusion assumes the form of a grandiose rumination on the divine yet indeterminate nature of love. Of course, such a passage necessarily moderates claims about the extent of realist reclamation in *Lighthousekeeping*. Whereas in *The PowerBook* a real meeting between Ali and her lover – in 'Meatspace not cyberspace' (2000: 189) – succeeds in banishing the postmodern and the hypertextual, in *Lighthousekeeping* the love between Molly and Babel Dark and (in a different manner) between Silver and Pew elides its narrativity *only* when Winterson suspends all postmodern irrealism.

After dramatizing an orgasm scene for Silver (2004: 217) that rivals Lily Briscoe's parallel ecstasy in *To the Lighthouse*, Winterson orchestrates a blissfully satisfying reunion between Silver, Pew and Silver's pet DogJim in the abandoned Cape Wrath lighthouse. This reunion aesthetically counterbalances the romantic tragedy of Molly and Babel Dark and symbolically rewrites, or revises, Ali's terminal isolation in *The PowerBook*. In blatant contrast to the endings of these books, Silver's return to the lighthouse provides closure and comfort, unifying fragmentation and disconnection in the 'jerky amphetamine world' (135). Although she twice articulates the ultimate literary cliché 'I love you' (230, 232), which stumbles as painfully as the same utterance in *The PowerBook* (2000: 129), the scene actually triumphs *because of* its sentimentality, which exists in the midst of postmodern exhibitionism, almost mocking it. Indeed, the ending of *Lighthousekeeping* furnishes the integrity and authenticity that Ali craved in *The PowerBook* and that Lily Briscoe only solipsistically achieved in *To the Lighthouse*. *Lighthousekeeping*'s final sentences – 'I love you. The three most difficult words in the world. But what else can I say?' (2004: 232) – displace the narrative boundaries of textual transmission and mapping and culminate in prayer-like silence. Crucially, Silver has succeeded in retrieving 'meaning' from its earlier classification as 'psychosis'[8] and, through her, Winterson is able to redeem subjectivity from postmodern relativism, ahistoricism and narrativity.

In short, *Lighthousekeeping* reveals the first example of a restrained and moderated, potentially new Wintersonian voice. She tempers her usual stylistics in her most Dickensian novel to date, and the result is as complex as one might expect. Evading fixed genre categories, the novel represents an unmistakable divergence from classical postmodernism yet ultimately halts short of complete rejection or realist affirmation. For now, *Lighthousekeeping* is perhaps best labelled a transitional work that might come to be viewed as the genesis of her mature phase. *Weight* stands as both a continuance and a complication of its achievements and limits.

'The hells we invent are the hells we have known' – mythologizing meaning and identity in *Weight*

If *Lighthousekeeping* is considered a transitional work, then the novella *Weight* must be seen as its companion text. Indeed, numerous similarities exist between the two works – and *The PowerBook* as well. Thematic correspondences are rife, especially boundaries and desire, and astrophysics and evolutionary metaphors reappear, juxtaposing Darwinian fossil records with quantum space-time. The linkages between naming and fate, character and destiny, are also consistently systematized: allegorical in *The PowerBook* and *Lighthousekeeping*, mythological in *Weight*. More important is the role of autobiographical narration, which dominates *Weight*'s introductory and concluding sections. Although her introduction tries to distance the novella from confessionalism or autobiography, Winterson has tolerated such approaches in interviews,[9] as well she should: *Weight* imparts a tale of liberation through relinquishment, and its biographical significance is vital to its impact. 'Of course I wrote it directly out of my own situation. There is no other way', Winterson remarks; 'Autobiography is not important. Authenticity is important' (2005: xiv). To achieve this authenticity, she creates a revisionist mythos for love and selfhood, composing the most stable ending in her oeuvre – one that also revisits the precipitate departure, in *Lighthousekeeping*, of Pew and DogJim from their reunion with Silver.

In many ways *The PowerBook*, *Lighthousekeeping* and *Weight* can be grouped as a triptych on the incumbencies of responsibility. In the first two books Winterson refracts this trope through the lens of extramarital desire and infidelity. In *Weight* she focuses it upon the narrative of Atlas, who assumes the 'impossible burden' of the world with 'infinite gentleness' (89), then equally as gently relinquishes it. The novel's ending derives its power not from Atlas's liberation *from his burden*, however, but rather his paradoxical freedom *from himself*. Similar to *Lighthousekeeping*, the novel commences with questions of parentage and belonging, occurring first in the context of Atlas's parents, then Heracles's. Later, Winterson couples Atlas's role as symbolic orphan with quantum theory, writing, 'Time had become meaningless to Atlas. He was in a black hole. He was under the event horizon. He was a singularity. He was alone' (123). Juxtaposed beside Heracles, his double or 'moving mirror' (13) – an echo of the 'shadow selves' of *Lighthousekeeping* (2004: 164) – Atlas seeks self-revelation rather than amnesia, belonging rather than exile, figuratively aligning himself with Silver instead of Ali. Indeed, he describes the central question of the novel when he describes his entrapment within limits:

> Why had he not recognised the boundaries of his life, and if he had recognised them, why did he hate them so much? . . .
> It is fit that a man should do his best and grapple with the world. It is meet that he should accept the challenge of his destiny. What happens when the sun reaches the highest point in the day? Is it a failure for morning to become afternoon, or afternoon to turn into peaceful evening and star-bright night?
> (2005: 71)

Bowing under the mythological architecture of *Weight*, character remains Heraclitean, tied to naming and fate. In Winterson's retelling, however, Atlas 'leans against the limits' (14) of himself until he is joined and thereby liberated by Winterson's authorial voice, an intrusion that severs Atlas from his destiny and reunites him, surprisingly, with postmodernism. Appropriating Atlas's words – 'leaning on the limits of self' (145) – Winterson reaffirms postmodern relativism by declaring that 'Now it seems there are no boundaries. The universe has no centre. Every limit can be crossed' (132). She then reiterates Lyotard's classic postmodern critique, stipulating that 'Science is a story. History is a story. These are the stories we tell ourselves to make ourselves come true' (145). Despite its classical foundations, in other words, and contradicting the realist flashes in *Lighthousekeeping*, *Weight* enlists and actually depends upon postmodern aesthetics for its structure and meaning. One hesitates to place too much significance upon such a slim novella, but it nonetheless exhibits the same degrees of authorial intrusion, dispersed textual frames, inverted meta-narratives and references to quantum physics that were last seen in *The PowerBook*.

Only after dismantling the conventions between author and character does *Weight* achieve closure, which Winterson models on *Light-*

housekeeping's all-too-brief reunion between Silver, DogJim and Pew. Atlas receives his epiphany in parallel fashion, beside the dog Laika, rocketed into space and presumptive death by the Russians. Saving this dog liberates Atlas from his personal limits, whether self-imposed or fated. He 'had long ago ceased to feel the weight of the world he carried, but he felt the skin and bone of this little dog. Now he was carrying something he wanted to keep, and that changed everything' (127). Ultimately this division between fate and self evaporates. *Weight* achieves, for Atlas and Laika, what Ali craves in *The PowerBook* and what Silver experiences only fleetingly in *Lighthousekeeping*: redemption through relinquishment, unification through self-awareness. The novella features some of Winterson's most poetic aphorisms encapsulated in one of her most concise plots, as though its mythological base helped mollify her usual stylistic bravura, weighing it down or – to borrow a metaphor from *Lighthousekeeping* – 'grounded' it.

At the end of *The PowerBook* and *Lighthousekeeping*, characters abandon the central protagonists, and nostalgia predominates. Although Winterson's novels end frequently in sadness and isolation, *Weight* ends triumphantly, as Atlas and Laika abandon one world to enter a better one together. This time one encounters no strained articulations of love. Instead:

> *Nothing happened.*
> *Write it more substantially – NOTHING.*
> Atlas raised his head, turned over, stood up, stepped back. The dog's nose lifted. Atlas looked back at his burden. There was no burden. There was only the diamond-blue earth gardened in a wilderness of space. (150)

After a quarter-page exegesis about dark matter, Winterson exits the text. By comparison with *Gut Symmetries* and *The PowerBook*, where quantum theory or astrophysics 'lend a scientific basis to nomadism, previously demarcated by the fantastic' (Meyer 2003: 221), *Weight* uses such metaphors simply to extend mythopoetic rationales. In brief, Winterson's textual mapping concludes for the first time on notes of affirmation, enlightenment and togetherness rather than exile, amnesia or nostalgia.

Like Silver's 'string of guiding lights' (Winterson 2004: 21), *The PowerBook*, *Lighthousekeeping* and *Weight* seem to forecast their author's evolving methods and styles. In these novels Winterson continues to chart the boundaries of the self, and though they are published only five years apart, they help frame the discussion surrounding her engagement with postmodernism, revealing how integral history, place, identity and love continue to be in her work. These contrapuntal tales probe the unstable relationships between myth and reality, exile and belonging, while seeking existential and ontological stabilities to rehabilitate postmodern crises of authenticity and subjectivity. Assailed by emotional absolutes, Winterson's orphic (and polymorphic) narrators crave integrity in the midst of indeterminacy and disconnection. They celebrate the ludic joy of definition-less space, the paradoxical freedoms of exile and alterity. Early in Winterson's career, that seemed to be enough; in the evangelical political climate of the twenty-first century, however, it may no longer suffice.

Concluding one sequence of novels and potentially inaugurating another, *The PowerBook* and *Lighthousekeeping* extend Winterson's experiments with postmodernism into the new millennium, confirming that, for this writer, no realist accommodation will ever come easy. Spanning the decades that marked the flourish of postmodernism as well as its flattening, Winterson's novels continue to elide the conventions of mimetic form. *Lighthousekeeping* commences a necessary reconsideration of postmodern orthodoxies, contemplating a revisionist model that redeems history, linearity and subjectivity from postmodern relativism. This novel couples *The PowerBook*'s narcissistic obsession with intrusive narration, self-reflexivity and hypertextuality with reconstituted formulations of plot, character and topography. Part-revisionist mythology, part-exegetical text, *Weight* is a fitting companion to these books, borrowing elements from each to illumine its author's postmodern loyalties and lamentations. From *Lighthousekeeping*, *Weight* inherits the renewed senses of history, character and allegory. From *The PowerBook*, it imports intrusive narration, quantum theory and meta-fictional instability. Tropes of doubling, exile and isolation predominate, and Winterson's narrators still embody the characteristics of the postmodern *flâneuse*: existential wanderers through boundaries of desire, navigators of conceptual space. Whether interior or external, virtual or real, such spaces require figurative mapping, as does the self. 'What landmasses are these, unmapped, unnamed?' Winterson queries in *Weight* (2005: 141), and while her narrators often conclude their quests at the symbolic Ogygia of this question, Atlas – and possibly Winterson herself – tenders a simple answer: that which can no longer be borne, which no longer holds true, must be relinquished. 'I realise now that the past does not dissolve like a mirage', she advises:

> I realise that the future, though invisible, has weight. We are in the gravitational pull of past and future. It takes huge energy – speed-of-light power – to break that gravitational pull.
>
> How many of us ever get free of our orbit? . . .
>
> The pull of past and future is so strong that the present is crushed by it. We lie helpless in the force of patterns inherited and patterns re-enacted by our own behavior. The burden is intolerable.
>
> The more I did the more I carried. Books, houses, lovers, lives, all piled up on my back . . .
>
> (2005: 99)

Postmodernism is unquestionably part of this 'intolerable' 'burden', as are autobiography, feminism, celebrity, and all the other labels that Jeanette Winterson has attracted. It has formed a large part of the 'orbit' of her past and her present, and it will take great effort to break its 'gravitational pull'. Only subsequent novels will determine the role postmodernism will play in her future.

Notes

1. Online, *http://www.jeanettewinterson.com/pages/content/index.asp?PageID=10*. Winterson's website ranks among the best authorial sites, and she's one of the few celebrities to triumph over a 'cyber-squatter', appealing to the World Intellectual Property Association to reclaim the rights to her domain-name, which had been registered by researcher Mark Hogarth.
2. This is one of the primary fault-lines in lesbian-feminist criticism of Winterson's work. In contrast to Doan, Roof and Moore, Lynne Pearce (1995) and Rachel Wingfield (1998) have argued that Winterson's humanism runs the risk of diluting sexual difference into a liberal individualism that thwarts feminist classifications.
3. Elias coins the phrase 'metahistorical romance' to describe the Western world's confrontation with post-World War II history as a 'post-traumatic imaginary' (2001: xii). Viewing this confrontation within the contexts of trauma and the sublime, she explores how it inspires fabulation, resists closure and empiricism, and suffers from repetition and deferral. Hutcheon's *A Poetics of Postmodernism: History, Theory, Fiction* (1988) and Elam's *Romancing the Postmodern* (1992) are more widely known.
4. Attentive readers will note that she ostracizes *Boating for Beginners*, even though its initial publication defined it as a novel.
5. These include Roy Bhaskar and Rom Harré's 'critical realism'; James Wood's 'hysterical realism'; Joseph Dewey's 'spectacle realism'; Ihab Hassan's 'fiduciary realism'; Bill Buford's 'dirty realism'; and John Somer and John Daly's 'deep realism'. 'Postmodern Realism' and 'neorealism' are more ubiquitous.
6. Numerous passages confirm this linkage, but one is particularly apt: 'This new aesthetic, which I term "hypertext" or "Net" aesthetic, represents the need to switch from the linear, univocal, closed, authoritative aesthetic involving passive encounters to that of the non-linear, multivocal, open, nonhierarchical aesthetic involving active encounters' (Odin 1997: 599).
7. Haraway's 'A Manifesto for Cyborgs' (1985) and the expanded version of that essay in *Simians, Cyborgs, and Women* contend that 'cyborg semiology' (1991: 163) poses the greatest challenge to the 'informatics of domination' created by 'a polymorphous, information system' (161). Analysing 'virtual corporeality' (1999: 55), Sofia is sceptical of *de facto* linkages of cyberspace with utopia, detailing the inherent misogyny and violence that undergird visual abstraction in virtual worlds. See also N. Katherine Hayles, *How We Became Posthuman* (1999).
8. After stealing first books, then a bird, Silver is ordered to see a psychiatrist, who suggests that 'An obsession with meaning, at the expense of the ordinary shape of life, might be understood as psychosis, yes' (2004: 195).
9. Her interview with Bill Moyers is but one example. After inquiring, 'But what is your Achilles' heel?', he asks her to read the ending of *Weight* before he proffers the obvious: 'So your Achilles' heel could be that you can't put the weight of the world down'. Winterson concurs. Online: http://www.pbs.org/moyers/portraits_winterson.html

Works cited

Andermahr, Sonya (2005), 'Cyberspace and the body: Jeanette Winterson's *The PowerBook*', in Nick Bentley (ed.), *British Fiction of the 1990s*. London: Routledge, pp. 108–22.

Belsey, Catherine (1994), 'Postmodern love: questioning the metaphysics of desire'. *New Literary History*, 25.3, 683–705.

Butler, Judith P. (1993), *Bodies that Matter: On the Discursive Limits of Sex*. London: Routledge.

Cronquist, Ulf (2005), 'Hypertext, prosthetics and the netocracy: posthumanist aspects of Jeanette Winterson's *The PowerBook*', in Carmen Rosa Caldas-Coulthard and Michael Toulon (eds), *The Writer's Craft, the Culture's Technology*. Amsterdam and New York: Rodopi, pp. 47–56.

Doan, Laura (1994), 'Jeanette Winterson's sexing the postmodern', in Laura Doan (ed.), *The Lesbian Postmodern*. New York: Columbia University Press, pp. 137–55.

Elam, D. *Romancing the Postmodern*. London and New York: Routledge.

Elias, Amy J. (2001), *Sublime Desire: History and Post–1960s Fiction*. Baltimore and London: Johns Hopkins University Press.

Ganteau, Jean-Michel (2004), 'Hearts object: Jeanette Winterson and the ethics of absolutist romance', in Susan Onega and Christian Gutleben (eds), *Refracting the Canon in Contemporary British Literature and Film*. Amsterdam and New York: Rodopi, pp. 165–85.

Geyh, Paula E. (1993), 'Burning down the house? Domestic space and feminine subjectivity in Marilynne Robinson's *Housekeeping*', *Contemporary Literature*, XXXIV.1, 103–22.

Haraway, Donna (1991), 'A cyborg manifesto: Science, technology, and socialist-feminism in the late twentieth century', in *Simians, Cyborgs and Women: The Reinvention of Nature*. New York: Routledge, pp. 149–81.

Hayles, N. K. (1999), *How we Became Posthuman*. Chicago: University of Chicago Press.

Lyotard, Jean-Francois (1984), *The Postmodern Condition: A Report on Knowledge*. Minneapolis: University of Minnesota Press.

Meyer, Kim Middleton (2003), 'Jeanette Winterson's evolving subject: "Difficulty into dream"', in Richard J. Lane, Rod Mengham and Philip Tew (eds), *Contemporary British Fiction*. Cambridge: Polity, pp. 210–25.

Moore, Lisa (1995), 'Teledildonics: Virtual lesbians in the fiction of Jeanette Winterson', in Elizabeth Grosz and Elspeth Probyn (eds), *Sexy Bodies: The Strange Carnalities of Feminism*. London and New York: Routledge, pp. 104–27.

Müller, Monika (2001), 'Love and other dismemberments in Jeanette Winterson's novels', in Beate Neumeier (ed.), *Engendering Realism and Postmodernism: Contemporary Women Writers in Britain*. Amsterdam and New York: Rodopi, pp. 41–51.

Odin, Jaishree K. (1997), 'The edge of difference: Negotiations between the hypertextual and the postcolonial'. *Modern Fiction Studies*, 43.3, 598–630.

Palmer, Paulina (2001), 'Jeanette Winterson: lesbian/postmodern fictions', in Beate Neumeier (ed.), *Engendering Realism and Postmodernism: Contemporary Women Writers in Britain.* Amsterdam and New York: Rodopi, pp. 181–9.

Pearce, Lynne (1995), '"Written on tablets of stone"?: Jeanette Winterson, Roland Barthes, and the discourse of romantic love', in Suzanne Raitt (ed.), *Volcanoes and Pearl Divers: Essays in Feminist Lesbian Studies.* Binghampton, NY: Harrington Park, pp. 146–68.

Purinton, Marjean D. (1998), 'Postmodern romanticism: the recuperation of conceptual romanticism in Jeanette Winterson's postmodern novel *The Passion*', in Larry H. Peer (ed.), *Romanticism Across the Disciplines.* New York and Oxford: University Press of America, pp. 67–98.

Roof, Judith (1994), 'Lesbians and Lyotard: Legitimation and the politics of the name', in Laura Doan (ed.), *The Lesbian Postmodern.* New York: Columbia University Press, pp. 47–66.

Sofia, Zoë (1999), 'Virtual corporeality: A feminist view', in Jenny Wolmark (ed.), *Cybersexualities: A Reader on Feminist Theory, Cyborgs and Cyberspace.* Edinburgh: Edinburgh University Press, pp. 55–68.

Wingfield, Rachel (1998), 'Lesbian writers in the mainstream: Sara Maitland, Jeanette Winterson and Emma Donoghue', in Elaine Hutton (ed.), *Beyond Sex and Romance: The Politics of Contemporary Lesbian Fiction.* London: Women's Press, pp. 60–80.

Winterson, Jeanette (1996), *Art Objects: Essays on Ecstasy and Effrontery.* London: Vintage.

—— (2000), *The PowerBook.* New York: Vintage.

—— (2004), *Lighthousekeeping.* New York: Harcourt.

—— Personal website. Available http://www.jeanettewinterson.com (accessed 16 September 2006).

—— (2005), *Weight.* London: Canongate.

Selected Works by Jeanette Winterson

Books

Oranges Are Not the Only Fruit (1985), London: Pandora.
Boating for Beginners (1985), London: Methuen.
Fit for the Future: The Guide for Women Who Want to Live Well (1986), London: Pandora Press.
The Passion (1987), London: Bloomsbury.
Sexing the Cherry (1989), London: Bloomsbury.
Written on the Body (1992), London: Jonathan Cape.
Art and Lies. A Piece for Three Voices and a Bawd (1994), London: Jonathan Cape.
Art Objects: Essays on Ecstasy and Effrontery (1995), London: Jonathan Cape.
Gut Symmetries (1997), London: Granta.
The World and Other Places (1998), London: Jonathan Cape.
The PowerBook (2000), London: Jonathan Cape.
Lighthousekeeping (2004), London: Fourth Estate.
Weight (2005), London: Canongate.
Tanglewreck (2006), London: Bloomsbury.

Scripts for television, theatre, film and radio

Static (radio play) (1998), J. Mortimer (ed.), *Young Playwrights Festival*, London: BBC Books.
Oranges Are Not the Only Fruit: The Script (1990), London: Pandora.
Shades of Fear (1993), director: B. Kidron.
Great Moments in Aviation (script) (1994), London: Vintage Film Scripts.
Text Message (2001), BBC Radio 4. 24 November. www.bbc.co.uk/radio4/woman'shour/2001 (accessed 20 July 2006).
The PowerBook (2003), Director: D. Warner.

Interviews and articles

Brooks, Libby (2001), 'Power surge'. http://www.jeanettewinterson.com/pages/content/index.asp?PageID=214 (accessed 28 September 2006).
Dougary, Ginny (1997), 'Truth or dare'. *The Times Magazine*, 4 January, 9–11.

Lambert, Angela (1998), 'Jeanette Winterson', *Prospect Magazine*, issue 27, February 1998, http://www.prospect-magazine.co.uk/article_details.php?id =4295

Marvel, Mark (1990), 'Jeanette Winterson: Trust me. I'm telling you stories', *Interview*, 20, 164–8.

Winterson, Jeanette (1990), 'Interview'. *Spare Rib*, 209, 26–9.

—— (1998), 'The art of fiction'. Interview. *The Paris Review*, 39, 68–112.

—— (1999), 'Introduction: Gulliver's wound', in Jonathan Swift, *Gulliver's Travels*. Oxford and New York: Oxford University Press, v–xii.

—— (2001), 'The pride, the passion and the problems of working with film moguls'. *The Times*, 6 January.

—— (2005a), Appendix interview with Louise Tucker, 'P.S. about the author . *Lighthousekeeping*. London: Harperperennial, p. 4.

—— (2005b), 'Endless possibilities'. Appendix essay to *Lighthousekeeping*. London: Harperperennial, pp. 18–23.

—— (2005c), 'Imagination and reality', in Becky McLaughlin and Bob Coleman (eds), *Everyday Theory: A Contemporary Reader*. Toronto: Pearson Longman, pp. 246–55.

Suggested Further Reading

Books

Acheson, James and Sarah C. E. Ross (eds) (2005), *The Contemporary British Novel*. Edinburgh: Edinburgh University Press, pp. 189–99.

Allen, Carolyn (1996), *Following Djuna: Women Lovers and the Erotics of Loss*. Bloomington and Indianapolis: Indiana University Press.

Armitt, Lucie (2000), *Contemporary Women's Fiction and the Fantastic*. London: Macmillan.

Bengston, Helene, Marianne Børch and Cindie Maagard (eds) (1999), *Sponsored by Demons: The Art of Jeanette Winterson*. Odense, Denmark: Scholars' Press.

Bentley, Nick (ed.), *British Fiction of the 1990s*. London: Routledge, pp. 108–22.

Childs, Peter (2005), *Contemporary Novelists: British Fiction Since 1970*. Basingstoke: Palgrave Macmillan, pp. 255–73.

Grice, Helen and Woods, Tim (eds) (1998), *Postmodern Studies 25: 'I'm telling you stories': Jeanette Winterson and the Politics of Reading*. Amsterdam/Atlanta, GA: Rodopi.

Makinen, M. (2005), *The Novels of Jeanette Winterson: A Reader's Guide to Essential Criticism*. Basingstoke: Palgrave.

Morrison, Jago (2003), *Contemporary Fiction*. London: Routledge, pp. 95–114.

Neumeier, Beate (ed.) (2001), *Engendering Realism and Postmodernism: Contemporary Women Writers in Britain*. Amsterdam and New York: Rodopi.

Onega, S. (2006), *Jeanette Winterson*. Manchester: Manchester University Press.

Palmer, Paulina (1993), *Contemporary Lesbian Writing: Dreams, Desire, Difference*. Buckingham: Open University Press.

Reynier, Christine (2004), *Jeanette Winterson: Le Miracle Ordinaire*. Bourdeaux: Presses Universitaires de Bourdeaux.

Reynolds, Margaret and Jonathan Noakes (2003), *Jeanette Winterson: The Essential Guide*. London: Vintage.

Rusk, Lauren (2002), *The Life Writing of Otherness: Woolf, Baldwin, Kingston, and Winterson*. New York and London: Routledge.

Tew, Philip and Rod Mengham, (eds) (2006), *British Fiction Today*. London: Continuum, pp. 139–50.

Watkins, Susan (2001), *Twentieth-Century Women Novelists: Feminist Theory into Practice*. Basingstoke: Palgrave.

Articles

Andermahr, Sonya (2006), 'Jeanette Winterson's *Lighthousekeeping*', in Philip Tew and Rod Mengham (eds), *British Fiction Today*. London: Continuum, pp. 139–50.

Bratton, Mary (2002), 'Winterson, Bakhtin, and the chronotope of a lesbian hero.' *Journal of Narrative Theory*, 32, (2), Summer, 207–26.

Burns, Christy L. (1996), 'Fantastic language: Jeanette Winterson's recovery of the postmodern word', *Contemporary Literature*, 37, (2), 278–306.

Cosslett, T. (1998), 'Intertextuality in *Oranges Are Not the Only Fruit*: the Bible, Malory and *Jane Eyre*', in H. Grice and T. Woods (eds), *'I'm telling you stories': Jeanette Winterson and the Politics of Reading*. Amsterdam: Rodopi, pp. 15–28.

Doan, Laura (1994), 'Jeanette Winterson's sexing the postmodern', in Laura Doan (ed.), *The Lesbian Postmodern*. New York: Columbia University Press, pp. 137–55.

Finney, Brian (2002), 'Bonded by language: Jeanette Winterson's *Written on the Body*', *Women and Language*, 15, (2), 23–31.

Ganteau, Jean-Michel (2004), 'Hearts object: Jeanette Winterson and the ethics of absolutist romance', in Susana Onega and Christian Gutleben (eds), *Refracting the Canon in Contemporary British Literature and Film*. Amsterdam and New York: Rodopi, pp. 165–85.

Hinds, H. (1992), 'Oranges Are Not the Only Fruit: reaching audiences that other lesbian texts cannot reach', in S. Munt (ed.), *New Lesbian Criticism: Literary and Cultural Readings*. Hemel Hempstead: Harvester Wheatsheaf, pp. 153–72. Reprinted in T. Wilton (ed.) (1995), *Immortal Invisible: Lesbians and The Moving Image*. London and New York: Routledge, pp. 52–65.

Marshment, M. and Hallam, J. (1994), ' "From string of knots to orangebox": lesbianism on prime time', in D. Hamer and B. Budge (eds), *The Good, The Bad and The Gorgeous: Popular Culture's Romance with Lesbianism*. London: Pandora, pp. 142–65.

Meyer, Kim Middleton (2003), 'Jeanette Winterson's evolving subject: "Difficulty into dream" ', in Richard J. Lane, Rod Mengham and Philip Tew (eds), *Contemporary British Fiction*. Cambridge: Polity, pp. 210–25.

Onega, S. (2004), 'Science, myth and the quest for unity in Jeanette Winterson's *Gut Symmetries*'. *Anglistik*, 15, (1), 93–104.

O'Rourke, Rebecca (1991), 'Fingers in the fruit basket: A feminist reading of Jeanette Winterson's *Oranges Are Not the Only Fruit*', in S. Sellers (ed.), *Feminist Criticism: Theory and Practice*. Hemel Hempstead: Harvester Wheatsheaf.

Shiffer, Celia (2004), ' "You see, I am no stranger to love": Jeanette Winterson and the extasy of the word', *Critique*, 46, (1), Fall, 31–52.

Web resources

The official Jeanette Winterson site: http://www.jeanettewinterson. com/

http://www.themodernword.com/scriptorium/winterson.html

www.uni-koeln.de/phil-fak/englisch/kurse/wintersn.htm

http://books.guardian.co.uk/authors/author

British Council, Arts website: www.contemporarywriters.com/authors/ ?p=auth100

The Jeanette Winterson readers' site. Anna Troberg, 1998: http://web.telia.com

Index

Lightning Source UK Ltd.
Milton Keynes UK
UKOW06f1222190816

281049UK00006B/59/P